W9-DAQ-987

THE LOST BOYS
OF MONTAUK

THE LOST BOYS OF MONTAUK

THE TRUE STORY OF THE WIND BLOWN, FOUR MEN WHO VANISHED AT SEA, AND THE SURVIVORS THEY LEFT BEHIND

AMANDA M. FAIRBANKS

THORNDIKE PRESS
A part of Gale, a Cengage Company

LIBRARY OF CONGRESS CIP DATA ON FILE.
CATALOGUING IN PUBLICATION FOR THIS BOOK
IS AVAILABLE FROM THE LIBRARY OF CONGRESS.

ISBN-13: 978-1-4328-9074-2 (hardcover alk. paper)

Published in 2021 by arrangement with Gallery Books, a Division of Simon & Schuster, Inc.

Printed in Mexico
Print Number: 01   Print Year: 2022

For Theo and Violet

"We all know that if we are to live ourselves there comes a time when we must relinquish the dead, let them go, keep them dead. Let them become the photograph on the table. Let them become the name on the trust accounts. Let go of them in the water. Knowing this does not make it any easier to let go of them in the water."

— Joan Didion, *The Year of Magical Thinking: The Play*

"If you want to keep a secret, you must also hide it from yourself."

— George Orwell, *1984*

The Lost Boys of Montauk:

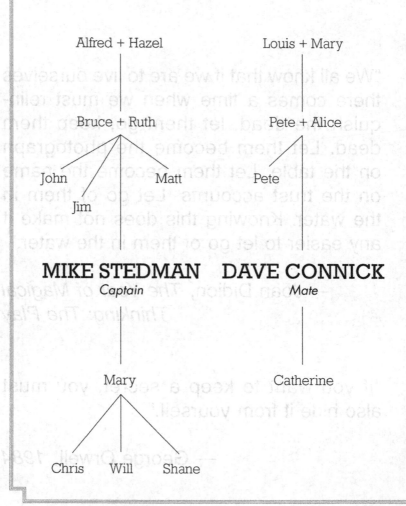

Alfred + Hazel   Louis + Mary

Bruce + Ruth   Pete + Alice

John   Matt   Pete
Jim

MIKE STEDMAN   DAVE CONNICK
Captain   *Mate*

Mary   Catherine

Chris   Will   Shane

Cast of Characters

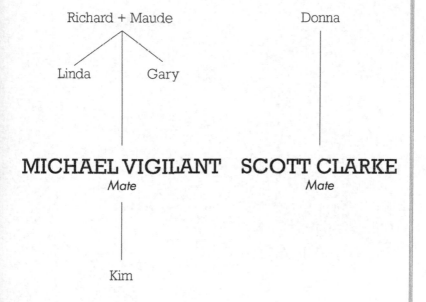

Richard + Maude   Donna

Linda   Gary

MICHAEL VIGILANT   SCOTT CLARKE
Mate   *Mate*

Kim

AUTHOR'S NOTE

This is a work of narrative nonfiction. This account is the result of interviews, oral histories, primary-source documents, books, and newspaper and magazine articles. A note of warning: I was at the mercy of either family histories that had been written down ahead of time, or family members and friends who were still alive and willing to speak with me. You will therefore come to know some of the four men who died aboard the *Wind Blown* and their survivors more deeply than others.

CONTENTS

■ ■ ■ ■

PART ONE:
BEFORE

■ ■ ■ ■

Captain Michael Stedman.

1.

THE LAST VOYAGE

On March 22, 1984, the *Wind Blown,* a commercial fishing boat, departed from Montauk Harbor on eastern Long Island around dusk to begin its first trip of the early-spring season. The four-man crew planned a weeklong trip to catch tilefish about 120 miles offshore.

It was a gray, frigid, forty-degree afternoon. A light easterly wind indicated the possibility of a brewing storm, but it was nothing that Captain Michael Stedman thought his sixty-five-foot, steel-hulled boat couldn't handle.

Back then, even vaguely reliable long-term weather forecasting didn't exist. Offshore fishermen received twice-daily weather updates on single-side-band radios. And if you weren't standing in your wheelhouse at five o'clock in the morning and eleven o'clock at night, your radio tuned to channel 2670, you missed it. For commercial fisher-

17

men, as Mike knew firsthand, a little weather was nothing to fear — an occupational hazard if ever there was one. Besides, if things got really bad, he could always run back to the harbor and ride out the storm.

It was Mike's fourth or fifth offshore trip aboard the *Wind Blown,* and the young, relatively inexperienced crew hadn't yet jelled. The foursome was still figuring out how best to work together. Mike had purchased the *Wind Blown* only months prior, after years spent working on other men's boats. At long last, he was the captain of his own vessel and in control of his own destiny — financial and otherwise. Captain Mike answered to no one but himself.

The year 1984 was the height of the commercial tilefishing boom — right in the sweet spot of a decade-long East Coast–fishing gold rush that spanned from the late 1970s to the late 1980s. Historic numbers of golden tilefish flooded the North Atlantic. It was pretty much a guaranteed bonanza for anyone who geared up, went out, and did it. Back in those days, baited circle hooks pulled in thirty- to forty-pound tilefish. It was like plucking money from the sea: soaking-wet dollar bills that reeked of rotten fish guts.

Depending on the going price and grade of tilefish, a successful offshore trip promised a longlining crew anywhere from $15,000 to $30,000. Once they pulled back into the docks, the crew filled cardboard cartons like bakers frosting a layer cake: ice, tilefish, ice, tilefish.

Whatever landed in Montauk traveled the length of fish-shaped Long Island by truck to the Fulton Fish Market in Lower Manhattan, where it was sold through brokers, mostly to Chinese and Korean buyers. What the commercial fisherman gained in freedom, he lost in transparency, since the pricing structure, like the catch, fluctuated according to supply and quality and freshness — to say nothing of the weather and proximity to holidays and school vacations. Though the Fulton Fish Market has since moved to the Bronx, nearly all of Long Island's annual catch still ends up there. Haggling was the name of the game; the difference of thirty cents a pound could make or break a twenty-thousand-pound haul. Decades prior, the Mafia had taken control of the Fulton Fish Market, seeing it as an ideal, all-cash business for laundering money.

The truck driver eventually returned to Montauk carrying thick wads of cash.

Receipts in hand, each boat owner first subtracted the cost of the trip. In 1984, a typical week offshore ran about $5,000 for food, fuel, and ice. No one got paid until the crew had hosed their vessel clean of blood, dirt, and rusted fishhooks. Cash was king. Some years, owners pulled in upwards of a quarter of a million dollars.

Then as now, commercial fishermen weren't salaried employees. Deckhands worked for a share of the catch — less the owner's and captain's slices of the pie (typically an equal split). Any fish that wasn't the target species (in this case, golden tilefish) went into a separate cardboard box the crew labeled SHACK MONEY. The deckhands kept the profits from whatever they caught that wasn't the target species. (A seventy-five-pound swordfish, at five dollars a pound, netted a sizable chunk of change.)

Two of the four men on the *Wind Blown* — Michael Stedman and David Connick — were an improbable pair to have joined forces on an offshore commercial fishing boat. Most Montauk fishermen come from working-class families. Few attend private schools. Blue-blooded pedigrees are rarer still.

Mike was the thirty-two-year-old son of a

20

Harvard-educated United Nations civil servant. Dave, his twenty-two-year-old mate, was the son of an affluent New York family who belonged to the Maidstone Club and owned a weekend house, south of the highway, in East Hampton.

Though separated by nearly a decade, Mike and Dave were like brothers, the privileged sons of powerful, domineering fathers. It was a different era, and their fathers had a lot in common. Both were white-collar men who liked to drink and had wandering eyes. For Mike and Dave, nothing was less appealing than the dry-cleaned suits and suspenders their fathers wore to the office every morning. Social climbing and cocktail-party banter made their skin crawl. The decision to become commercial fishermen was an act of defiance, a discarding of their inheritance. Mike and Dave showed their rebellion by growing chin-length hair, streaked by the sun. Unlike their fathers', their athletic, sinewy bodies were the result not of playing regular games of tennis or golf, but years of riding waves.

Most Montauk fishermen don't surf. Some don't even know how to swim. In that regard, Mike and Dave were outliers too. If they weren't offshore fishing and the surf

David Connick.

was breaking, they could be found at Georgica Beach in East Hampton or Ditch Plains in Montauk — out in the water, straddling their surfboards, their torsos facing the horizon, waiting for another set to roll in — part of a small, insular tribe of eastern Long Island surfers.

The two other men on the *Wind Blown*'s final voyage, Michael Vigilant and Scott Clarke, were young, enthusiastic deckhands from scrappy, hardscrabble families. They were busy sharpening their skills and putting in their time, eager to someday become captains of their own vessels.

Michael Vigilant, the nineteen-year-old son of a commercial fisherman, was a familiar face around the docks but new to

Michael Vigilant.

the *Wind Blown* crew. He was filling in until Tom McGivern, one of the original *Wind Blown* crew members, returned from a surfing trip to the Canary Islands. At eighteen, Scott Clarke was the fourth and youngest crew member. A relative newcomer to Montauk, Scott was already well on his way to cementing his reputation as a young man with an ironclad work ethic who wasn't afraid to get his hands dirty.

As lowly deckhands, Michael and Scott were enticed by the cash they might make. Every offshore trip was a bit like gambling, albeit with the advantage of a stacked deck. Each crew member stood to make between $2,500 and $5,000 for a week of work. With three to four trips each month, the money added up. Even so, the three youngest members of the *Wind Blown* crew (lacking mortgages and young mouths to feed) could easily drink through it in a week's time. Already the father of three sons, Captain Mike didn't have the luxury of pissing away a week's worth of wages. He occupied a separate tier of the hierarchy altogether. As owner and boss, his rank entitled him to an additional percentage of whatever he and his crew hauled back to shore.

But the pull wasn't only about the money. It was about the spirit of the thing. Hundreds of miles offshore, different rules applied. Aboard the *Wind Blown,* no matter the foursome's divergent social classes, a brotherhood had started to form. And not by accident, but on purpose: their very lives depended on it.

Commercial fishing has always been a young man's game. Few fishermen work past the age of fifty. For some, the older they get, the more the close calls accumu-

Scott Clarke.

late. And the baton eventually gets passed from one generation to the next. Every offshore trip is an endurance test. Each crew works to the brink of exhaustion — and often well past that. Commercial fishing is all about pushing boundaries. It becomes a point of pride, the ability to ignore all indications that your body needs to *stop* and *sleep*.

Offshore, the mentality is to fish until you simply cannot fish any longer. With a fatality rate twenty to thirty times higher than that of other occupations, commercial fishing is among the most dangerous jobs in the nation. Sinking vessels cause the greatest number of fatalities, followed by fishermen falling overboard. After tabulating annual fatal workplace injuries, the Bureau of Labor Statistics consistently ranks commercial fishermen above timber cutters (second) and airline pilots (third). For purposes of survival, fishermen (and deckhands especially) develop a remarkable sense of timing and balance. But the danger of the work rarely registers for young men, whose whole lives are stretched out ahead of them, like so many miles of monofilament fishing line.

"A fisherman is like a good cheese," Hilda Stern, the wife of Richard Stern, a legendary character among the Montauk fleet, said in a profile about captains' wives that appeared in 1976 in the *East Hampton Star,* the local newspaper. "He just goes on forever."

Mike Stedman was one such fisherman who was sure to get better with age. Longevity coursed through his bloodline. A confident man in the prime of his life, Mike had a smile that radiated contentment. As captain, he relished the healing solitude of being out on the water, the quiet hours alone in his wheelhouse to sit and think, with only the natural world to keep him company, and nobody to bother him. Mike probably never said as much out loud, but he was driven to prove something. *It was time to make something of himself.*

Deep in the recesses of his mind, though, it's possible that Mike had started to second-guess himself. The rumors swirled around the docks. Originally a Long Island party boat with a plywood pilothouse and four fish boxes cemented to its deck, the *Wind Blown* wasn't built for the fierceness of the North Atlantic. The fifteen feet added onto her stern by a previous owner had created a destabilizing weakness. Cruder still: several members of the fleet said she was an unseaworthy piece of shit.

"I remember when Mike brought that boat into the harbor, and seeing that it was a steel hull with a plywood structure," Rick Etzel, a Montauk commercial fisherman who now owns the *Breakaway,* told me. He remembered thinking: *Man, that's not a good combination.* For Rick, the addition of the longline drum, which Mike and a friend had bolted onto the roof of the *Wind Blown*'s wooden pilothouse, was but "another head-scratcher."

At the time, the *Wind Blown* was all that Mike could afford. She was a starter boat, a common first purchase among members of the Montauk fleet. Back then, many starter boats were made of wood. In fact, given the *Wind Blown*'s steel-hulled underside, Mike was doing better than many of his peers. But with a mortgage, three children, and a $7,000 insurance payment due in a week's time, any repairs or modifications to Mike's brand-new acquisition would have to wait until he owned more of the *Wind Blown* than the bank did.

Mike was easy to love. He was the cool guy. Everyone wanted to be around him, whether as his friend, as a fisherman, or as a surfer. But his steely will was as strong as his body, and people innately sensed that it was better not to cross him.

Early Wednesday, the day before their March 22 departure, the crew began cleaning and refueling the boat at Montauk Harbor, just off West Lake Drive. Dave and one of the younger men went "grub shopping" at the IGA, a grocery store in East Hampton on North Main Street. They filled three or four shopping carts with $800 worth of calorie-dense groceries — enough food to fuel four men working eighteen- to

28

twenty-hour shifts for the next five to seven days.

Six dozen eggs. Loaves of wheat bread. Gallons of orange juice. Packages of English muffins. Containers of oatmeal. Boxes of spaghetti. Jars of Ragú tomato sauce. Strong coffee. Everything except for three things: fish, bananas, and alcohol. Fish you can always catch. Bananas are bad luck on fishing boats, a long-held superstition dating back to the slave trade when banana boats were struck by tropical hurricanes — and sank. (Another story goes that a boat carrying a shipload of bacteria-laden bananas killed everyone aboard.) As for alcohol? Once offshore, even beer is technically forbidden.

Most offshore fishermen, the *Wind Blown* foursome included, more than made up for weeklong periods of forced sobriety once they were back on dry land. The air would smell sweetly of freshly rolled joints. Miller High Life, "the champagne of beers," flowed like water. Silver cans of Pabst Blue Ribbon did too.

On Thursday afternoon, Mike kissed and hugged his wife, Mary, and their sons goodbye. His departure that day was nothing out of the ordinary. There was nothing romantic about it. Mike was the provider. It was time to get back out on the water so he could feed his family.

For the three months she called Montauk home, the *Wind Blown* docked in a slip behind what was then Christman's Restaurant and Bar. Once Mike made his way to the boat, he brought on board the broccoli and tuna-fish casserole Mary had topped with bread crumbs and freshly grated cheddar cheese.

By afternoon, Dave and Scott were already on the *Wind Blown,* readying supplies, loading ice, and tossing pieces of squid and mackerel into a plastic bucket to use as bait. Once offshore, they'd supplant it with any eel or trash fish they caught. Mike stood watch from inside his wooden wheelhouse, double-checking gear and stowing away an extra full-body survival suit a fisherman friend had loaned him, just in case.

Fueled up and ready to go, the *Wind Blown* was prepared for just about anything that came her way. She had a VHF radio, a single-side-band radio, radar of at least twenty-five miles, a Loran-C (a hyperbolic radio navigation system), paper charts, and a magnetic compass. A US Coast Guard inspection from Star Island, Montauk, on February 23, 1984, had confirmed the "presence of proper lifesaving equipment" on the boat. In 1984, few Atlantic fishermen, Captain Mike included, had yet to invest in weather-fax machines, which, at the time, measured a little larger than briefcases.

Michael Vigilant was the last to board the *Wind Blown* that Thursday afternoon. He wore black rubber boots, jeans, a blue flannel button-down shirt, and a denim jacket. Although no one knew it at the time, he had just proposed to his girlfriend.

Young and in love, Michael and Kim Bowman, an eighteen-year-old senior at East Hampton High School, kissed passionately on the docks that afternoon, their bodies pressed tightly together. Moments earlier, hoping to repair a recent argument, Michael had impulsively offered his hand in marriage. Kim didn't give Michael an answer to his proposal. She promised him they'd talk more about getting married in a week's time, when he got back.

Finally Michael disentangled himself. Kim and her younger brother, Frankie, waved good-bye from the docks. They watched as the *Wind Blown* steamed down the narrow, rocky inlet, past Gosman's Restaurant. The boat turned right, out toward the Montauk Lighthouse, and headed southeast into the vast Atlantic. Minutes later, the *Wind Blown*

31

reached the edge of the violet-streaked horizon, and quickly motored out of sight.

On Friday, March 23, the sun was not yet an hour high when the men, dressed in foul-weather gear (typically chest-high rubber waders held up with suspenders), went about the tricky task of setting their lines amid the rolling, churning seas. Fish usually bite best at first light, dusk, and high tide. When fishing with a drum, the hooks are typically set over the stern and hauled in at either port or starboard. (When facing toward the bow, or front, of a boat, *port* and *starboard* refer to the left and right sides, respectively.) The *Wind Blown* crew was longlining for tilefish at the edge of the continental shelf, near Veatch and Atlantis Canyons. Down below, hundreds of fathoms beneath the inky-blue, rumpled surface, vast underwater mountain ranges teemed with fertile marine life.

The crew set out dozens of miles of galvanized steel cable, which fed out from the longline drum fixed to the roof of the *Wind Blown*'s plywood deckhouse. About thirty feet separated each prebaited circle hook. After the snap-on gear had soaked in the water for a few hours, or overnight, it was time to test it out — and if the fish were biting, to start pulling it back in. The first mate worked the rail, hauling in the yellow-speckled tilefish, alive and squirming, from the ocean floor. The second mate removed the hooks and then, knife in hand, slit the throat of each fish; when they had bled out enough, the third mate would gut them and pack them on ice. It was teamwork, and the *Wind Blown*'s foursome would not yet have been wedded to their particular roles in the way that some more seasoned crews are; the men willingly alternated roles until they found their groove, until they found the rhythm of the sea. If the fish were biting, the crew easily cycled through thousands of baited hooks each day.

Longlines can be set near the surface to catch swordfish or tuna — or near the bottom to catch monkfish or tilefish. The *Wind Blown* crew, hunting golden tilefish, sank the heavy lines near the ocean floor, marked off by aluminum poles with radar reflectors, strobe lights, and flame-orange, inflatable high-flyers (a type of buoy) at either end. With thousands of dollars of gear soaking in the water, the foursome shared a meal Dave had prepared in the galley using a propane stove.

The men needed food that stuck to their ribs. Dave might fry up a steak with baked potatoes. Other nights, dinner looked like grab-and-go sandwiches, piled high with deli meat and generous dollops of mayonnaise, or plate-size squares of Mary's tunafish casserole. After dinner, they'd take turns getting a few hours' sleep, interspersed with two-hour shifts in the wheelhouse. The men learned to tell time based on the phases of the moon and the height of the sun at noon. On clear nights, constellations illuminated the night sky. Once dawn came, the smell of freshly brewed coffee stood in for alarm clocks.

Day after day, the pattern repeated itself. Though monotonous, a repetitive, predictable routine was what the men needed to transform steel fishing lines into a paycheck substantial enough to be split four ways.

The *Wind Blown*'s first few days offshore on this March trip weren't especially fruitful. Fish aren't dispersed in equal numbers throughout the ocean. The act of catching them is both an art and a science, requiring that fishermen be acutely attuned to the present moment. A quarter-degree change in water temperature can shift their migratory patterns — as can shifting tides, wind, the time of day, and a whole host of unpredictable factors. It's often a game of luck and instinct, predicting where exactly they'll congregate next. All that week, the crew persevered. Captain Mike eventually hit the jackpot. He transformed the *Wind Blown* into a fish-catching machine. His crew started hauling in thousands of pounds. Tilefish were coming up on every hook. Fishermen describe such conditions as "boiling hot."

As the week wore on, the weather worsened. Late March in the North Atlantic is unpredictable and often brutal. Storms can well up overnight. The wind rarely stops blowing. The air is bone-cracking cold, the kind of chill you can't shake, no matter how many cups of coffee you've drunk. Though technically springtime, late March on the East End of Long Island can feel as bitter and raw as January.

On Wednesday, March 28, at two o'clock in the afternoon, the National Weather Service in New York City posted a gale warning. Back in Montauk, Chuck Weimer was out day-fishing for flounder on his forty-two-foot boat, the *Zeda,* in Block Island Sound. He noted in his red leather logbook: "Really pretty rough in the late afternoon," and observed that winds were blowing easterly at twenty to thirty miles per hour. "All boats on their way in."

Later that evening, the NWS upped the ante, issuing a winter storm warning. But the forecasters gravely missed the mark. As the mass headed north, it formed an eye, around which the wind flowed east to west, with the northwest quadrant headed straight for eastern Long Island. Winds picked up from thirty to fifty to seventy-five miles per hour. The Montauk Point Lighthouse eventually reported wind gusts of over a hundred miles per hour.

Any Montauk-based fishing vessels that were still out had started making their way back toward land. Each captain adopted a different strategy for navigating the pitch-black, angry seas. Some docked to the north in Stonington, Connecticut, for the night. There are worse ways to spend a stormy, early-spring evening than saddled up to a bar, a few drinks in.

Kevin Maguire had been out fishing for yellowtail flounder aboard his boat, the *Pontos,* a fifty-five-foot steel-hulled vessel with a plywood wheelhouse, before taking shelter in Stonington. That night, when he and a group of his buddies walked toward the Portuguese Holy Ghost Society, a popular watering hole among Connecticut fishermen, the wind was blowing at eighty to ninety miles per hour and kept pushing him backward. Kevin felt weightless. "It was like you were flying," he recalled. With his arms outstretched, only the tips of his toes clung to the pavement. All these years and hurricanes later, try as he might, Kevin has never been able to replicate that feeling of weightlessness.

Richie Rade, the captain of the *Marlin IV*, had been out in Atlantis Canyon, near the *Wind Blown,* longlining for tilefish. Atlantis Canyon is about 120 miles southeast of Montauk Point. Richie and Mike made radio contact around nightfall. High winds made the rain blow sideways. Richie's men couldn't see a thing. Mike informed Richie that he was heading back. Richie took the long way home. Rather than risk the treacherous sliver of ocean that divides Montauk Point and Block Island, he headed north around Block Island. With the inlet into Montauk Harbor impassable because the water was so high, a dozen other vessels dropped anchor in Fort Pond Bay, a large body of water a few miles west of the Montauk Point Lighthouse.

Low and slow was the name of the game. In theory, if a vessel stays low in the water, crashing waves break over rather than overturn it. No captains I interviewed panicked enough to dump their catch. One vessel, caught in a rip current, sent out a Mayday alert; the US Coast Guard (the nearest headquarters were in New Haven, Connecticut) sped to its rescue. Sensing danger, some captains headed in the exact opposite direction — farther offshore. It's the counterintuitive notion some seamen believe carries the greatest likelihood of survival: pointing the bow of a boat toward oncoming waves is a safer bet than if the vessel's stern (or rear) is the first point of contact.

With thousands of pounds of sweet, buttery tilefish stored inside wooden boxes packed on ice, the *Wind Blown* careened up the East Coast; the eastern tip of Long Island was square in her path. The *Wind Blown* soon confronted not just a storm, but a dreaded nor'easter. The National Weather Service later described it as "one of the most severe general cyclonic storms in recent history."

From the Carolinas to New England, warm, moist air from the Atlantic collided with cold air descending from Canada to create a degree of atmospheric instability and intensity few, if any, weather forecasters had predicted. Thirty-six thousand Long Island residents lost power that evening, as surging tides flooded basements and hurricane-force winds downed trees.

Out east, as the far end of Long Island is known to locals, duneland and beach grass didn't stand a chance. The sea swallowed half a dozen homes along Dune Road in Westhampton Beach, and residents of low-lying areas, such as Gerard Drive in Springs and Lazy Point in Amagansett, evacuated their homes because of rising water. In Sag Harbor, the water went all the way up to the front door of the American Legion. The Dory Rescue Squad, experienced ocean fishermen wearing bright-orange life vests, evacuated nine Cape Gardiner residents using the same type of plywood boat made popular by prior generations of whalers and haul-seiners (a type of fisherman who used a dory to haul nets out to sea and a truck to pull the nets back to shore). It was the worst squall to hit eastern Long Island since the notorious Ash Wednesday Storm of 1962.

In New Jersey, powerful gales buckled the Atlantic City boardwalk and torrential rains flooded casino lobbies. Blizzard-like conditions blanketed Connecticut in eighteen inches of fresh snowfall. Farther north, two Massachusetts residents lost their lives as the weather made landfall. A fallen electrical wire and a tree falling on a van were to blame.

The Dory Rescue Squad helps evacuate stranded residents.

On Cape Cod, eighty-mile-per-hour winds blew the *Eldia,* a 473-foot steel freighter, ashore; the US Coast Guard evacuated its twenty-three crewmen via helicopter. The savage, unnamed storm, which meteorologists described as a "springtime freak," toppled the Great Point Light on the northernmost tip of Nantucket Island. The force of the 1984 gale reduced the stone lighthouse, built in 1818 on the site of the original 1784 light, to a pile of rubble.

Once morning dawned and President Ronald Reagan assessed the damage, he pledged federal disaster relief. But the boys aboard the *Wind Blown* were still out. They were in the fight of their lives.

On Thursday, March 29, Chuck Weimer was safely back home in Montauk. He noted in his logbook that hurricane-force winds had picked up, blowing east to northeast at fifty to seventy-five miles per hour. Offshore, the sea's surface became unreadable through blowing spray and foam. "DID NOT SAIL," Chuck wrote in all-caps of the fateful day that he, and so many others on the East End, have since committed to memory. "WIND BLOWN WENT DOWN OR IS LOST. REALLY BAD NEWS."

Richard Stern, the captain of the *Donna Lee,* a dragger, last spoke with Mike Stedman on a VHF radio early Thursday, around seven o'clock in the morning, from the comfort of his Montauk living room. Mike sounded relatively okay, despite the horrific winds and thirty-foot waves. He conveyed a sense of optimism. Richard expected the *Wind Blown* to roll into Montauk no later than eleven o'clock that morning.

Standing six feet seven, Richard was a legendary fisherman. His hands were the size of baseball gloves. He predicted the weather using two techniques: looking up at the sky and reading his barometer. Over the years, Richard had lost two trawlers to weather-related incidents. Earlier in the week, he had rightly forewarned members of the Montauk fleet that a storm coming up from the Carolinas spelled trouble: "I don't give a fuck what the weatherman says. It's a major storm. People are going to die."

Mike's call to Richard around 7:00 a.m. placed him twelve nautical miles south of the Midway Buoy, the marker dividing the fourteen miles of ocean between Montauk Point and Block Island. Richard assumed the *Wind Blown* was navigating the deep water south of the Midway Buoy. "Deep water is safer in bad weather because there is less chance a boat will be hit by large or unexpected waves," the *East Hampton Star* wrote in one of its two front-page, above-the-fold stories, which ran the following week. The boldface headlines read:

Fishermen Feared Lost in Storm
Off Montauk
The Town Is Battered

Kevin Maguire, the *Pontos* captain, spoke with Mike on channel 67 of a two-way VHF radio late Wednesday night and again early Thursday morning. Mike had just hung up with Richard Stern. Gale-force winds and crashing waves were hammering the *Wind Blown* from all directions.

Depending on sea conditions, tilefishermen usually made it back from the canyons in twelve to eighteen hours. By Thursday

morning, the *Wind Blown* crew had sur-
passed twenty-four hours in transit, finally
approaching Montauk when the northeast
wind and rising tide were perilously at their
highest. At the time, Mike told Kevin that
the *Wind Blown* was about a dozen miles
southeast of Montauk Point. A natural-born
stoic, Mike was letting Mother Nature run
her course. *What other choice did he have?*

Captain Mike possessed the hard-won
bravado of a man who had successfully
charted the exact same course dozens of
times before. The trick was staying steady
and calm. Panic was for amateurs. Once he
made it home to East Hampton, sitting on
his couch with a cold pint of beer in hand,
the whole thing would make for an epic
story. It was a tale as old as time: a young,
heroic captain had faced the inhumanity of
the sea — and persevered.

But early Thursday, Kevin heard something in his friend's voice he had never
heard before. Mike's voice trembled when
he spoke.

"Please tell my wife I love her," Mike said.

"Mike, you're going to come in and tell
her yourself," Kevin responded.

It was the last time anyone heard Mike
Stedman's voice.

When Mike Stedman went off to sea, he left behind his wife, Mary, and their three sons: Christopher, William, and Shane. The past few years of the couple's marriage had been rocky ones — the arrival of three boys in nine years; the emotional and financial strain that raising young children places on even the strongest relationships. The relentlessness of his work, and his frequent absences, had driven an undeniable wedge between husband and wife. Of the pair, Mike was the anchor, the stable, reliable parent.

Dave Connick's last few conversations with his mother, Alice, had been strained. She had frequently expressed her disapproval of the dangerous work her son had chosen. But life at sea fed his restless, fearless soul, and he refused to back down. Upon his return, he also had plans to meet up with his girlfriend, Catherine Cederquist.

Scott Clarke had been raised by a single mother. For years it had been Donna and Scott against the world. Scott had left home at fourteen, and a pack of commercial fishermen had become the father figures he never had. Scott needed to test out his sea legs. He'd promised his mother that he'd be careful.

Michael Vigilant, too, had a single mother waiting for him back at home. Maude had been widowed six years earlier: her fisherman husband drowned in November of 1978 in the Gulf of Mexico. Like his father, Michael had never learned to swim. After Michael proposed to Kim, he had asked her to wait for him until he came back. It was impossible to imagine that Michael would never pull into the docks again, his jean jacket smelling sweetly of fish scales.

The Wind Blown *sitting in Montauk Harbor.*

2.
THE BOAT

Mary Stedman believes that when people are about to die, they leave behind a series of clues. Looking back now, the signs were all there, plain as day.

In late September of 1983, Mike was sitting on his rattan couch, a pillow wedged behind his lower back. Mary had sewn the pillows using a brightly colored striped Mexican fabric. They had recently built their saltbox house on Stephen Hands Path in East Hampton. Mike worked six days a week. Sunday was the one day he could give his swollen, callused fingers a rest. The day before, because his family's livelihood depended on it, he had cleaned the *Marlin IV*. It was a Montauk-based party boat primarily used as a seagoing taxi to escort day-tripping fishermen in search of a few hours on the water. As captain, Mike spent his Saturdays hosing the *Marlin IV* clean of blood and fish guts, and gave a crew mem-

47

ber a wad of cash to go grocery shopping in preparation for another trip offshore.

At first, that particular Sunday afternoon was indistinguishable from any other. Mary, whose dark, wavy hair framed her pale face, stood nearby in the kitchen, laser-focused on getting a healthy supper on the table. She busied herself chopping up ginger and onion for one of her legendary stir-fries served over brown rice. Mary fed her growing family well: steamed artichokes drenched in butter, breaded bluefish cheeks when they were in season, eggs Benedict with homemade hollandaise sauce.

In the Stedman household, white sugar and processed foods were forbidden. Most days, Mike subsisted on coffee and a banana until dinner. They were self-described "granola-heads," with Provisions, the newly opened health food store in Sag Harbor, a frequent destination. Only two years prior, Mike and Mary had finally caved, allowing a television to invade their living room. But rather than stare at a screen, their boys were encouraged to play with LEGO sets and Lincoln Logs, Twister and Chutes and Ladders. Or, better yet, to go outside and run around.

Mike had his legs splayed out across the wooden coffee table. In between sips of

Canadian beer, probably a bottle of Molson or Moosehead, he flipped through classified boat advertisements in *Boats & Harbors.* Printed on yellow newsprint, and now billed as "The Commercial Marine Marketplace," it included page after page of ads for fishing vessels from all over the United States — from the East Coast to the West Coast, from the Gulf Coast to the inland waterways.

Each advertisement foretold a different destiny: "Motivated seller! Must sell!" Mike started to hoot and holler. Upstairs in their attic, he had been filling a brown box with cash. After every offshore fishing trip, he'd set aside a few hundred dollars, earmarked for the boat he'd eventually call his own.

Throwing a fistful of walnuts and pecans into her seasoned wok, coated in a thin layer of coconut oil, Mary looked over at Mike and asked him what all the fuss was about.

"This is the boat I want," Mike said, his finger glued to one of the advertisements. He pointed to a $170,000 fishing boat named the *Wind Blown* based in Freeport, Texas.

"Wait a second. You've never even seen it," Mary countered. "You have to see another boat and compare them. You can't just buy the first boat you see."

He and Mary went back and forth that

Sunday afternoon as their boys played in the backyard, out of earshot. Each round became more and more contentious. A "heavy-duty" feeling of discord — of separation — had started to come between them, Mary recalled later.

"You wouldn't buy the first car or the first house you looked at. Why would you buy the first boat?" Mary demanded. Her cheeks grew flushed. She felt her words, the voice of reason, falling flat. "Why would you go all the way to Texas, when there are dozens of boats for sale within fifty miles of here?" But despite her pleas to reconsider, Mike refused to back down.

Once Mike made up his mind to do something, Mary had learned, there was no point in wasting her time trying to dissuade him. Mike and Mary were two strong-willed Capricorns, born in early January, one day apart. The nitpicking spouse always had the opposite of the intended effect. She was similarly hardwired. Mike would eventually come around, she thought. He almost always did. The two might even have a laugh about it.

For nearly a decade, Mike had worked on other men's boats, whether aboard the *Viking* fleet, or the *Marlin IV* and *Marlin V*. All were party boats, which, unlike charter boats, charged each individual passenger, instead of small groups, for half days or full days at sea.

Party boats have a rich Long Island history. Starting in 1932, the Long Island Rail Road ran routes dubbed the Fisherman's Special from New York City to Montauk. You couldn't beat the price. In the 1950s, the six-hour, round-trip fare was $2.75. The Fisherman's Special originated in Manhattan at Pennsylvania Station. From there, it traveled to Jamaica Station in Queens, where passengers from Manhattan, Queens, Brooklyn, the Bronx, and Staten Island scurried across the platform to secure a spot. Since passengers couldn't reserve seats ahead of time, it was every man for himself. When the fish were biting, the train ran from Friday to Sunday and had three hundred seats. Latecomers either stood or squatted in the aisles until they reached the end of the line.

During the 125-mile-long trip, the train passed through suburbs and farmland until it crossed over the Shinnecock Canal at Hampton Bays. Once it stopped in Southampton, its passengers had officially arrived on the East End. They next passed through Bridgehampton, East Hampton, and Ama-

Mike filleting fish.

gansett. Montauk was finally within reach
when the train hit the pitch pines of
Napeague (a narrow, low-lying strip of land
sandwiched between the Atlantic Ocean and
Gardiner's Bay). Glancing out the window,
as the seventeen miles that separate Amagansett from Montauk Point whizzed past,
one could plainly see that nature, not man,
had the upper hand — from the wind-
hollowed dunes to the green-gray beach
grass, from the stunted evergreens to the

beach plum bushes. Known as The End, Montauk is the easternmost point in all of New York State. As the train steamed north toward Fort Pond Bay, it signaled its arrival by tooting its horn.

All hell broke loose once everyone disembarked. Montauk felt like another planet. The fishermen breathed in the salty sea air. Just as they'd done when first boarding the train in New York City, the men made a mad dash to secure a seat aboard their party boat of choice. Some captains and their vessels were thought to have better luck finding fish than others.

Starting in the mid-1970s, Mike Stedman was one such captain. "1/2 DAY FISHING CAPT. MIKE STEDMAN 668-2885" advertised a photograph of the *Marlin IV*. By 1983, Captain Mike had worked aboard the vessel, a well-known Montauk party boat, for several years. During the summer months, Mike and his young crew helped passengers set their lines, untangle their lines, and fillet their catch — always in sight of land. But once the summer people had gone, the real fun began. Come September, Mike and his crew retrofitted the *Marlin IV* and steamed hundreds of miles offshore: the gold rush for bottom-feeding tilefish was well underway.

53

Captain Stedman's advertisement aboard the Marlin IV.

During the summer of 1983, the *Marlin IV,* painted a bright shade of turquoise with white trim, had broken one of the ribs inside her hull. Once the insurance money came in, Mary recalled, Richard Rade, the boat's owner, apparently bought a condominium in Florida rather than repair the *Marlin IV,* on which her family's livelihood depended.

"I'm going to die on that boat," Mike repeatedly said to Mary. "I need my own boat." Mary didn't disagree. It wasn't that she didn't want her husband to own his own boat. It was the next logical step. But Mary, who is a deeply intuitive person (several people described her to me as "witchy"), had a bad feeling about the *Wind Blown*

54

from the very start. She felt a heavy, sinking feeling, a *knowing* in the pit of her stomach most of all.

Mike was becoming a man and doing so on a wing and a prayer. Unlike many of their peers, he and Mary had married young. By 1983, at thirty-one and twenty-eight respectively, they felt the responsibilities of parenthood weighing heavily on their shoulders. And unlike their friends with trust funds or families with two steady incomes, Mike was the sole breadwinner. Though his parents, Bruce and Ruth Stedman, were capable of coming to their son's financial rescue in the event of an emergency, Mike couldn't stomach the humiliation of asking them to bail him out. From his father in particular, Mike knew better than to ask for help. It was the equivalent of admitting defeat. With three young sons and a wife to provide for, the time was ripe for Mike Stedman to strike out on his own.

It was now or never.

Two more signs spelled trouble.

Later that fall, on Sunday, October 23, two officers from the East Hampton Police Department pulled up in front of the Stedman home. Two-and-a-half-year-old Shane had broken his leg while roughhousing with his older brothers at East Hampton High School's football field, not far away. Shane was in agonizing pain, lying in the back of an ambulance headed to Southampton Hospital. Chris was nine; Will was seven. The incident traumatized Chris, and afterward he vowed to himself that he'd never let anything bad happen to his two younger brothers again.

Keep in mind that parenting in the early 1980s was generally less paranoid and anxiety-ridden than today, when helicopter and snowplow parents hover around their progeny well into adulthood. Back then, mothers routinely left their children sitting in the backseats of their cars while running errands. Tylenol had just introduced tamper-resistant packaging. Helmets were unheard of when roller-skating or riding bikes. And as in most small towns in America, in East Hampton it wasn't considered parental neglect to let a young child roam free, particularly when he had two older, protective brothers keeping watch.

That afternoon, hoping to reach one of Shane's parents at home, the two police officers knocked on the front door. While waiting for someone to answer, the officers spied a cluster of tall, leafy marijuana plants growing in the backyard. The Stedman garden was particularly lush and verdant, given its steady diet of fish carcasses, which Mike and his sons buried deep in the sandy, porous soil from time to time. The cannabis garden Mike had planted was a symbol of his adoration for Mary, who loved nothing more than a little ganja. Mike too. He tilled the soil and monitored each plant, making sure it had the proper amount of water and sunlight. In a few weeks, just before the first frost, they would harvest the plants and put them to use.

After obtaining a search warrant, four officers wielding flashlights returned to the house around dusk. Officers confiscated fourteen marijuana plants in all, including four that had been drying out, upside down, in the basement. They also confiscated marijuana from the kitchen, along with a pipe and a used joint. Detective Francis Mott arrested Mike and charged him with criminal possession of marijuana (in those days, a class A and B misdemeanor offense in New York State).

Back at police headquarters, Mike admitted that the marijuana plants were indeed his. Town Justice Shepard Frood released him on his own recognizance, directing him to report back to the East Hampton Justice Court in a week's time.

This wasn't Mike's first brush with local law enforcement. In his late twenties, he'd been charged for driving with a suspended license, the result of several unanswered traffic warrants.

But a slap on the wrist this was not. The threat of possible jail time hung in the balance. For Mike Stedman, it was time to finally grow up and get his act together, to stop playing things so fast and loose.

Detective Mott concluded the arrest report by writing: "Investigation continuing at this time."

A few weeks later, in mid-November, Mary contacted Mike using a friend's ship-to-shore communication system. For the Stedmans, investing in their own offshore communication system seemed a frivolous expense the family could surely do without. It was the middle of the week, and Mike was away on a five-day fishing trip. When Mary finally reached him, she sounded uncharacteristically frantic. She asked that her husband return home.

Mike always cleaned up for Mary after he'd been offshore. Once home, after tackling his sons, he'd make his way to the upstairs master bathroom, where he'd shower and shave. Using a jar and a brush to create a foamy lather, Mike would cover his tanned face in a thick layer of shaving cream. Though his face was usually clean-shaven, he occasionally left a mustache behind, like Tom Selleck, the handsome star of *Magnum, P.I.,* the popular TV show that had premiered in 1980.

As he stepped into the hot, steaming shower, the smell of Dr. Bronner's peppermint soap wafted through the Stedman house.

For Chris, Mike's eldest son, the sharp, familiar scent was like a smoke signal. Dad was home again. All felt right with the world.

In late afternoon, around sunset, Mike drove his three sons to Georgica Beach. It was a warm night when they all piled into their father's two-seater, seafoam-green pickup truck, which smelled of bait, beer, fish, fuel, and grease. Ready to deploy at a moment's notice, the truck's bed contained a mishmash of fishing line, net, and rubber boots. The fish oil penetrated everything it touched. Even the dollar bills in their father's wallet had a fishy odor.

The foursome headed south of the highway, past dark, shuttered mansions and manicured hedgerows that lined the asphalt roads. The rose-bushes and thorny branches were empty of the blush-pink blossoms, two or three to a stem, that the boys surreptitiously picked and brought home to surprise their mother every June.

But unlike most trips to Georgica, where they'd instinctively head right to watch their dad surf the three rock jetties that jut out into the Atlantic Ocean, Mike made a sharp left.

Chris recalls that the mood was unusually solemn as Mike dropped to his knees and began digging a hole in the sand. He explained to his sons that their mother had just suffered a miscarriage. The three boys sat in silence as Mike gathered enough driftwood to build a small fire. He pulled out a lighter. They watched as their mother's white cotton nightgown went up in flames. Chris believes it contained a bloody four-month-old fetus. A sibling who would have been born the following May.

No one said a word as they left the empty beach around nightfall. Mike hoisted Shane up on his shoulders. His strong, determined legs led the way.

"She's the wrong boat. She's the wrong boat. *She's the wrong boat!*" Mary repeatedly warned Mike, her voice rising until she screamed to be heard. But her husband's stubborn shell was impenetrable to her hysterical pleas. Over the years, Mary had had inchoate feelings about all sorts of things. Maybe in spite of her instinctive misgivings about the *Wind Blown,* Mike refused to back down. He asked his wife to have faith in him.

The day after Christmas, once Santa Claus had come and gone and the boys had unwrapped their presents, Mike kissed his wife and sons good-bye and headed to Kennedy Airport. He had booked a one-way ticket to Houston, Texas. Mike was off to make his longtime dream of owning his own boat come true. He was off to meet his bride, so to speak.

In Quintana, Texas, about an hour's drive from Houston, he met up with Tom McGivern, who had spent the Christmas holiday at his family's condominium in Palm Beach, Florida. Tom, the son of a prominent Manhattan judge, had a patrician pedigree. Like Dave, Tom was an East Hampton summer kid from a well-to-do family. Tom had fallen in love with fishing during his summers home from Harvard. Working at the docks alongside Mike, who was like an older brother to him, Tom earned $100 a day and a bag of fresh fish to take home each night for supper. By summer's end, his savings

Tom McGivern aboard the Marlin
IV.

account had grown some eightyfold. Plenty
of money to survive the Cambridge winter
once back at Harvard.

"His passions were Shakespeare and
Churchill and his family," read the obituary
of Tom's father, Owen McGivern, which ran
in the *New York Times* on July 8, 1998. The
son of Irish immigrants, Owen became
presiding justice of the Appellate Division

of the New York State Supreme Court. In that obituary, Edward Koch, the former mayor of New York City, described the elder McGivern as a "master raconteur." Koch said: "He had the gift of the leprechaun. He beguiled audiences with his humor and intelligence."

As with his gravestone, located on a plot of land picked out and paid for years earlier, Owen McGivern didn't leave any details of his funeral to chance. About a year before he died, he gave Joan McGivern, his wife of forty-three years, explicit instructions: "A low Mass with no incense; a eulogy by one daughter and one son, not to exceed five minutes each; the singing of two hymns, 'Amazing Grace' and 'A Mighty Fortress Is Our God,' followed by a reception at the Union Club." At the Church of St. Ignatius Loyola on Park Avenue, two Jesuit bishops and six priests stood at the altar, looking down at his coffin. Before Owen took his last ride out to his beloved East Hampton (a burial followed at the Most Holy Trinity Roman Catholic Cemetery on Cedar Street), a bagpiper serenaded the judge with "Danny Boy." A second reception followed at the Maidstone Club.

Joan told the *New York Times:* "He was afraid I wouldn't get it quite right. He

63

would say, 'You can't leave it to chance.' "
The maniacal wrangling of detail was the
exact sort of thing Mike's father, Bruce,
might have done. Even after they were dead
and gone, both men had a difficult time
relinquishing control.

Owen McGivern was a judge. Bruce Stedman was a civil servant. It's safe to say
neither of these fathers imagined their sons
would work as commercial fishermen. A
summer job during college was one thing.
But making your career as a commercial
fisherman — *actually choosing it* — seemed
about as likely in 1983 as the Berlin Wall
coming down.

Mike often picked up Tom at his family's
1860s three-story cedar-shingled summer
home on Dunemere Lane in East Hampton.
Arriving well before dawn in his green Wil-
lys Jeep, Mike would signal his arrival by
lightly tapping his horn, so as not to awaken
the entire neighborhood. Tom slept in the
front bedroom to hear Mike's arrival. After
exchanging brief pleasantries, Mike and
Tom often sat in silence during the thirty-
minute drive out to Montauk. Meanwhile,
Tom's younger brother, Morgan, a fellow
surfer and burgeoning photographer, stayed
home, logging a few extra hours of sleep.

Morgan was best friends with Dave Connick.

Tom, his sisters, and their mother, Joan, still use the main house; Morgan and his college-aged son call the modest guest cottage home. Morgan McGivern possesses the only known photograph of the *Wind Blown* once she made it from Texas to Montauk in 1984. Morgan has digitized the original Kodachrome slide, along with two dozen other images; taken together, they document a bygone era.

Dunemere Lane, across the street from the East Hampton Library, sits south of New York State Route 27. In the other direction, if you keep driving east down Dunemere Lane, where the tops of giant elm tree branches have grown together to form a makeshift tunnel, you'll eventually run right into the Maidstone Club. The McGiverns and the Connicks are longtime members. Otherwise known as Montauk Highway, Route 27 is the main highway that courses east to west; it divides the South Fork into haves and have-nots. The Stedmans lived on the opposite side of the tracks, in Northwest Woods, a densely wooded section of East Hampton, about ten minutes away. Nowadays, tens of millions of dollars separate homes located on either side of Montauk Highway. Owning a house in the estate section, "south of the highway," is still an undeniable status symbol linked to the astounding price of oceanfront real estate.

In early December of 1983, Mike had taken out a $135,000 loan from the Bank of the Hamptons. Before Mike embarked for Texas, a number of friends helped him scrape together the money he needed for the $35,000 down payment. Tom, who loaned Mike around $5,000, slept aboard the dry-docked *Wind Blown* with his friend that first night in Quintana.

At daybreak on December 27, Mike and Tom scraped barnacles from her underside. A dark, weather-beaten shade of maroon, the *Wind Blown* was in desperate need of a fresh coat of paint. The advertisement had neglected to mention that she had seen better days. Mike vowed to restore her to her former glory with some tender loving care. And he wasn't alone in the monumental undertaking. His friends willingly shed their blood, sweat, and tears to make Captain Mike's dream come true. They had his back. His dream of owning his own boat had become theirs too.

Over the next few days, Dave Connick and Scott Clarke met up with Mike and Tom in

Quintana. Scott, the young Montauk deck-hand whom Mike had recently taken under his wing, hailed from the opposite end of the Long Island hierarchy. While Tom and Dave had attended Choate, the Connecticut boarding school, Scott had gone to Ocean-side High School. Hampered by an undiagnosed learning disability, he'd eventually dropped out of school. His mother worked for TWA at LaGuardia Airport. His father was never in the picture. And once his mother remarried, Scott and his stepfather didn't exactly get along.

While not precocious in the classroom, Scott excelled at commercial fishing. At the docks, many of his peers were also breaking free from their fathers — if they even had fathers in the first place. Fishermen were Scott's people. They were his chosen family. Despite his youth, with a mature, hardworking, easy-to-please disposition, the teenager passed for a man well into his twenties.

David Connick grew up splitting his time between a Park Avenue penthouse apartment in Manhattan and a weekend house in East Hampton. The Connicks spent every July and August at East Hampton's exclusive Maidstone Club. The family tradition started back when David's grandfather, a successful New York City litigator, became a member in the 1930s. It was a lavish life of tennis on grass courts, golf overlooking the Atlantic, and themed cocktail parties. Nothing about the *Wind Blown* — with its chipped paint and crew members who sometimes went a week without bathing — was what the Connicks had imagined for their well-bred son.

Tom McGivern should have been on the *Wind Blown* when she went down a few months later on March 29, 1984. And he would have been, had he not decided to go on a last-minute surfing trip to Tenerife, the largest of the Canary Islands. Tom planned to be gone a month, give or take. The winter surf in Tenerife was world-class. There was no point in rushing home — Tom would be back on the *Wind Blown* alongside Mike and Dave soon enough, doing the work he loved best.

Survivor's guilt — *Why them and not me?* — plagues Tom still. Now approaching sixty, he lives in San Francisco and works in finance. Wearing a five-millimeter-thick winter wetsuit, Tom surfs at nearby Ocean Beach whenever the opportunity presents itself. Tom has a wife and two school-age children, plus two adult children from a previous marriage. Unlike Chris, Will, and Shane Stedman, who grew up without their father, Tom's four children got the lucky roll of the dice. Though all three Stedman sons are now grown men, Tom keeps an eye on "the boys," knowing Mike would have done the same had their fates been reversed.

In 2017, sitting in a café with me in San Francisco and reflecting on the incident all these years later, Tom grew teary-eyed. During their voyage home from Texas to Montauk, Tom built wooden fish boxes that they later cemented and welded onto the *Wind Blown*'s deck. He can't help but think now that those boxes resembled small coffins — both for the thousands of pounds of golden tilefish they eventually caught, and also for the four crew members who vanished at sea.

Maybe it really was as simple as Mike picking a different boat.

As with buying a used car, when you buy a secondhand boat, it comes with a history — a series of previous lives, if you will. The transaction from old owner to new owner is often an act of obfuscation. Mike Stedman never got the whole story.

In fairness, he didn't exactly do his due diligence. It was a decision guided not by his head but by his heart. Given his years as a waterman, Mike probably should have known better. He purchased a boat that some rightly predicted was never built to withstand violent seas. Mary knew it was the wrong boat. The fishermen who had examined the *Wind Blown* up close, shaking their heads, knew it was the wrong boat. Hell, all of the fleet knew it was the wrong boat. For the survivors, the guilt crept in afterward. Few, if any, had spoken up beforehand.

But what is it to be a friend? Do you support a man and his dream and his quest to prove his father wrong — or do you speak up, insult a man's judgment (bad as it may be), and risk your friendship? Nice as he was, Mike had an intensity that you didn't necessarily want to cross.

"Boat Quality Rests with Buyer as Much as Builder," read a headline from the July 1980 issue of *National Fisherman.* The story explained: "Sometimes the fishermen don't understand they're making a substantial business investment. They think they're simply buying a boat, and assume too much." Like many would-be boat owners, Mike must have figured that hiring a naval architect or a marine surveyor for a professional assessment was an extravagant expense, and one he could easily forgo.

But first, back to the boat itself. Over the course of her eighteen-year life-span, the

Wind Blown had three different owners.

She started out in 1966 as the *Capt. Scotty.* Based in Babylon, New York, she was a party boat, painted a cheerful combination of bright red and crisp white. In her prime, she resembled a striped candy cane, ferrying day-tripping fishermen in search of a few hours on the water. Her first owner, George Tweedy Sr., who ran Babylon Open Boats, put together her plywood wheelhouse and her engines himself, after purchasing the steel hull from Gladding-Hearn Shipbuilding in Somerset, Massachusetts.

Three years later, in August of 1969, Tweedy sent a postcard to Preston Gladding, who ran Gladding-Hearn, asking to order the "C872c Model," presumably a type of replacement part. The postcard captured the *Capt. Scotty* on a bright summer's day; on the back of the postcard, it advertised: "Bay and ocean fishing. Complete electronic equipment. Tackle available. Accommodations for ladies."

In 1974, Tweedy retrofitted the modest fifty-foot fishing vessel. Like Mike Stedman a decade later, Tweedy had young mouths to feed; he needed a bigger boat. Tweedy brought the *Capt. Scotty* up to Massachusetts, where Gladding-Hearn welded a fifteen-foot extension, later inspected and

71

The Capt. Scotty *in 1969.*

The Capt. Scotty *in 1974.*

approved by the US Coast Guard, onto her existing hull. Now, at nearly sixty-five feet and fifty-odd tons, with three Detroit Diesel engines at her disposal, the *Capt. Scotty* could carry more passengers and steam up to twenty miles offshore, making each trip more lucrative.

Tweedy eventually parted ways with the Long Island–based vessel. In 1981, he sold her to Robert E. Everett, president of Windward Boats in Freeport, Texas. Windward Boats took out a $125,000 mortgage. Tweedy's two sons drove the *Capt. Scotty* down to meet her new owners. Shortly after, Everett rechristened her *Wind Blown* (to better reflect the name of his company). Along with a new name, her employment switched from "party fishing" to "oil exploitation."

From the time she left George Tweedy until Mike Stedman brought her back to Long Island two years later, the *Wind Blown* roamed around the Gulf of Mexico. Docked in the nearby port of Galveston, she had a second life as an emergency standby boat, traversing the waters around the offshore rigs that extracted oil and natural gas. But she was born a Long Island fishing boat and she would die a Long Island fishing boat, biding her time in Texas until a fisherman in East Hampton saw a grainy picture of her on an ordinary piece of newsprint, fell in love, and wagered his life savings to call her his own.

Mike planned to rename the *Wind Blown.* He even had a new name picked out: *Sinbad.* The name came from *Sinbad the Sailor,* a Technicolor film from 1947 about a fictional Middle Eastern mariner that starred Douglas Fairbanks Jr. (my great-uncle) in its title role. From time to time, whenever the movie came on TV, Mike and his son Chris would sit on the couch and watch it together, enraptured.

On December 27, 1983, Mike filed paperwork with the US Coast Guard to update her "ownership, home port, and name change." But he left WIND BLOWN painted in white block letters on her port side, so everyone in Montauk called her by what was technically her former name. A new paint job could wait. Putting her to work — and fast — was Mike's main objective.

Many mariners warn that renaming a boat can be bad luck. Some partake in elaborate rituals when changing the name of a vessel, often breaking a bottle of champagne across its bow to appease Neptune and Poseidon, the all-powerful Roman and Greek sea gods. Fishermen tend to be a relatively superstitious bunch. Some believe it's bad luck to whistle while aboard a fishing boat because whistling brings the wind; others refuse to shave during a time of drought.

The US Coast Guard's Certificate of Documentation revealed that the name change to *Sinbad* didn't become official until July 9, 1984 — four months after she sank, with all hands, at sea. Two years later, in October of 1986, the Coast Guard officially struck the vessel from its records for "failure to surrender or renew."

During the return trip from Texas, the four men who sailed the *Wind Blown* back to Montauk — Mike, Tom, Dave, and Scott — encountered a series of obstacles. Reflecting back, Mary described the mechanical difficulties as yet another portentous omen.

First Captain Mike lost steering in the Gulf of Mexico. The crew stopped near Sabine Pass, on the Texas–Louisiana border, to fix the steering wheel. One night, to kill time, they meandered into a local honky-tonk bar to grab a few beers. Docked beside Vietnamese shrimp boats with whole families living aboard, they felt like they were a long way from Montauk.

The men journeyed onward. The *Wind Blown* next looped around Sanibel Island and headed up Florida's inland waterways to cross Lake Okeechobee. At nightfall, while passing through the St. Lucie Canal, they encountered a small gill-net fishing boat; while making room in the canal, the *Wind Blown* unknowingly struck bottom, bending both the three-blade propeller and the shaft. Hours later, they were finally back in their beloved Atlantic. Come morning, the Gulf Stream was a brilliant shade of turquoise, as fevers of stingrays swam underneath. But once at full steam, a slow, foreboding thump echoed from the belly of the boat. The crew stopped to survey the damage. They ducked into Cape Canaveral to make the necessary, and costly, repairs.

Coincidentally, Russell Bennett, a childhood friend of the Connick brothers, was down in Jupiter, Florida, about thirty miles away from the St. Lucie Canal, with Dave's older brother, Pete. He and Pete drove up to meet the injured *Wind Blown.* Russell recalled that Mike took off in Russell's two-seater Triumph TR6 sports car, painted British racing green, to drive across the state to Tampa, and returned with a brand-new propeller and twenty-foot shaft. The mood was lively and upbeat. The men bid each other farewell. Russell, later a longtime employee of the *East Hampton Star,* remembered it as the last time the two Connick brothers saw each other — a statement echoed by their mother, Alice Connick, in a *Star* story published shortly after Dave's disappearance. "The brothers have not seen one another since," she was quoted as saying.

But memories, especially when recalling incidents nearly forty years in the past, are tricky, malleable things. Tom McGivern had a completely different recollection of what transpired. Tom said the foursome never crossed paths with Russell and Pete in Florida. Rather, Mike and Tom rented an industrial van in Cape Canaveral and embarked on the four-hour-plus drive across Florida to Tampa, where Mike bought a new propeller and drive shaft to the tune of several thousand dollars. On the return trip to Cape Canaveral to link up with Dave and Scott, Tom and Mike stopped at a roadside McDonald's, where each man inhaled a Filet-O-Fish sandwich and an order of french fries.

However they got to Tampa and back, the mechanical issues that had plagued the start of their journey finally righted themselves. Captain Mike just needed to get the kinks out. Now equipped with a new propeller and shaft, with the wind at her back, the *Wind Blown* steamed up through the Carolinas. Ducking under Cape Fear, they took the Intracoastal Waterway until they hit the Chesapeake Bay. From there, it was a straight shot up to Montauk. All told, the two-thousand-mile-long winter journey took the better part of a month. Mary remembered that the *Wind Blown* finally pulled into her new home port of Montauk, New York, on January 21, 1984. Tom recalled that it was a few days later: January 25 or 26.

Before Tom headed off to the Canary Islands in early February, he loaned Mike his 1976 brown Ford Ranger pickup truck. When Mike disappeared aboard the *Wind Blown,* leaving Tom's truck sitting at the docks, everyone assumed Tom was dead too. In the bed of the two-seater truck, Tom had stored the *Wind Blown*'s broken propeller. Although he intended to eventually remove it, the added weight of the thirty-two-inch-wide steel propeller helped stabilize the rear of his truck when the roads were snowy or slick with ice.

Some forty years later, the faded maroon-and-gray propeller still survives, nestled between piles of freshly chopped oak and cherrywood behind Morgan McGivern's cottage. Much like the surfboards and wetsuits he saves that have seen better days, Morgan can't bring himself to get rid of it. To someone stopping by, it might look like a piece of detritus in need of being hauled off to the dump. But for Morgan, it's his last connection to Dave, his childhood best friend.

When Mike Stedman got back to Montauk, everything had started falling — albeit imperceptibly — like a house of cards.

The Wind Blown's *broken propeller.*

Chris Schumann, a Montauk commercial fisherman, ran into Mike shortly after the *Wind Blown* pulled into her narrow slip behind Christman's Restaurant and Bar for the first time. Chris and Mike were longtime fishing buddies. He remembered Mike as a man of substance. "I just want to see my bride," Chris recalled Mike saying, eager to be reunited with Mary. Since the beginning of their courtship twelve years earlier, four weeks was the longest period of time Mike and Mary had ever been apart.

It was December 24, 1972. Mary Cavagnaro was in East Hampton at a holiday party with her mother, Cletus, who was chain-smoking Salems and already blitzed. Mary felt the room spinning on her mother's behalf. She longed to be anyplace else.

"Can I use the car?" Mary asked her mother.

"Go ahead," Cletus said, slurring her words.

Mary drove her mother's sedan to the Shagwong Tavern. In operation since 1936, the Shagwong is an iconic, wood-paneled bar in the heart of downtown Montauk; even in the dead of winter, its red-and-green neon sign glows along the easternmost stretch of Montauk Highway.

Three days before, Mary had run into a man named Mike Stedman at the Shagwong. She had been wearing an A-line dark-brown jumper with a turtleneck, green tights, and Frye boots. "It was a hippie kind of a thing," Mary recalled. "I looked like a pixie elf."

Mike liked what he saw. He hadn't wasted any time making small talk. He walked up to Mary and told her he loved her. The daughter of an alcoholic, Mary figured it was the beer talking and headed straight for the ladies' room to collect her thoughts. She slammed the bathroom door in Mike's face. But Mary had felt it too. Their connection was undeniable.

"Hi, Maz," Peter Hewitt, the bartender, said to Mary when she walked into the

Young Mary (at right) and friend.

Shagwong around eleven o'clock on Christmas Eve. "Mike Stedman is in the kitchen making avocado sandwiches."

Mary froze.

Mike started screaming, unable to contain his excitement. He ran over to Mary. "I knew you'd come back for me," he said.

Outside, snowflakes had started to fall.

"I'm in love with you," Mike said, his hazel eyes catching the light. "Come home with me."

It was not unlike the first time Mike saw the *Wind Blown.* Mike was a man of action. In Mary, Mike saw what he wanted. And he went after it.

"It was like fireworks," Mary said. It didn't hurt that Mike was drop-dead gor-

Young Mike.

geous. His "perfect hair," which effortlessly fell across half his face, was the first thing that caught her eye.

Based on past experiences, Mary knew that people who will alter your destiny have a powerful way of announcing themselves. There's rarely anything subtle about their arrival. Only days prior, Mary had dropped out of college, sold all of her worldly possessions, and subjected herself to the required immunizations to make a pilgrimage to Goa, India, with an on-again, off-again boyfriend.

But life, it seemed, had other plans.

Standing four inches taller, at five feet ten inches and 165 pounds, Mike carried Mary out of the Shagwong Tavern and drove her to his nearby apartment. Drunk guys, hoping to get laid, had told Mary they loved her before. But this was a wholly different attraction. Making love with Mike was unlike anything she had experienced, or would experience again. The admission, all these years (and two husbands) later, made her wince. But it was true.

"It was the magic of being young," Mary said, "when the whole world is your oyster." A whirlwind courtship ensued. A week later, Mary turned eighteen and Mike turned twenty-one. On January 20, 1973, Mike and Mary drove to Washington, DC, to protest President Richard Nixon's second inauguration. Six months later, on June 30, 1973 — the day of a total solar eclipse — a priest at the Most Holy Trinity Roman Catholic

83

Mike and Mary Stedman on their wedding day.

Church in East Hampton declared Mike, in a white tuxedo, and Mary, in a white veil, husband and wife. Susan Coursey was the maid of honor. Bart Stuart was the best man. During his toast at the reception, which was held in the backyard of Mary's childhood home on Route 114, attendees recalled that Bart quoted a line from the Grateful Dead: "We can share the women, we can share the wine."

Theirs was an immediate synergy, an instant joining of two lives. To Mary, it felt like she had found a missing puzzle piece, the way their irregular edges formed a circle. It was impossible in those first months and years of new love to imagine the secrets each would withhold from the other, the lies they would tell — the ungraspable parts of two people, no matter their physical and emotional intimacy.

Mike and Mary didn't waste any time. The birth of their son Chris made her a mother at nineteen. At twenty-one, she gave birth to their second son, Will. And their third and final son, Shane, arrived when she was twenty-six. "Everyone told me not to get married, to get an abortion, to go back to school and become a photojournalist," Mary explained to me. "There was huge pressure to conform to the women's movement. I felt really judged."

During the sixties and seventies, a time of fragmentation and upheaval, though feminists had fought for a certain kind of emancipation, Mary didn't have any role models she could emulate who had personally paved the way. Maybe if she had been born a decade later, the feminist movement would have catapulted her into another sphere. But Mary was born a few years too

85

early to take such a daring leap.

Like her mother and her grandmother before her, she soon fell into the gendered norms of the era: Mary Stedman became a wife and a mother. Mama Mary presided over the home front like a powerful lioness. And yet, her identity as a mother never captured the totality of who she was as a woman. At the height of her female power, a group of young men were drawn to the powerful force field that surrounded her. They couldn't help themselves. Mary emitted the kind of magnetism that had prompted Mike to profess his love to a complete stranger. One thing was for sure: Mary Stedman was way more interesting than your average East Hampton housewife.

But there was always a sense that, if given a more forceful nudge, she might have chosen a different path. Hers was a great, untapped intellect. Over the years, nearly every person I interviewed who knew Mary, whether during her childhood, adolescence, or adulthood, relayed a slightly different version of her. Every marriage contains multitudes, and it's quite likely that Mike never fully grasped his wife, whose intellect ran circles around him, in all of her complexity. She kept her private life closely guarded. Mary's inherent unknowability had an intoxicating effect: you couldn't help but want to figure her out.

Twelve years later, in 1984, Mike was back in Montauk and beaming with pride. He couldn't contain his excitement. Just like convincing Mary to come home with him all those years ago, he had done the thing he'd set out to do: he'd returned home behind the wheel of his very own boat. It was no small victory. Chris Schumann drove Mike to East Hampton. With the familiar crunch of his gravel driveway again underfoot, Mike flashed him a wide smile.

A few weeks later, Chris approached Mike about working as a crew member aboard the *Wind Blown.* But Chris was too late — Michael Vigilant had already agreed to fill in while Tom McGivern went on his surfing trip. Michael was already a known entity around the docks. He had a hardworking, reliable disposition that Mike had seen firsthand, when he busted his ass aboard the *Viking,* day in and day out.

Chris, as it turns out, had caught a lucky break. By March, a vacancy opened up on the *Provider III,* a boat owned by Lance Hallock. Later that month, when the *Wind Blown* went missing, Lance and Chris went out searching from dawn to dusk for the missing foursome. Despite all the evidence, it was impossible to believe the crew would never pull into the docks again.

The *Wind Blown* had vanished without a trace.

"You just have to accept what comes and you can never know what the next day will bring," Hilda Stern said in the story about captains' wives that appeared in the *Star* in January of 1976. "Sometimes my husband will leave at six in the morning, sometimes at midnight. He tells me when he expects to be home, but I never really know until he walks in the front door." Richard Stern's schedule reigned supreme. All year, there were only three days Hilda could count on her fisherman husband being home: Thanksgiving, Christmas, and New Year's Day.

The Sterns didn't have a radio that connected Hilda to Richard when he was offshore. "My husband gets involved in his work and I get involved in mine and I want to be free to go when I have to for the children, to do my work as a class mother, at the church, and the PTA," she said. In this way, Hilda Stern, a mother of three, didn't see her daily life as altogether different from that of her neighbor, whose husband commuted every morning from Montauk to his office job in East Hampton. In both instances, the wives were more than capable of handling any crises that arose.

"I have to have faith that my husband will use his judgment about winds, tides, and weather, and not put himself or his crew in danger," Hilda said. "Sure, there are plenty of things that happen out there that I don't know about. Sometimes months or years later I will overhear my husband relating some close call. And maybe it's better I don't know." For fishermen's wives, a heightened state of anxiety goes with the territory. Hilda pointed to a wind gauge near the kitchen door: "I worry every time the wind blows."

If the wives or girlfriends were really in a pinch and urgently needed to reach their husbands or boyfriends, they might try reaching out to Sand Dollar, the radio name of Mary Louise Cook. Starting in the seventies, from her dining room in Harvey Cedars, New Jersey, Sand Dollar kept her VHF and single-side-band radio turned on seven days a week from 8:00 a.m. to 11:00 p.m. (except on Thursday mornings, when she abandoned her volunteer duties to do her weekly grocery shopping). Twice a day, she'd phone the National Weather Service and supply offshore fishermen with reports on marine conditions and pending storms.

Like a new mother suddenly attuned to the faintest sound of her crying baby, Mary Cook had trained her ear to hear her call number through any amount of static: "KZJ 332. Come in, Sand Dollar, come in." She leapt into action, connecting sick deckhands with emergency room physicians, alerting crew members whose wives had gone into labor, or reassuring anxious mothers whose sons were stuck offshore longer than anticipated. She would even order flowers for Mother's Day, help make dentist appointments, or coordinate the delivery of extra cigarettes and cough medicine — the little things that help make an offshore trip a bit more pleasant. Fifteen to twenty boats, from clammers to scallopers, would be tuned to channel 4125. The whole fleet, from New Jersey to Montauk, listened in. Nothing was private.

Like Richard and Hilda Stern, when Mike and Mary Stedman married, they had an unspoken agreement. By marrying a fisherman, Mary accepted — even welcomed — their regular periods of separation. During his weeklong trips offshore, she became a single parent. The independence suited her temperament. Mary was the opposite of a needy spouse. Their time apart didn't make her bitter or angry; she possessed a prideful resourcefulness. Still, his monthlong trip to Texas was the longest he'd ever gone without seeing his family.

In late January of 1984, when Mike walked through the front door, the outside world was fast asleep, deep in hibernation. The same seemed to be true inside the house. His family had quarantined themselves beneath thick, quilted blankets. It was the first time all the Stedmans had simultaneously gotten sick. A virus accompanied by a high fever had rendered everyone unresponsive. Mary's immune system, typically impervious to the routine maladies that plague school-age children, had finally given way. The stress, the worry about her absent husband, had proved too much for her.

Mike had gone off to achieve his lifelong dream of buying his own boat and come home to celebrate with his family, only to find them barely able to lift their heads off the couch — let alone muster a congratulatory smile. Once they had recovered, Mike drove Mary out to Montauk. He was eager to show off the new lady in his life. From the second Mary saw the *Wind Blown* sitting in Montauk Harbor, she realized her husband had made a fatal miscalculation. In the clear light of day, the *Wind Blown* looked even worse than she had in the black-and-white ad.

Granted, Mary didn't know a whole lot about fishing boats. But walking alongside the boat's exterior — a shade of maroon so dark she might as well have been painted black — she asked Mike why the *Wind Blown* sat so low in the water. Nothing, it seemed, could make Mary happy. She sensed that Mike viewed her disapproval as a personal betrayal.

Though she thought the boat didn't seem sturdy enough to weather offshore conditions in the North Atlantic, Mary decided to keep her mouth shut. Money had already changed hands. For better or for worse, the paperwork had been signed. It was a done deal. The *Wind Blown* belonged to the Stedmans now.

But everyone also knew Mike was operating in the red and that after his first, hopefully lucrative season, he would make the necessary fixes. Mike wasn't reckless — he was just hustling to make a buck. "He was such a sweet, hardworking guy," Phil Berg said.

As twentysomethings, Phil Berg and Mike Stedman converged in Montauk. They had known each other since they were teenagers, when the two boys lived a few towns away.

Before Mike met Mary, he and Phil crewed together aboard the *Flying Cloud,* a party boat. By the end of the day, after helping passengers untangle their lines and fillet their catch, if Phil had made enough money to buy a steak and a six-pack of beer, he was living the good life.

In January of 1984, after the *Wind Blown* arrived in Montauk, Phil used his crane (back then, he installed cesspools) to bolt the longline drum to the roof of Mike's new boat. Mike was working his way up the ladder and finally in possession of his own vessel; Phil eagerly lent his assistance. But with space at a premium, the longline drum wouldn't fit on the rear of the *Wind Blown,* where, on most vessels, it would typically go. The roof of the wooden wheelhouse was the only available space. Despite their ingenious solution, the 2,200-pound addition (and that's without any fishing line on it) only added to the vessel's unseaworthiness.

The *Wind Blown*'s January arrival soon became the talk of the docks. Heather Hallock remembers going with her husband, Lance, to see the *Wind Blown* for the first time. When she and Lance got a closer look, Heather shook her head in disbelief: "I mean, who puts the longline on top?"

Captain Lance Hallock at docks with tilefish.

Stu Foley, who owns Air and Speed Surf Shop in Montauk, also knew Mike. The two men first met in 1976, when they worked aboard the *Viking* fleet. As commercial fishermen who also surfed, Mike and Stu became fast friends. Stu also eventually befriended Scott Clarke, a happy-go-lucky, goofy newcomer to the East End.

Like Mike and Stu, Scott had grown up closer to the city, on western Long Island. Out east, the transplanted up-islanders stuck together. Stu soon hired Scott to work aboard his lobster boat. Everyone called Scott by the nickname Oswald, but Stu couldn't remember exactly why. In 1984, when the men were lost at sea, Stu mailed any photographs he had of "Oswald" to

Scott's mother, Donna Llewellyn, who lived up-island. Rescuers had never found her son's body. It felt like the least he could do.

When Stu and I sat down together in Montauk, on a wooden bench outside his surf shop in the fall of 2017, I asked him for his honest assessment of the *Wind Blown*. Maybe ten minutes into our first and only conversation, he leveled with me: "The *Wind Blown* was a disaster. The whole boat was cockamamie. She had a plywood wheelhouse. There was an addition on the back. The boat was totally unseaworthy. We were all, like, 'Mike, if you put the *W* upside down, it would be *Mind Blown.*'"

On Tuesday, March 27, 1984, Mary woke up screaming in the middle of the night. Mike had been offshore aboard the *Wind Blown* for five days. Their three sons were fast asleep, Shane in the upstairs bedroom next to theirs, Will and Chris in their bunk beds downstairs.

Mary had dreamed she was visiting a northern European country, maybe Switzerland or Germany. It was midnight, dark and cloudless, and she stood overlooking a frozen lake. Mike was beside her, daring her to step out onto the frozen pond. Standing beneath the winter stars, he promised her an unobstructed view of the Big Dipper.

A wolf howled, emitting a bloodcurdling wail, scaring Mary into running out onto the ice. She screamed for Mike to come to her rescue. Moments later, she heard a crack: a perfect circle had formed around her feet. Down she plunged into the frigid water. She felt her lungs burst and saw a supernatural green color. An endless downward spiral.

Over the years, as a child of the sixties and seventies, Mary had done her fair share of hallucinogenic drugs. But she'd never had a dream in which she herself had died.

Mary woke up sweating, feeling her heart beating through her chest. She buried her face in the pillow next to hers — breathing in the familiar scent of her husband. The morning would arrive soon enough, filled with the comforting routine of her boys filing into the bedroom demanding breakfast, the brushing of teeth, the packing of lunches.

She eventually fell back to sleep, but the dream had unsettled her. It seemed too vivid, too real. It was the first ominous sign in a week that forever altered the course of her life.

The next day, Wednesday, felt scattered.

Mary snapped at her dentist for no reason. She felt lost driving the familiar streets of her hometown. Stopping in to buy a bottle of grape juice for Shane at Bucket's Deli, she ran into Matt Norklun, a close friend. He described to her a haunting dream he'd had in which four angels had died, and said that upon waking, Mary came immediately to mind.

As she drove home, the approaching storm had an eerie, foreboding quality. Mary made it home just before the powerful March nor'easter started making landfall. The trees shook, their spring branches still bare of leaves. An inch of snow began to accumulate. By nine o'clock that night, when the telephone rang, it felt like hurricane-force winds might uproot the house from its foundation.

The caller was Maude Vigilant, the mother of crew member Michael Vigilant.

"Have you heard from Mike yet?" Maude demanded. "Why are they still out?"

Maude started screaming and swearing at Mary. She wanted to know why the Stedmans hadn't invested in a ship-to-shore communication system. Six years earlier, Maude's husband had died in a fishing accident. It was inconceivable that her son would meet the same fate.

"I'm worried too. But I believe everything is going to be okay," Mary said. She hoped by saying it aloud, she might will it to be true.

The line went dead.

Maude had hung up on her.

Or maybe the weather was to blame.

Mary stayed awake all through Wednesday night in a state of constant prayer. At one point, she heard something in the TV room adjacent to the kitchen. She walked downstairs and saw her three children piled on top of each other like a litter of puppies, fast asleep on the couch. The front door was wide open. Rain flooded the entryway. Wet leaves covered the floor.

Mary shut and locked the door, and carried each boy back to bed.

Early Thursday morning, Kevin Maguire, the *Pontos* captain, phoned Mary with an update. He had just spoken with Mike on the two-way radio. Kevin said they expected the *Wind Blown* and her four-man crew, though badly shaken up, to pull into the docks by lunchtime.

Later that morning, after dropping her sons off at school, Mary returned home, where she picked up her copy of the *New York Times*, which had been flung across her driveway around sunrise, landing with a comforting thud. Reading the newspaper was her daily ritual. As she sipped black tea, she tried to quiet her racing, anxious mind, but her eyes couldn't focus on the headlines. A sickening taste sat wedged at the back of her throat. She needed to get out of the house.

Mary got into her Subaru station wagon and drove over to visit her childhood friend Susan Coursey. At the time, Susan was renting a place in East Hampton on Miller Lane. Susan and Mary had known each other all their lives. Susan's two daughters and Mary's three sons were like cousins.

As girls, the two women had attended the Most Holy Trinity School together, where the nuns favored Susan because of her goody-two-shoes, eager-to-please demeanor. Mary, on the other hand, had earned a reputation for being wild and rebellious. The girls proved useful foils to each other: Mary coaxed Susan out of her shell; Susan made sure that Mary's inherent distrust of authority didn't get her expelled. Both girls came from dysfunctional families whose parents had long since checked out. Their mothers didn't sip wine; they went for the harder stuff. Vodka was their drink of choice.

Once at Susan's house, Mary paced back

and forth, unable to sit still. As the storm raged, the floorboards of the house creaked like a wooden boat at sea. (Later on, Susan became the friend whom Mary relied upon in the months and years that followed, the friend who thought to send in Mike's overdue life insurance payment, the friend who made sure that grief didn't get in the way of clean laundry and home-cooked dinners. Over and over, Susan was the friend who tried to scotch-tape Mary back together again.)

Leaving Susan's house, Mary got back into her car and drove to East Hampton's Main Beach on Route 27. Hers was seemingly the only vehicle on the road. At the beach, she parked in a small lot facing the ocean and cracked open her car door. Strong winds kept slamming it shut. Through the windshield, the ocean looked gray and cold; giant, foamy swells kept crashing onto the sand, one after another. The waves didn't come in predictable sets that morning. There was no lull.

From Main Beach, Mary turned left, heading west onto Montauk Highway. Moments later, she saw a bright bolt of lightning strike a group of elm trees, across from where the Red Horse Market now stands. She closed her eyes and pressed down on the accelerator. Just east of Jericho Road, a giant branch landed with a thud across the front of her 1983 Subaru, smashing the windshield. Covered in glass shards, Mary thought she had been killed.

But where's the tunnel? Where's the light? Where are the angels? Mary wondered. A lifelong, devout Catholic, she thought she'd not only died but was also going straight to hell. Her immediate thought was of Shane. She breathed a sigh of relief when she turned around and saw that his car seat, covered in broken glass, was empty. If Shane had been in the car, he would have been seriously injured, or worse.

A few minutes later, an ambulance arrived, and paramedics safely extracted Mary from the car. For the next hour, East Hampton Village's police chief, Glen Stonemetz, held Mary's hand. "It was close, very close," he said. Staring at the dented hood and cracked windshield, he tried to reassure her, repeating over and over: "We can fix cars, but we can't fix people."

They sat in his squad car, watching as firemen in black foul-weather gear used chainsaws to dismantle the giant elm tree, which blocked both lanes of Montauk Highway. The volunteer firemen reminded Mary of her fisherman husband, of how during the

Mary Stedman's injured Subaru.

cold months he and the others would layer long underwear, which buttoned up the front, beneath wool sweaters and chest-high yellow and orange Grundéns waterproof fishing bibs, held in place by suspenders.

Mary kept flashing back to Mike standing in his wooden wheelhouse, holding steady under pressure. She knew about their survival suits. But her husband needed more than a thick layer of inflatable black neoprene if he was going to survive this storm. What Mike needed was a miracle.

Chief Stonemetz drove Mary to her aunt Peggy's house on nearby Dayton Lane Extension. A few minutes later, Mary's mother, Cletus, stormed through the front door.

"Mary, the boat is missing. The boat is missing. Mike's boat is missing!" Cletus screamed, again and again.

"Get some Valium, Peggy," Cletus yelled to her sister. "Find the brandy."

Although another week and a half would go by before they knew for sure, it was at that exact moment that Mary's powerful intuition took over.

Despite the chaos surrounding her, she didn't panic.

She knew her husband wasn't just missing. The ten-day search that followed was a fool's errand.

She knew that Mike was already dead.

The East Hampton Star *on Main Street*

3.

THE BACKSTORY

The beginnings of this book started taking shape five years ago, during the winter of 2016. At the time, I was working as a staff reporter at the *East Hampton Star*. Needless to say, it's been a tough century for print journalism. Since 2005, some two thousand small towns across America have lost their local newspapers. Located on the easternmost tip of Long Island, the *Star* is one of the last remaining small, family-owned newspapers in the country.

For me, the East End wasn't home. Or not yet, anyway.

As New York City residents, my husband and I were trying out life on the East End — some sort of cross between city people and year-round residents. *Interloper* is probably a more accurate description.

A little more than a year into our courtship, we bought a three-bedroom house together in East Hampton. Located in

Northwest Woods, it was primarily our summer and weekend retreat. After battling long workweeks, and enduring a two-hour drive on the Long Island Expressway (when the traffic cooperated), my husband and I would arrive at the house late on Friday evening.

Most weekends, I ran a circular, three-mile course that looped through the woodsy residential neighborhood. Trees outnumbered houses. Mary Stedman's home, I later discovered, was just down the road, maybe a half mile away. Unbeknownst to me, I had run past her forest-green shutters and gravel driveway more times than I could count. The great, hulking evergreen tree that sits at the corner of Mary's driveway, and which now stands taller than the house itself, I later learned, Mike had bought the Christmas before he disappeared and planted in the soil.

After graduate school, I had landed a plum position working alongside Gail Collins in the editorial department of the *New York Times.* Each columnist had his or her own researcher, and Gail graciously gave me two days each week to pursue my own stories. It was 2008 and the start of a troubled era in print journalism. The Internet had disrupted the business model, whereby newspapers relied upon a steady stream of advertising dollars and paying subscribers to stay afloat. A consulting firm deemed the *New York Times* too top-heavy. Each year, layoffs threatened to decimate the newsroom.

With a new job offer in hand, I eventually fled the comfort of the mother ship. I first worked as an editor at a now-defunct start-up magazine, and later as a reporter at the *HuffPost.* My husband, meanwhile, as a tenured professor of sociology at Columbia University, had the job security of a bygone era.

East Hampton was where we rested our weary bones before the siren song of Manhattan summoned us back to the city once more. On Sunday nights, our entire street went dark. As if on cue, our neighbors (composed almost entirely of second-home owners) packed up their station wagons and rolled back to the concrete jungle.

But having children, I soon learned, changes everything. With the birth of our son, Theo, in 2012, we began to feel that a slower-paced version of life was a better fit. We liked East Hampton so much that in January of 2013, we committed to a one-year experiment, testing out life as year-round residents. By the end of it, we figured we'd come to a decision: we'd either love it or hate it. Over the next few years, after a daughter, Violet, joined our family, we gave up our city way of life and became full-time, year-round country mice.

At a professional crossroads, I eventually went to work at the local weekly newspaper. The Rattray family has owned the *East Hampton Star* for some eighty-five years. Since its inception 135 years ago, the newspaper has had three successive owners: the Rattrays purchased the newspaper from the Boughtons, who had bought it from George Burling, its founder, in 1890 for $100, as the story goes. The *Star*'s motto, located under the masthead, reads: SHINES FOR ALL. The print edition, which costs one dollar and comes out every Thursday, is still a six-column broadsheet, despite the potential cost savings of switching to a narrower format.

Each week, the bare-bones editorial staff writes a dozen or so obituaries. David Rattray, the *Star*'s editor, ensures that each letter to the editor is printed in full (to the delight of the writer but often to the frustration of the reader). Helen Rattray, David's mother, now in her eighties, is the *Star*'s publisher. Helen is a ferocious copy editor.

She takes no prisoners — hers is the final word. Reporters who don't learn to abide by her idiosyncrasies typically seek employment elsewhere. Over the past century and counting, the *Star* has weathered the invention of the radio, movies, television — and, the most challenging of them all, the Internet.

Working at a local newspaper was something I had never done before. I had grown accustomed to the anonymity of working in New York City. At the *New York Times,* I worked on the thirteenth floor of a see-through, steel-and-glass skyscraper designed by Renzo Piano. Soaring high above Eighth Avenue, the building felt like an impenetrable fortress. An army of uniformed security guards stood watch in the lobby. Telephones were our protective shields. The caller ID on our landlines displayed 111-111-1111. While working in the editorial department, I regularly filed stories for the Metropolitan and Sunday Styles sections of the newspaper, preserved my anonymity, and largely flew under the radar.

But East Hampton in the off-season was another universe altogether. Once the summer people left, it felt like the town could breathe again. Full-time residents included families who had lived there for generations.

Everyone knew each other. But I was an outlier. Three generations of my ancestors had settled in Southern California. Despite our familiarity with the area as city transplants, my husband and I were the newest of newcomers.

Every week, I ran into the people whom I had quoted in my *Star* stories at Mary's Marvelous (a popular East Hampton coffee shop on Newtown Lane) and politely listened to their litany of likes and dislikes — what I had gotten wrong and what I had gotten right. There was no escaping them. The lack of anonymity made me a better, more careful reporter. The pattern, which repeated itself every Thursday when the paper came out, had a predictable, small-town charm.

The *East Hampton Star*'s newsroom, virtually unchanged since the turn of the 20th century, was unlike anyplace I had ever set foot. I can remember ascending its creaky wooden staircase for the first time and being stunned by the presence of laptop computers. It was like stepping inside a time machine, whisking me back to an era when journalism was considered a public service. I half expected to see typewriters still in use and reporters at their desks encircled by plumes of cigarette smoke, sipping scotch.

I soon discovered the Rolodexes were doing more than just gathering dust. Irene Silverman, the paper's editor-at-large, an incomparable line editor, has worked there since 1968. Jack Graves — a prodigious workhorse who covers local sports and writes multiple stories each week in addition to penning a weekly column — arrived around the same time as Irene and still occupies the upstairs corner office. Back when I started, Morgan McGivern worked as a staff photographer. During the weekly staff meetings, although I didn't know his backstory at the time, Morgan, with his surfboards sticking out the back of his pickup truck and a camera haphazardly slung around his neck, seemed like an idiosyncratic character plucked out of small-town newspaper central casting. I liked him right away.

In 2016, Biddle Duke joined the staff. As editor-in-chief, he had just launched a new glossy magazine called *EAST*. It was February when the two of us first collided in an office on the second floor. A few inches of fresh snowfall blanketed Main Street, where the *Star*'s building has sat, sandwiched between the East Hampton Library and the East Hampton Historical Society, for more

Morgan McGivern and Chris Stedman circa 1978.

than a century.

From our very first encounter, Biddle and I shared an easy, effortless rapport. He had grown up spending his summers in Southampton, the son of Angier Biddle Duke, the former ambassador to El Salvador, Spain, Denmark, and Morocco. During the Kennedy and Johnson administrations, the elder Duke served as chief of protocol. In his midfifties, Biddle had a boyish charm that belied his age. Tall and good-looking, he couldn't help but catch your eye.

Our talk soon turned to story ideas. It was a casual conversation between two journalists first becoming acquainted. Just like the relationship between a journalist and a source, trust undergirds the relationship between an editor and a reporter. Though it was unspoken, Biddle and I were sizing each other up. His arrival and the launch of *EAST* coincided with my frustration with weekly newspaper deadlines and stories that merely skimmed the surface. Each week, just as things were getting interesting, it was time to file another story and move on. There were never enough inches. I longed for meatier, more time-consuming assignments.

During maybe our second meeting, Biddle casually mentioned what he described as "one of the great untold stories of the Hamptons." Something about tilefish and 1984 and a fishing boat, the name of which he couldn't immediately recall. The cadence of his voice started to shift. His pale-blue eyes widened. Time seemed to slow down.

It soon became clear to me that this was more than just a passing story. Something had clearly struck a nerve in him.

"But why don't *you* want to write it?" I asked, genuinely curious to hear his response.

"I'm way too close to the story," Biddle said, explaining that the social aspect was too messy for an insider to navigate. His wife, Idoline Scheerer Duke, had grown up as an East Hampton summer kid alongside Dave Connick. The potential for personal fallout was all but guaranteed. It was best in all respects — for his marriage, his reputation, his surfing buddies — that Biddle stay away.

"You should talk to Mary," Biddle said.

He was, of course, referring to the captain's widow. As Biddle kept talking about Mary, I grew intrigued. I wanted to learn more. Little did I know that I would spend the next few years of my life trying to understand Mary's many contradictions.

When taking on complicated stories, journalists look for a way in. Generally speaking, one source leads to another. The story needed Mary's blessing (at least) and her participation (at best) — and ideally some combination of the two.

Biddle eventually sent an e-mail to Mary. The two had overlapped decades before at the *Southampton Press,* he as a reporter, she as a photographer. In the e-mail, Biddle vouched for my credibility. Mary responded quickly. Her tone was cordial, but the timing wasn't right. And for that summer, other stories and other assignments occupied my time.

That August, my husband, newly enamored of Silicon Valley, took a two-year sabbatical from his position at Columbia, and we moved to Northern California to test the waters on the West Coast. But even from 3,500 miles away, I couldn't quite let go of something about the story of those four lost boys.

The East End of Long Island had captured my heart. The shifting, magnificent light. The wide expanse of sea and sky. Out east feels as close to God's country as anyplace I've encountered. Looking back, I realize my inability to relinquish the story was also about my fondness for the place — a place I missed and to which I dearly hoped to return.

Decades ago, the East End was a largely blue-collar community from October to May. For summer kids, as Biddle Duke and Dave Connick had been, it was acceptable to fall in love with the place; but it was another, altogether rarer thing to call it home for twelve months out of the year. Back in the eighties, surfing was a locals-only pastime. Until surf schools started sprouting up on the South Fork, the surfers were all local working people — fishermen, plumbers, carpenters, teachers, and such. If you surfed, and you really took to it, your fellow surfers became your tribe.

In 1987, Biddle first crossed paths with Alice Connick. It was three years after her son, whom she called Davey, had died aboard the *Wind Blown*.

At the time, Biddle had just started dating Idoline Scheerer. The four Scheerer siblings had grown up alongside the two Connick brothers. Both families were Maidstone Club members. Idoline, the youngest daughter, was a catch. Everyone, Alice most especially, knew it.

Alice had dropped by the Scheerer place, one of the original shingled summer cottages located in the dunes near Georgica Beach. To readers unfamiliar with the astounding cost of East End beachfront real estate, "summer cottage" is a bit of a misnomer. In 2021 dollars, the cottage would fetch a pretty penny: $15 to $20 million.

Back in 1987, Biddle was living in Southampton year-round and, like Alice's dead son, had earned a reputation as a surfer with a bit of a rebellious streak.

Alice had a discerning eye. She sized up Biddle, looking him up and down. "What do you do?" she asked him.

"I'm a reporter for the *Southampton Press*," he responded.

"You won't make any money that way," Alice snapped back.

In that moment, Biddle felt the acuteness of Davey's pain. Alice's words cut deep. Biddle remembered thinking that Davey must have been similarly belittled by his mother for his choice to become a commercial fisherman, and not once, but *many times.* Davey's response had been to run as fast as he possibly could in the opposite direction — *out to sea.*

Biddle's passion for the story notwithstanding, I needed to find my own way in. I was four years old in March of 1984, when the *Wind Blown* went down off the coast of Montauk. I grew up in a suburb of Los Angeles, about as far away from the eastern end of Long Island as you can get on the mainland of the United States. I was an outsider if ever there was one. And my outsider status allowed me to approach the story with fresh eyes, beholden to no one's version of what had transpired but my own.

Nine months after moving to Northern California, in the spring of 2017, I struck up a casual e-mail correspondence with Mary. I figured it was worth one last shot.

On May 1, 2017, in an e-mail titled "Interview Request," I wrote:

Hi Mary,
I hope your spring is off to a lovely start.
I wanted to touch base with you and see if you might have time for a quick phone call. Maybe later this week or early next? Kindly let me know when you can. Looking most forward!

Amanda

When it comes to reporting, the phone is useful for many things, but there's no replacement for sitting down in the same room with someone and making eye contact. If Mary was going to trust me to tell her story, she first needed to size me up. My family had planned a two-week visit to Sag Harbor that summer, and I asked if she'd like to meet when I was back in town.

We agreed to get together in the basement of the East Hampton Library on Main Street. It seemed as quiet and private a place as any to talk. At first, Mary was difficult to pin down. I worried she might cancel. But we finally met up on a Sunday afternoon in late July of 2017. I've always been fascinated by complicated women, and quickly fell under her spell. There was an

118

immediate depth to her, a palpable warmth. Mary was a talker. We spoke, uninterrupted, for nearly three hours.

Over the coming months, I spoke with her for dozens more hours and accumulated tens of thousands of interview notes. I soon learned to allocate at least two- to three-hour chunks of time whenever I phoned Mary. She and I talked about our respective marriages, astrology, witchcraft, and our shared affinity for New Age spirituality and Eastern religions. One Christmas, she even sent me a present.

As I dove deeper into the story — a story that time had nearly buried — I discovered I had been right to follow my intuition. This wasn't simply a narrative about a fishing boat that had gone down in 1984. It was a look at the improbable way in which these four men's lives collided aboard the *Wind Blown,* and at the survivors who were left behind. And there was the unspoken sense that complicated bonds between fathers and sons lay at the center of this whole, meaty thing. The foursome aboard the *Wind Blown* were part of a long, noble lineage of men who had gone to sea to battle the elements, a primal struggle of man versus nature. No matter their divergent social classes, the four men had more in common than they likely ever knew. Besides a love of fishing and a search for identity, all had complicated relationships with their fathers — whether their fathers were alcoholics, absent, distant, or dead.

More compelling still, I wanted to understand how tragedies become imprinted in our memories, how trauma and grief wend their way through generations and become a kind of inheritance bequeathed to our descendants. And why had this particular tragedy lodged itself in the psyche of the local townspeople, dozens of whom, well into the twenty-first century, recalled to me the exact date that the *Wind Blown* went down?

In October of 2017, I left my family behind in California and took a reporting trip to gather material.

I met Mary in East Hampton for lunch at a restaurant that has since shuttered. I went porgy fishing at five o'clock in the morning, the only woman alongside day-tripping fishermen aboard one of the *Viking* boats. It took some convincing that my incessant questions weren't the province of a federal agent looking to bust their chops but of a journalist who had never been on a fishing boat before.

The next day, accompanied by an old

friend, I toured the Montauk Lighthouse and visited the Lost at Sea Memorial.

I stayed nearby in a one-room cottage on Old Montauk Highway, about two miles from downtown. A two-lane highway separated the cottage from the ocean. On my last morning, with a return flight to San Francisco booked later that afternoon, I decided to go for one final swim.

It was an unseasonably warm, early fall day. I crossed the highway where the asphalt walking path led to a narrow dirt road. On one of the trees, a sign read: CAUTION PROCEED AT YOUR OWN RISK. A few hundred feet below, the ocean appeared. Maybe fifty steps down the winding staircase, I stood on the sand and took off my running shoes, disrobed, and set a white bath towel down next to my belongings. I walked into the ocean, held my breath, and quickly submerged myself. I swam fifty feet out and back again. Maybe five minutes later, I came out of the water and started drying off.

Sitting right next to my towel was a large clamshell, a little larger than the palm of my hand. Written inside the shell in blue, red, and pink crayon was an inscription: FOREVER IN OUR HEARTS. On the exterior of the shell, someone had drawn what appeared to be a sunset, with overlapping

Clamshell found on sand in Montauk.

colors of light blue, dark blue, yellow, and orange.

I looked around, wondering if someone had jokingly placed the shell near my towel. But the beach was empty. Only a few seagulls stood watch.

Returning to the cottage, I tucked the shell into my suitcase for safekeeping. Once I made it home to California, I mentioned it to Mary when I resumed my conversations with her. She believed the shell's placement was a clear sign — as if the spirits, the ghosts of the men who'd died aboard the *Wind Blown* (if you believe in that sort of thing, as Mary and I do), had granted me their permission to share their story with the world.

"Invoke all ocean spirits," Mary told me. "Ask for blessings from the angels."

I dug into the details in the obsessive-compulsive way of an investigative journalist hot on the trail of a great story. It had ignited a degree of curiosity that soon consumed me. I attacked the story from all possible angles, paying little mind to how I would weave all the elements together later on. I became entwined in its many threads, which spun out in more directions than I could possibly have predicted. I asked questions that made people feel uncomfortable at best and enraged at worst. More than a few sources hung up the phone on me; many never returned my calls.

"Has Mary told you the secret yet?" Chris Stedman asked me pointblank, during one of our first telephone conversations in the spring of 2018. Chris and his two brothers called Kauai, one of the Hawaiian Islands, home. The following month I had planned a reporting trip to finally meet them face-to-face.

My mind raced back to the many personal matters Mary had divulged to me. Little things that accumulate over the course of an ordinary life. Some of which she told me off the record, and these, I assured her, would have no place in my manuscript.

"I don't think so," I responded. It seemed there was something bigger I hadn't yet discovered. I was reminded of the way certain sources had politely tiptoed around my questions or refused to return my calls. My heart started to race.

The revelation that Chris shared with me altered the landscape of the story. More skeletons, from different families, soon spilled forth. And they deepened my understanding — both of the young men lost at sea and their survivors.

Over the coming months, Mary became increasingly upset. She had lost control of the story. She eventually stopped speaking with me. Meanwhile, another source, involved in one of my new lines of inquiry, threatened a lawsuit. And both of Chris's brothers, Will and Shane, decided not to speak to me.

As a journalist, I had been clear from the outset about my intentions. I sought to tell the full story, not the fairy-tale version, of what had happened. Not an easy or always pleasant task. Collateral damage and frayed boundaries are almost guaranteed outcomes.

Most people reveal themselves in layers — calculated little bits at a time. But even after dozens of hours of interviewing Mary, who was as discerning a source as I had ever encountered, I always came away with the exact same feeling. No matter how deep we went (and her photographic memory seemingly knew no bounds), I always felt like I was only ever scratching the surface.

She reminded me a little of Edie Sedgwick, whom Jean Stein described in her captivating biography of the model and Warhol muse: "Edie was very elusive . . . trying hard not to let anybody ever get close to her in any real sense; she would throw up these giant clouds of camouflage." Like Edie, Mary had a chameleonlike quality. She seemed a master at emotional compartmentalization. *Who,* I began to wonder, *had Mary ever really let in?*

Over time, I've come to believe that Mary would have refused to cooperate if some part of her didn't want the essential elements of the story to eventually come out. Why else do you welcome a journalist into your life?

■ ■ ■ ■

PART TWO:
DAVE CONNICK

■ ■ ■ ■

Dave Connick surfing at Egypt Beach.

4.
THE SUMMER PEOPLE

"They are here for the weekend. You are here for life," Mary Cavagnaro would tell herself as a young girl coming of age in East Hampton. At first, it was a helpful reminder, albeit one she couldn't help but flout. The boundary between the locals and the summer people was one Mary eventually learned the hard way not to cross. She had an untamed quality about her. In her mind, it was better to beg for forgiveness than ask permission. Or more fun, anyway.

The summer people occupied an altogether different stratum. They drove fancier cars, wore more expensive clothing, and seemed to breathe more rarefied air. Once Labor Day came and went, the summer people left the South Fork and returned home to the city, where second lives welcomed them back into the fray. When September rolled around, it was almost as if they had never left the familiar constraints of the Upper East Side.

For a century now and counting, the summer people have had a unique relationship to the community of year-round families who call the South Fork — in all of her seasons — home.

Dave Connick should never have been on the *Wind Blown*. He was born into a family whose wealth had afforded him the privilege of choice, and grew up spending his summers at the Maidstone Club in East Hampton. (Maidstone was the original name of East Hampton, after the town in Kent, England, where the town's first settlers originated centuries ago. The club that carries its name boasts five hundred members, most of whom are second- and third-generation legacies, descendants of some of East Hampton's oldest and wealthiest families.)

With its starched tablecloths, formal dress code, and private cabanas, the Maidstone Club, designed by architect Roger Bullard, is about as far from the Montauk docks as you can get. Commercial fishermen occupied a separate underclass altogether. The two worlds never mixed.

The Connicks are multigenerational summer people. Their family's seasonal lineage stretches back nearly a hundred years. The tradition started when Dave's grandfather, Louis Connick, a partner at the New York City law firm Simpson, Thacher & Bartlett, became a member of the Maidstone Club in the 1930s. The Connicks were one of the first Irish Catholic families deemed worthy of acceptance. Well into the twentieth century, the Maidstone Club, founded in 1891, didn't admit Blacks or Jews. Even by modern standards, it's far from a melting pot. Racial and economic segregation is still alive and well within its walls.

A front-page story from September 5, 1940, in the *East Hampton Star* described a six-hundred-person gala that had recently taken place at the Maidstone — at the time, the largest event in the private club's history. The festive end-of-summer party had a South American cruise theme; its members played the role of seagoing passengers. Some attendees wore sequined costumes. Mrs. Louis Connick, Dave's grandmother, dressed up as a Puritan. The following year, on July 17, 1941, the *New York Times* ran a story titled "Parties Planned at East Hampton" on page sixteen of the society section. Beneath the headline, bold letters announced that Mrs. Louis Connick would chair an upcoming summer benefit. On the same page, readers were brought up to speed on new styles of hats, hairstyles, social activities, engagements, and nuptials.

The 1980s were an undeniable turning point on the South Fork, a resort destination since the early twentieth century, and one where the Maidstone Club occupies acres of prime oceanfront real estate. The eighties were a boom time. City slickers with gigantic Wall Street bonuses arrived with checkbooks in hand and bought up land that had once belonged to resourceful farmer-fishermen. By the twenty-first century, a new type of conspicuous consumption emerged. Self-made billionaires started tearing down modest single-family homes and replacing them with ten-thousand-square-foot McMansions. The current price of real estate is such that many locals can no longer afford to buy homes in the bucolic beachfront towns where they grew up.

But the foursome aboard the *Wind Blown* never witnessed Black Monday or the stock market crash of 1987, let alone the invention of the World Wide Web. Years before their time, they sensed the inherent emptiness of the "greed is good" mantra that swallowed a generation whole. They headed it off at the pass.

There's a hilarious essay about the Maidstone Club that Peter de Jonge wrote in 2005 for *New York* magazine. Titled "Barbarian at the Tee," it chronicled de Jonge's attempt to golf at the Maidstone's eighteen-hole private course, despite being neither a member nor accompanied by one.

"Even if my outrage at Maidstone's archaic membership policies is a bit forced, there's something gratifying about mocking an institution that derives such satisfaction from its exclusivity and whose labyrinthine admissions process is designed to exclude bad eggs like me," de Jonge wrote.

Public and private golf courses are worlds apart. Since I'm not a golfer, let's rely on de Jonge's description to explain the difference: "The dirt on a public tee is hard and baked, and what little grass still clings to it is sprinkled with busted tees and cigarette butts. A Maidstone tee looks like a just-vacuumed Persian carpet; the spongy turf is so moist that inserting a tee is a tender, consensual act."

During de Jonge's hours-long round, though he had prepared himself for his forceful removal, he encountered no such thing. Civility, in the form of polite waves and respectful nods, reigned supreme. His daring reportorial stunt revealed a startling truth: "As long as you're willing and able to keep your bilious thoughts to yourself and arrive in the right clothes, just about any white person can pass as a member of the privileged class. Maybe that willingness and ability to pass is all wealth is."

On January 1, 2020, I paid a visit to the Maidstone Club. Morgan McGivern had graciously extended an invitation to join him for New Year's Day brunch. Walking me through the property, Morgan explained that his maternal grandmother formerly owned the dark-brown, thatched-roof, Elizabethan-style house across the street from the club. The twenty-room residence on Old Beach Lane, which sits atop a steep pitch of sand, has since changed hands; heirs to the Johnson & Johnson fortune now own it.

During our New Year's Day brunch, not one person of color, besides the Jamaican waitstaff, was present. Once we had ascended the staircase and taken our seats in the dining room at a table with a placard labeled MCGIVERN, it felt like Morgan and I had unwittingly boarded a festive cruise ship, still decorated in red and green for the Christmas holiday. Sitting high above the dunes and beachfront, we were afforded a wide, sweeping vista: a breathtaking expanse of ocean, from east to west, as far as your eye could see. As we left, the staff bid him farewell with a polite nod. A check never materialized.

We collected our coats and went outside for a brisk walk. The McGiverns have a cabana adjacent to the kiddie pool and the saltwater swimming pool, covered in a forest-green tarp for the wintertime. Past the dunes, where a sandy walkway leads directly to the ocean, a lifeguard will sit, like an eagle-eyed headmaster chaperoning a middle school dance, come Memorial Day. A few yards away, we passed a cabana whose black-and-white placard read A. J. CONNICK — Dave's father. Two doors down from the Connicks' cabana, I stumbled across another familiar surname: A. D. DUKE — Biddle's late uncle, Tony, who founded the Boys & Girls Harbor, a local summer camp that served more than fifty thousand disenfranchised children. One summer when Morgan was fourteen, Tony Duke asked him to paint the inside of his cabana the darkest shade of blue imaginable. Morgan happily pocketed $250.

First built in the 1920s, the white wooden cabanas that surround the pool and beachfront are a rare commodity. Despite their rustic, simple charm, each one costs around $15,000 a year to maintain. The 100-

square-foot spaces offer little more than a private enclosure in which to use the restroom, apply a coat of sunscreen, and rinse off the sand, but they change hands with remarkable infrequency. Having one at your disposal is an undeniable, albeit unspoken, status symbol. Especially among the new-money set, a beachfront cabana is a sign of having arrived. Maybe one or two beach-front cabanas become available each year — and that's only after someone dies or a couple divorces.

Mary Anne Miller, who grew up in East Hampton, spent her summers at the Maidstone Club. The Miller family settled in East Hampton around 1650; her father is a tenth-generation Miller. In the 1920s, her maternal and paternal grandmothers arrived on the East End from Ireland. As young women, both worked as housekeepers for wealthy summer families not unlike the Connicks.

But the Millers weren't Maidstone members. They were the hired help. During high school, Mary Anne, now in her fifties, and her three brothers all got summer jobs at the Maidstone Club. Though Mary Anne officially got her working papers at fourteen, she was already a known, trusted commodity among Maidstone families; since the age of twelve, she had babysat their children. During the day, Mary Anne tended the snack bar, dispensing hot dogs, cheeseburgers, grilled cheese with sliced tomatoes, and the world's most perfect tuna-salad sandwich, while her brothers worked as lifeguards and beach attendants.

Mary Anne watched, transfixed, as the wives paraded past the snack bar, decorated in the club's official colors of blue and yellow. The women took seats at one of the navy-blue tables flanked by daffodil-yellow wooden chairs; blue and yellow umbrellas shielded pale-skinned lunch patrons from the sun. Each woman wore a version of the same uniform: a Lilly Pulitzer sleeveless sundress with sandals and a small handbag. Everyone was a size zero. For lunch, the women ordered salads with a glass of Tab — a popular diet soda — over ice. If you were wearing your mother's floral Lilly Pulitzer dress, passed down from one generation to the next, it was but another indication of your superior position in the preppy hierarchy. Wealthy WASPs love nothing more than overt displays of frugality.

Once the lunch tables had been cleared, Mary Anne steadied herself for what came next.

"Oh my God, there he is," she would mutter to herself. Dave Connick's afternoon arrival felt like a jolt of electricity coursing through her body. Though they were roughly the same age, Mary Anne's lowly position in the social hierarchy rendered her invisible. Dave always wore the same uniform: bright-orange Birdwell Beach Britches (a type of nylon board short with a lace-up closure), brown-leather flip-flops, and a Sex Wax T-shirt. Every July and August, Mary Anne watched as, like clockwork, Dave's chestnut-brown hair turned a subtle, reddish hue. Super tan, skinny, and ripped, he was difficult to miss. Sometimes he'd show up after a long day of surfing still wearing his O'Neill wetsuit, which left little to the imagination. Dave was the polar opposite of his brother, Pete, who had a mop of curly blond hair and who, like his mother, Alice, pranced around the club in head-to-toe tennis whites.

Dave and his crew generally showed up late in the afternoon. They were too cool for school. He and his pack of friends made themselves right at home at the bar, which overlooked the swimming pool. When the teenagers ordered a Southside, the Maidstone's official drink, the bartender never carded them. Described by *Town and Country* magazine as the "summer drink of the country club set," the Southside is synonymous with the Maidstone Club. Using a base of gin (though rum or vodka can be substituted in a pinch), the bartender combined mint simple syrup, mint leaves, the juice of one lemon, and a splash of soda. The lemony, minty, fizzy concoction tasted like summertime in a glass. Club rules dictated that money never changed hands. The teenagers simply signed their last names on the tickets. At summer's end, their parents paid all outstanding balances in one lump sum.

Once evening came, Dave and his crew decamped. They had better, more interesting places to be. Their parents, meanwhile, headed home to shower and shave. Couples often met up at each other's homes for cocktail hour. The Maidstone's dining room, where groups might sit six or ten to a table, was next on the itinerary. Club members abided by its strict dress code. In the dining room, jeans were forbidden and jackets were required. Even if you wanted to grab fries and a Coca-Cola from the snack bar, you had to put on shoes and a cover-up. At the Maidstone, the Connicks would socialize with the other Irish Catholic families who similarly split their time between the city and the country: the

Mahoneys, the McGiverns, and the Raymonds, among others. Within their social circle, most of the men had served in the Second World War and, thanks to the GI Bill, had gotten their shot at the good life with degrees from Harvard, Princeton, or Yale. By contrast, most of the other Maidstone members were white, elite, East Coast WASPs. Homosexuals and people of color were personae non gratae.

The real fun began in the evening, for both the staff and the club members. Mary Anne and her brothers changed out of their casual daytime uniforms and into more formal attire to wait tables. The young staff took particular delight in watching the wives enter the dining room like peacocks with their tail feathers on display. Since the afternoon, they had all dialed up the glamour, wearing the latest Pucci prints and diamond rings the size of ice-skating rinks. Their husbands, meanwhile, sported a different sort of summer uniform: madras pants, tasseled loafers, and pastel sport coats. Other couples might grab dinner in the more casual, wood-paneled Tap Room.

During my visit to the Maidstone, Morgan pointed out two black-and-white framed photographs of the Connicks hanging in the club library. In one photo, Dave and Pete's parents, Alice and Peter Connick, stood among a group of members to perform a rendition of "Maidstone's My Silver Lining," in celebration of the club's seventy-fifth anniversary. The year would have been 1966. The women wore ball gowns; the men wore tuxedos. Alice and Pete were a sharp-looking pair. That night, they looked especially radiant.

Names are curious things. And the one belonging to Andrew Jackson Connick, Dave's father, contains multitudes. The story goes that Andrew was named after his paternal grandfather. When the elder Andrew Connick emigrated from Ireland to the United States, he randomly inserted Jackson in between his first and last names. Everyone in America had a middle name; assimilation was the name of the game.

Dave's father, Andrew, was the second and final son of Louis Connick and Mary McGuire. Shortly after Andrew was born, Louis pleaded with Mary to name him after Louis's father, Andrew Jackson Connick. Mary agreed to name her son Andrew, albeit on one specific condition: *her son would only go by the name of Pete.* Apparently her father-in-law was quite a tyrant. So every Sunday, when the extended Connick clan met for lunch, Pete went by Andrew. But for the rest of the week — and for the rest of his life — Andrew was known as Pete. Or AJC, for short.

Later on, after naming his own eldest son Peter, AJC happily adopted the nickname of Big Pete. The family tradition didn't stop there. Little Pete, Dave's brother, eventually married and had two sons of his own: Andrew McGuire Connick and James David Connick.

In East Hampton, the Connick family started out as summer renters. Beginning in the 1930s, Louis and Mary drove out east from the city every Memorial Day weekend. They'd book a hotel room on Main Street at the Maidstone Arms, which is now the Maidstone Hotel. The couple and their four children relished the annual, frenzied ritual — figuring out which house they'd occupy until summer's end.

The Great Depression had left an indelible mark on all Americans. Even though Louis Connick was a successful Park Avenue attorney, he was reluctant to mortgage his life savings on a country house. It seemed a frivolous, unnecessary expense. Money had a quicksilver quality, and Louis had learned that the future was impossible to predict. Despite his success, he never knew what the coming year might bring.

At the start of every summer, an "annual cottage list" used to run in the *East Hampton Star*. Some years (presumably during slow news weeks), the list appeared above the fold, splashed across the newspaper's front page. A more civilized precursor to Airbnb, the house-renting website, the *Star*'s alphabetical list provided names of lessees and owners of various East Hampton properties. Presumably to avoid any confusion, it also listed the names of people who planned on occupying their own homes for the duration of the summer. In May of 1927, Louis Connick rented a house from a "Miss Marie S. Heiser" on Lily Pond Lane.

Once Louis died (in a rental home he and Mary were occupying on Dunemere Road, just down the street from the McGiverns), his wife decided she'd had quite enough of moving houses every summer. Shortly thereafter, she purchased an eight-bedroom summer house on The Crossways. The location couldn't be beat. East Hampton's Main Beach was but a five-minute bike ride away.

This was back when potato fields blanketed much of the South Fork, and decades before Goldman Sachs money transformed Sagg Pond in Sagaponack into Goldman Pond. Those who own or rent homes south of the highway today generally fall into two categories: new money and old money. The Connicks were old money, south-of-the-highway people. Dave's father, Big Pete Connick, grew up on tree-lined Park Avenue and attended Phillips Academy Andover in Massachusetts. Like his own father, Louis Connick, Pete went to Yale University, where he joined Skull and Bones, a secret society formed in 1832 that remained fully male until 1992. Upon graduating from Yale Law School, Pete rose through the ranks at Milbank, Tweed, Hadley & McCloy, a Manhattan law firm — eventually becoming partner.

The youngest of four children, Big Pete spent every summer of his eighty years on the South Fork. East Hampton was where he learned to bodysurf and played endless rounds of golf and tennis. Once he became a father, it was where Pete shared with his two sons the same annual rituals that had defined his own boyhood. At the Maidstone Club, sitting beneath a bright-blue beach umbrella, Big Pete watched as his younger son, Dave, took to the water like no Connick had before him. It was plain to see that, unlike his grandfather and his father, Dave wasn't going to become a corporate lawyer. Dave was a waterman. It was written in the waves.

"Then the gunning season was over, and the long quiet winter set in. Even those city people who came out from New York for Thanksgiving or Christmas were gone until late spring; Main Street was empty," Peter Matthiessen wrote in *Men's Lives: The Surfmen and Baymen of the South Fork*. "To the local people, all of us were 'people from away,' the forerunners of many still to come." The book's title comes from the famous Sir Walter Scott quote: "It's no fish ye're buyin, it's men's lives."

Published in 1986, Matthiessen's beautiful book includes a brief mention of the *Wind Blown*. "In early spring I had visited Bill Lester, who shook his head over the loss of four draggermen in the wild storm of March 29 that had raised winds up to eighty miles an hour and oceans thirty feet in height," Matthiessen wrote in the penultimate chapter. "The whole community had responded to the tragedy."

Matthiessen, too, had started out as a summer person. As a Manhattan transplant who worked for a time as a commercial fisherman, he described the eastern end of Long Island as a land of plenty — back when its robust sea life revealed little in the way of natural limits. Matthiessen grew up in a Fifth Avenue apartment overlooking Central Park. The Plimptons lived in the same building; they had a son named George who was born the exact same year as Peter.

The Upper East Side was home. The two boys attended St. Bernard's School, an all-male prep school on East Ninety-Eighth Street. After graduating from Yale in 1950, Matthiessen worked as an undercover agent for the Central Intelligence Agency based in Europe. While living abroad, Matthiessen founded the *Paris Review* in 1953, alongside Harold "Doc" Humes and Thomas Guinzburg. The men soon hired George Plimpton to take over as editor.

Before returning stateside, Matthiessen resigned from his CIA post. His next stop: the East End. By the mid-1950s, he had moved to Springs, and later to Sagaponack, where he studied Zen Buddhism, and became a Zen priest — writing some thirty books (a mixture of fiction and non-fiction) all the while. Although he was technically an outsider, Matthiessen's naturalist sensibility and quiet charisma were such that many year-round residents embraced him as a native son.

Like Matthiessen, both Connick brothers attended St. Bernard's. It was familiar territory for the Connick family: their father, Pete, had also gone there before attending Phillips Academy. In 2021, St. Bernard's will celebrate its 117-year anniversary. Tuition now runs $50,000 a year. Unlike some of its glitzier, tech-savvy competitors who teach coding and Mandarin, St. Bernard's culture and curriculum remain unchanged: blue blazers and penmanship, mandatory French and Latin. By the time its alumni — dubbed Old Boys — enroll at some of the best boarding and day schools money can buy, they will have mastered (after practicing several hundred times) the skill of a firm, solid handshake. Starting as early as kindergarten, these soon-to-be Old Boys are being fast-tracked to someday rule the world.

At St. Bernard's, around the age of seven or eight, Dave Connick and Andrew Greenebaum took an instant liking to each other. Partway through first grade, the boys became inseparable. Dave grew up at the corner of Eighty-Second Street and Lexington Avenue, Andrew at the corner of Eighty-First Street and Park Avenue — so close they could visit each other's apartments without crossing the street.

By third or fourth grade, Dave and Andrew had already established reputations for being troublemakers, good athletes, and decent-enough students. Their older brothers, Pete and Jimmy, were also best friends — and still are, to this day. From time to time, their parents also socialized. Andrew distinctly remembers when Alice Connick met his mother for the first time. Mrs. Connick told Mrs. Greenebaum she was the first Jewish woman she had ever met. Like most of the boys at St. Bernard's, Andrew came from good stock. Andrew's grandfather, Leon Greenebaum, was the chairman and CEO of Hertz, the rental car company. At St. Bernard's, Andrew was one of three Jews. At thirteen, Dave attended Andrew's bar mitzvah at Temple Israel, located on Seventy-Fifth Street between Park and Lexington Avenues. Fascinated with Judaism, Alice came along to hear Andrew chant the ancient tones of the Hebrew Bible.

Their wiseass, prankster fathers took a particular liking to each other. "Both fathers liked to drink like fishes," Andrew explained. It was the *Mad Men* era, and Andrew rarely saw Big Pete without a cocktail in hand. But Dave's father held his liquor well; Andrew never saw Big Pete drunk.

Every May, Andrew's parents allowed him

to bring a few friends to New Jersey, where the Greenebaum family had a weekend house, to celebrate his birthday. The boys squeezed into the backseat of the Greenebaums' Cadillac. They spent the weekend going bowling and playing softball. And then, around fourth or fifth grade, Andrew started accompanying Dave to his family's house in East Hampton on The Crossways.

At the Maidstone Club, Andrew became self-conscious about his darker features. Most of the kids had blue eyes and white-blond hair. Jews constituted "zero-point-zero percent," as Andrew noted. Despite his outsider status, he was excited to play a game of tennis on one of the Maidstone's pristine grass courts. At his family's country club in New Jersey, Andrew played on clay courts. Grass courts, which require constant maintenance, were a novelty. Even the tennis balls were a different color. When he swung his wooden Wilson racquet at the Maidstone, the white tennis balls bounced lower and faster.

Andrew sent me a black-and-white photograph from 1972 of nearly two dozen fourth-grade boys standing at the entrance to St. Bernard's. Dave Connick stood at the center of the pack, wearing a crew-neck T-shirt. To his left, in a fringed jacket, was

St. Bernard's boys.

Andrew. A few of their classmates even wore ties. Unlike most Upper East Side private schools, St. Bernard's didn't require a uniform, though jackets or collared shirts were mandatory. Levi's jeans and Chuck Taylor All Star sneakers were strictly weekend attire.

When Andrew turned ten, eleven, and twelve, his parents gave him concert tickets, usually two seats together at Madison Square Garden. Andrew always gave Dave the second ticket. Together the boys saw the Rolling Stones, David Bowie, and Led Zeppelin. By fifth or sixth grade, they started skateboarding and smoking weed. "I had posters of Elton John and David Bowie. Dave had pictures of Bob Marley and Bob Dylan," Andrew said. At one point, Andrew even wore a little leather bracelet in a failed attempt to mimic Dave's effortless bohemian style. "He was always a lot cooler."

In the Connicks' palatial apartment, they played three-on-one games of pickup basketball. It was always the Connick brothers plus Andrew against Big Pete, who would have just walked in the door from work, already unbuttoning his collar and loosening his tie. The apartment had a long hallway, and Alice would yell once the housekeeper had dinner waiting on the table. Andrew recalled that when the boys were in the seventh or eighth grade, the Connicks upgraded to a "super-nice" penthouse apartment (specifically PHB) at 1060 Fifth Avenue between Eighty-Seventh and Eighty-Eighth Streets that overlooked Central Park.

One night when Andrew slept over at Dave's apartment, the boys waited until Alice and Pete had gone to bed, then mimicked their sleeping bodies by stuffing lumpy pillows beneath the navy-blue quilted comforters. They sneaked out and headed

151

over to a nearby apartment, where two girls from Spence, an all-girls Upper East Side private school, awaited their arrival. The foursome played a round or two of spin the bottle. They eventually paired off and started making out, until one girl's mother emerged from her bedroom, saw what was going on, and threatened to call everyone's parents.

In gym class, Dave possessed the cool, easy confidence of a gifted, coordinated athlete. He wasn't a great sprinter, but he could run like the wind for miles at a stretch. At St. Bernard's, the boys ran around the Central Park Reservoir, just a stone's throw from the entrance to the school. One loop of the jogging track around the reservoir is about a mile and a half. After school, the gym coach lined the boys up and timed them from start to finish. Andrew was generally dead after about two hundred yards, right around the time that Dave was just hitting his stride. For years, Dave held the school's record. No one could beat him.

By the fifth grade, Dave ran the Central Park loop in ten minutes and thirty seconds (or thereabouts). The best part was Dave's signature move. They called it the "Prefontaine Psych-Out" — named after Steve Prefontaine, the legendary Olympic long-distance runner. Once Dave started running, he never made eye contact with his classmates. Unlike his peers who constantly looked over their shoulders, eyeing the competition, Dave stared straight ahead — laser-focused on crossing the finish line first.

Dave was an expert at evading punishment, but in time, both Andrew and Dave were suspended for relatively minor infractions. During an eighth-grade camping trip, when boys from St. Bernard's accompanied girls from Nightingale-Bamford, another Upper East Side private school, teachers caught Andrew with tightly rolled joints. Nine in the class of twenty-eight boys were barred from participating in the graduation ceremony.

By the fall of 1976, both boys were fourteen and headed off to New England boarding schools — Andrew to St. Paul's School in Concord, New Hampshire; Dave to Choate-Rosemary Hall in Wallingford, Connecticut. Boarding school marked the beginning of their separation. Socially, the boys had started heading in different directions. Dave increasingly spent a good deal of his free time in East Hampton, where he fell in with a group of surfers. "Dave started out like Mick Jagger and became more like

Keith Richards — and it happened pretty quickly," Andrew recalled. The two friends eventually lost touch altogether. "I can run hot. Dave ran wild. And neither one of us was going to back down."

From the age of about fifteen on, Andrew estimated that he and Dave crossed paths three to five times altogether. They never drove in a car together, with one of them behind the wheel. They never sat in a bar together. They weren't old enough.

"He was too cool, and I was too nerdy," Andrew said. He had his sights set on attending Dartmouth College, where his father and grandfather had both gone. Dave, meanwhile, had little interest in college. He figured there had to be more to life. The Ivy League, even if he could weasel his way in, felt like a claustrophobic, robotic training ground. Unlike many of his peers, who were being groomed for high-powered careers on Wall Street, nothing interested him less than stocks, bonds, and commodities. Whether slide-tackling during a soccer game or hanging from a jungle gym by one foot or climbing a tree so high it seemed impossible he'd ever make it back down in one piece, Dave was an adrenaline junkie. Unlike the more mild-mannered Andrew, Dave quickly lost interest in anything that

Dave taking flight.

didn't make his heart race. He never jettisoned Andrew; there was never a big, dramatic falling-out. As he grew older, Dave simply chose to surround himself with friends who, whether skateboarders or surfers or commercial fishermen, shared the same thrill-seeking gene.

Peter Matthiessen was quoted, in his 2014 *New York Times* obituary, as saying he suffered from a lifelong "uneasiness about unearned privilege." At sixteen, or thereabouts, he requested his name be dropped from the *Social Register,* a semiannual publication that indexes members of American high society.

In Dave, Matthiessen would have likely recognized an old soul who, having similarly relinquished the suffocating constraints of the material world, wasn't just catching fish. For Dave, it was never really about the paycheck. Out on the water, testing his limits, he was a young man on a path of self-discovery.

Like Matthiessen, Dave had grown frustrated by his fancy pedigree. Both men had shunned the starched khaki pants and chauffeured Lincoln Town Cars that were practically their birthright. The summer people, with their endless talk of credentials and clubs and connections, made them uncomfortable. As young men, they were seekers in pursuit of a different way of life. They found it on the South Fork, where both men embarked upon a certain kind of reinvention.

5.

CHOATE

"In Room 210 in Memorial House, David Connick, a fifteen-year-old Choate freshman, rocked — shirtless — in his chair, and pushed aside the last of a French assignment that did not appear a likely candidate for completion," Joyce Maynard wrote in a *New York Times* article titled "Choate-Rosemary Hall — Boys and Girls Apart" that appeared in December of 1976. Maynard, who'd joined the *Times* the year before as a general assignment and features reporter, later went on to become a successful novelist and memoirist. "He dreamily surveyed a wall of surfing posters tacked up next to a life-sized Jimi Hendrix and a photograph of his Aunt Nancy that Dave had put up recently 'because she just sent me 10 bucks.' "

Nineteen seventy-six was an interesting time to be at Choate. Two years prior, in 1974, Choate, the all-boys prep school, had merged with the all-girls Rosemary Hall. Maynard wrote that Rosemary Hall was a "somewhat less-distinguished grooming place attended, primarily, by the daughters of the rich." Such exclusivity came with a steep price tag. By 1976, tuition at the coed campus had soared to $5,200 a year, among the highest of top-tier prep schools in the nation. Its student body comprised the sons and daughters of the East Coast aristocratic elite, largely legacies. Choate, which President John F. Kennedy had attended, was but another rung on the calculated ladder they needed to ascend before becoming investment bankers, corporate attorneys, or politicians. As for the young women, if they didn't have high-minded career aspirations, they were at least expected to marry well.

In her *New York Times* story, Joyce Maynard zeroed in on Dave Connick with her reportorial spotlight.

"A wiry young man with a fast-talking, wisecracking manner, Dave came to Choate last fall, he said, because it was the best prep school that admitted him — the notion that he go to some boarding school a foregone conclusion," Maynard wrote. " 'Some of the rules here are a drag,' he said cheerfully, raking through a nearly surfable sea of pants, T-shirts and underwear with the handle of his hockey stick and coming up with a somewhat down-trodden-looking tie, compulsory dinner attire at Choate."

For Dave, who described the girls as "bopped out" and the boys as "prepped out," the adjustment from Fifth Avenue living to the Choate dormitory was "no hassle"; he added, quite philosophically for a mere teenager, that "you just keep on living." Still, his main problem with the school "is the unlikelihood of students from Choate and Rosemary Hall 'getting it together.' "

A new administration had tried clamping down on what it described as the big three — drugs, drinking, and sex, "none of which, students say, is an uncommon occurrence in the school," Maynard reported. More than three-quarters of the student body (Dave Connick surely included) had admitted to occasional marijuana use.

As December break beckoned, one of Dave's classmates said that "getting kicked out of a school like this can really ruin a guy's life." Dave, meanwhile, filled a laundry bag with dirty clothes and dreamed of getting a new O'Neill wetsuit for Christmas. In Connecticut, he left any concerns about social climbing to the more straitlaced members of the opposite sex who favored L.L.Bean hiking shoes with argyle socks, straight-legged corduroy pants, and gold hoop earrings. " 'Here's my advice for the Rosebuds,' Dave said, stroking his chin. 'Don't be so uptight. Life's beautiful.' "

Once finals were over and winter break began, Dave's next stop was East Hampton — where he'd surf at Georgica and catch up with a few of his buddies, who were similarly spending the Christmas holiday with their families at their second homes out east. Morgan McGivern was also at Choate. Sometimes the two friends hitched a ride to East Hampton together. Though they were roughly the same age (their birthdays were only four months apart), by the time Dave arrived at Choate, Morgan was already a sophomore. Both Dave and Morgan had the advantage of older, popular brothers who were upperclassmen; Pete and Tom helped ease the rocky transition. From time to time, Owen McGivern would tease his two sons that the Protestants who ran Choate threatened to ruin their good Catholic upbringing.

"His mother was, at best, difficult," Thorson Rockwell, another of Dave's childhood friends, said to me by way of introduction. Most sources politely tiptoed around my questions. Thorson dove in headfirst.

Many of Thorson's earliest memories were of Dave trying to rid himself of his Upper East Side trappings. The Upper East Side was familiar territory to both boys. Thorson grew up in a building next to St. Bernard's and met Dave during first grade, right around the time he and Andrew Greenebaum became inseparable.

Barry Augus, who went to St. David's, a rival Upper East Side private school, was another close friend. During grade school, Barry and Dave would round up a pack of boys in Central Park to play tackle football games with no pads. Once they both enrolled as freshmen at Choate, they'd meet at Vaz Place, a street with a decent-size hill a half mile from campus, contentedly skateboarding its "perfect pavement" until nightfall. Barry recalled that Dave had a sense of joy, a real ease, about him. He relished the experience of being alive. Dave soon coined the term "cosmic debris." Such things — and people — were to be avoided at all costs.

Sometimes all you need is one friend in a place in order to survive. Despite their shared affinity for hoarding surfing and skateboarding magazines, midway through their sophomore year at Choate, Dave and Barry had come to the same conclusion:

they were both miserable. Neither young man could call his parents and expect a wellspring of empathy on the other end of the telephone line. Their fathers, who had come of age during the Second World War, weren't emotionally accessible. The idea that their sons wouldn't graduate from Choate and go on to the Ivy League was an unthinkable break from the master plan. Alice Connick was especially livid.

But Dave was resolute in his need to shift gears. Despite his parents' misgivings, he eventually transferred to Friends Seminary, a private Quaker day school on Sixteenth Street in Gramercy Park. Back then, most people in his social circle considered Friends a second-tier school, a safe harbor after having suffered a few hard knocks — and certainly several notches beneath their status as Old Boys.

Once Dave transferred to Friends from Choate, he and Thorson Rockwell became reacquainted. Both were skateboarders who, when they weren't smoking weed, started experimenting with various hallucinogens: peyote, mushrooms, and LSD. In Manhattan during the mid- to late 1970s, if you walked down the steps of the Bethesda Fountain in Central Park — basically an open-air drug market — and didn't score any weed, acid, or cocaine by the time you made it to the other side, you were a unicorn. Some in Dave's peer group, who observed him at parties from a distance, recalled that he seemed like a cool guy, and, for a teenager, oddly spiritual. Even as a young kid, Dave was dialed into the thrum, the frequency of the universe. And if you weren't tapped into his "spiritual surfer wavelength," as Thorson recalled, Dave had little use for you.

During high school, Thorson routinely slept over at the Connicks' Fifth Avenue apartment, a block away from the Guggenheim. PHB had a giant wraparound terrace. Once the sun came up, the boys would take a few hits from a joint and put on a little Bob Marley.

"Stark-ass naked, Dave walked along the stone guardrail, maybe eight to ten inches wide," Thorson recalled. Dave, who was in ridiculously good shape and fairly well endowed, pranced along the terrace like a Siamese cat. Over the ledge, Eighty-Seventh Street was a straight drop, fifteen stories down. Upper East Side housewives, unaware they were gawking at a teenager, stared out the windows in disbelief, binoculars at the ready. Dave shot Thorson a sly, devilish look. Thorson laughed until his belly ached.

On weekends, Dave took Thorson out to Montauk, slowly indoctrinating him into the mariner culture. In the summer of 1980, shortly after graduating, when Dave went to Central America on an extended surf vacation, Thorson took Dave's place aboard the *Marlin IV.* Thorson helped Captain Mike Stedman escort fishermen on all-night bluefishing excursions. Mike's charisma, equal parts friendly and authoritative, left an impression. There was a heft to him that felt solid and trustworthy. His disposition put Thorson at ease. "Everyone wanted to be like Mike," he said. "Like a good general, he led from the front." Once Dave came back and they worked together aboard the *Marlin IV,* Thorson observed the close bond Mike and Dave shared. It was the genuine article. "Mike was a father figure to a band of misfit children, Dave included. Most skippers weren't nearly as sweet as he was."

Out east, Dave was busy putting down roots of his own. Thorson recalled that Dave moved out of his parents' penthouse apartment the day after he graduated from Friends. Unshackled from the golden handcuffs, he never looked back.

Once Dave became a full-time Montauk resident, Barry Augus saw a more reclusive, private side to his formerly easygoing friend. Walking into his modest, freestanding bungalow, which overlooked Fort Pond, was like walking into the home of a stranger. Dave's boyish enthusiasm, his trademark lightness, had evaporated. Montauk felt like Siberia. The summer people were nowhere to be found. Out back, Dave had parked his motorcycle and a Volkswagen bus a cousin had given him, where he stored his surfboards. The tan Volkswagen had several coats of primer on it. Once the weather got a bit warmer, Dave intended to repaint it.

Though Barry never told him as much, Dave seemed lonely and troubled. Dave had a passion for the sea, to be sure. But the last time the two men spent an afternoon together, he didn't seem quite like himself. It was plain to Barry that Dave had started down a different, self-destructive path. That day, Barry came away thinking that Dave was hiding out in the world of deep-sea fishermen, where no one from his past could find him. Dave had always been prone to taking unnecessary risks. He never outgrew it. As a boy, he'd done it with joy. Now his steely demeanor, coupled with the increasing time he spent aboard a commercial fishing boat, made Barry wonder whether, consciously or not, Dave had made peace with his ultimate destiny of someday dying at sea.

Several years later, Barry was living in Oakland, California, when Thorson Rockwell phoned and informed him of the *Wind Blown*'s sinking. A few days prior, Barry had been cooking when he felt a strong sense of Dave's presence nearby, as if his childhood friend were standing in the kitchen right next to him. After hanging up the phone with Thorson, Barry realized Dave had come to say good-bye. To be sure, the news of Dave's disappearance shocked Barry, but he was in no way surprised.

Thorson also described a similar shift in Dave's temperament near the end of his life. "He was losing his marbles a little bit," Thorson recalled of the last time he saw Dave. Wads of hundred-dollar bills sat crumpled up on the kitchen countertop. "He had gotten blue-collar tough. He was living life on the edge. He thought he was bulletproof."

In 1984, Thorson was working at an art gallery on Fifty-Seventh Street when he found out that Dave Connick had been lost at sea. He cried for three days straight. "The sea had its way with them, and they went down hard and fast," Thorson surmised. "Water engulfed the boat, and they went

166

straight down. I doubt they lived much longer than sixty seconds."

Thorson's guess is as good as anyone's, really. The precise ending, whatever transpired in those final minutes and seconds, is unknowable.

6.
MAHONEYVILLE

The Mahoneyville barn.

At fifteen, right around the time he went off to Choate, Dave Connick radically altered the course of his life. A lifelong downhill skier — his family vacationed in Aspen and Telluride each winter — Dave took to surfing with ease. Next, he learned to fish.

As a teenager, Dave became a regular presence at Mahoneyville, an epicenter for

East Coast surfing. A block away from Georgica Beach in East Hampton, Mahoneyville was a local compound frequented by affluent, wayward young men who generally had way too much free time on their hands. Because he was always so eager and "stoked" to go surfing, friends started calling him Stoker.

While at Mahoneyville, either during the summer of 1976 or 1977, Dave began spending more time with Tom McGivern. He was already best friends with Tom's younger brother, Morgan. Tom, who had recently graduated from Choate and enrolled at Harvard, drove Dave out to Montauk when the waves fell flat. And he was the one who introduced him to his friend: a fisherman named Michael Stedman.

It wasn't long before Dave caught the fishing bug. Aboard the *Marlin IV,* Tom and Dave worked as Captain Mike's trusty mates. Sometimes Morgan would tag along with his Nikon camera in tow. At Boston College, Morgan's senior portfolio featured documentary-style, black-and-white photographs of Montauk commercial fishermen hard at work.

Mahoneyville played a critical role in Dave's maturation. If Dave had never started hanging out at Mahoneyville, it's entirely possible — likely, even — that he would never have made his way out to Montauk. It was a series of fatal miscalculations that led to such a tragic end. Or maybe not. Maybe not even close. Maybe, all along, Dave Connick had the courage and conviction to follow his heart.

Philip Sprayregen was an East Hampton summer kid who came of age at Mahoneyville. In the early sixties, after his father died and his mother remarried, this time to a wealthy Manhattan lawyer, Phil and his family occupied a summer house south of the highway, at the intersection of Lily Pond and Hedges Lanes. Though he didn't know it yet, Mahoneyville was right down the road. Fifty some years ago, automated gates, landscape lighting, and security cameras didn't exist. The overall vibe was friendlier and more intimate, with the estate section kids free to roam from house to house. It was a *neighborhood,* plain and simple, and one where families often disguised their wealth rather than flaunted it.

It was the summer of 1963 when Dennis Mahoney, the eldest of the four Mahoney sons, first spotted Phil at Georgica Beach. At twelve, and already six feet tall and 150 pounds, Phil was hard to miss. Dennis soon recruited him to hang with the rest of the

Mahoneyville crew. The gang of boys, who rode their bikes until the tires wore out, took ownership of Lily Pond Lane. It was the pure freedom of youth. The Mahoneys' two-acre property — affectionately dubbed Mahoneyville — became the de facto estate section meetup spot. The O'Connells lived on the opposite end of Lily Pond Lane, with the Sprayregens conveniently sandwiched in between.

When friends drove out from the city to Mahoneyville for the first time, Phil directed them accordingly: "Take the Long Island Expressway. When you get to the East Hampton Airport, make a right onto Georgica Road. If you can't find Mahoneyville, just ask anybody you see for directions; they will know where you should go to get there." Once out east, city dwellers were always surprised that random passersby did indeed know Mahoneyville's precise coordinates.

On the South Fork during the 1960s and 1970s, Mahoneyville was where middle-school- and high-school-aged kids drank beer, smoked weed, and experimented with LSD for the first time. It was a seasonal affair: Mahoneyville came alive from Memorial Day to Labor Day. The shingled barn, painted with a giant white peace sign, contained dozens of O'Neill wetsuits. Surfboards of every size and shape leaned against all available wall space. Bob Marley and Peter Tosh records played on a near-constant loop. Mahoneyville was a primitive, primal scene. It was like living inside a commune while the rest of East Hampton went about its preppy, buttoned-up business.

Mahoneyville's best feature was its location: walking distance from Georgica Beach. Surfing was the tribe's main activity. Georgica's dunes and jetties were home turf. The boys stumbled out of bed early most mornings and wandered down to the beach to check out the surf conditions. That time of day was best because the wind hadn't yet picked up; by afternoon, sea breezes changed the face of incoming waves.

Unlike surrounding sandy-bottomed beaches, Georgica Beach has three jetties — man-made structures constructed of large rocks that run perpendicular to the beach. The sand along Long Island's south shore is dragged east to west, pulled by a powerful current that originates in Montauk and moves in the direction of New York City. One story goes that in the early sixties, Juan Trippe, the founder of Pan American World Airways, used his political clout to persuade

Suffolk County and the US Army Corps of Engineers to build the jetties as a way of protecting his beachfront estate.

The jetties were thought to minimize erosion by trapping sand as it flowed past. In 1968, the Army Corps of Engineers warned that the East End "will continue to erode and recede unless protected and nourished." At the time, attitudes were changing, along with increased environmental awareness. Some locals were vocal in their opposition. Activists distrusted engineers who advocated synthetic solutions meant to thwart naturally occurring phenomena.

Environmental politics aside, the man-made jetties created an unintended consequence: suddenly, the waves broke differently. Once the three jetties were built, the waves peeled off, rather than crashing directly onto the sand. To the delight of local surfers, the federal government's environmental intervention had created three new breaks. When the conditions were just right, the boys could catch a clean swell from the tip of the first jetty and ride it all the way to the parking lot. They could, and did, dance across the water.

Barbara Mahoney, the mother of four sons, was Mahoneyville's matriarch. Like Alice and Pete Connick, she and her husband, Dennis Sr., split their time between an apartment on Manhattan's Upper East Side and a summer house by the beach. In 1955, shortly after marrying, they plunked down $25,000 for a farmhouse and a series of adjoining buildings on Lily Pond Lane. In time, the East Hampton property became known as Mahoneyville.

The Mahoneys socialized with a group of close-knit Irish Catholic families who all owned summer houses nearby, the Connicks included. Once school let out in June, the wives stayed in East Hampton until Labor Day. Their husbands, who commuted back and forth by railroad into Manhattan, spent the workweek in the city. On Friday evenings, everyone reconvened out east. At the Maidstone Club, where the Mahoneys became members, several of their peers had similarly transcended, through hard work and determination, the social class into which they were born. The O'Connells, the Raymonds, the Shamashes, the Sprayregens, and the McGiverns rounded out their social circle. Many of the Irish Catholic families had between four and six children; there was always someone close in age to play alongside.

During the sixties, among married couples

in their social circle, sexual boundaries had started to loosen, and the nightly ritual of cocktail hour helped move things along. One drink always led to two. And two more after that. For the wives in particular, cocktail hour was a welcome respite from the monotony of domestic life as characterized in Betty Friedan's 1963 best seller *The Feminine Mystique,* which gave voice to "the problem that has no name." With the first crisp, cool sip of a gin martini, the day's worries started to vanish. Finally, they had a break from their young, cloying children. Child-rearing was mostly a task left to the mothers, albeit one that many of the women had deftly outsourced. Still, someone had to keep an eye on the hired help.

In *A Sensitive, Passionate Man,* Barbara Mahoney's memoir about her husband's alcoholism, she described Dennis this way: "My Harvard Law School graduate, my Phi Beta Kappa, had set out on the road to the top, Wall Street, the Establishment, the green pastures of the legal trade, the golden mecca for the class of 1950, and somewhere along the line he had lost his way. At forty, Sean was lost, but we were still locked into the life, set up for it, the apartment in town, the house in the country, children in private schools." Throughout the book, because of the stigma surrounding addiction and alcoholism, Barbara substituted "Sean" for Dennis's name. It was a brave book, particularly for the era in which she wrote it. In 1974, when *A Sensitive, Passionate Man* came out, *alcoholism* was still a dirty, little-used word. The book became a best seller, and was later made into a TV movie starring Angie Dickinson and David Janssen.

After graduating from Ivy League law schools, both Pete Connick and Dennis Mahoney went to work at prestigious Wall Street law firms. The goal was always to make it within the Establishment. But although they looked the part, Dennis and Barbara were quasi-interlopers. They hadn't been prep-school educated. Their bank accounts weren't padded with the security of family money. Even though the East Hampton house was a stretch, its purchase was symbolic: the Mahoneys were living the American dream. Decades before it became a cauldron of calculated chic (the right house, the right club, the right friends, the right parties), the couple fell in love with East Hampton because of its rural, simple charm.

In May of 1965, Barbara dropped off her four sons at their Park Avenue elementary school. She paid particular attention to the fathers. "They looked so pulled together, so purposeful, striding along in their neatly pressed suits, Brooks Brother-ed for the day, armed with attaché cases and the *New York Times*," she wrote. The orderly scene stood in stark contrast to the one at home. Increasingly, her husband lay sprawled across their bed, wearing wrinkled white undershorts, sleeping the day away.

By the late 1960s, Barbara was attending Al-Anon meetings in Bridgehampton, searching for a viable path forward. "In the rooms," as the saying goes, she sought camaraderie to support her through the illness that threatened to tear her marriage asunder. Alice Connick frequented similar meetings. The two of them sat alongside the wives of fishermen and farmers. No matter their class differences, they all shared the same shameful secret. Drinking had ravaged their families.

Out east, Dennis Mahoney staggered around the Maidstone Club, forever in search of another cocktail. Sadly, no amount of intervention did the trick. But it wasn't for a lack of trying.

What Barbara's memoir left out was that her husband was a World War II combat veteran. A sniper had shot through both his legs. Although Dennis went on to graduate second in his class from Harvard Law School before starting a successful legal career, his demons — specifically, untreated post–traumatic stress disorder (a diagnosis that didn't yet exist) — eventually consumed him.

In 1970, Dennis Mahoney lost the battle. He died of alcoholism.

Before their father died, Mahoneyville was heaven on earth for the four Mahoney sons: Dennis, Curtis, Nicholas, and Seamus (in birth order). The family's two-acre property came with a house, a cottage, and a barn. The front house had five bedrooms. The boys eventually took over the barn and a nearby cottage. Sleeping in the barn, with its flimsy walls and dirt floors, was akin to camping in a tent beneath the stars.

Friends who had embarked on pilgrimages to India mailed the boys bricks of hash hidden inside the bindings of hardcover books. "It was definitely a cannabis-infused situation," Dennis Mahoney, the eldest brother, recalled. Stoned and ravenously hungry after hours spent surfing, the boys walked across the barn's lawn and into the nearby potato fields. In the semidarkness, they dropped to their knees, digging up potatoes from the sandy, porous soil. Back at the barn, standing beneath the warm outdoor shower after swimming in the cold ocean was among the great pleasures of their boyhood. On the stove, someone would have already started boiling a huge pot of salted water to cook the freshly harvested potatoes. They also drank beer. A whole lot of beer: Labatt Blue, Heineken, Miller High Life.

Girls came and went. In those days, HIV and AIDS didn't exist. Young lovers spent the night together, and apart from the danger of getting pregnant, there wasn't a whole lot else they had to worry about. The uninsulated barn was made of tongue-and-groove boards. Its loft had large open spaces that were shady and cool. Dennis remembered sitting on one of the crossbeams with his legs dangling off the ledge. He would roll a joint, separating out the buds and tossing the seeds onto the floor below. Unbeknownst to him, the ritual resulted in little marijuana plants — needing no water and barely any sunlight — sprouting up from the cracks in the wooden floorboards.

After the elder Dennis Mahoney drank himself to death, the family lost their Upper East Side apartment. Barbara and the boys moved out to East Hampton year-round for a time, and she enrolled the boys in public school. In those days, East Hampton could have been any ordinary small town in America. Unlike now, when the Hampton Jitney runs upscale buses almost every hour, it wasn't an outpost of New York City. At East Hampton High School, Curtis Mahoney and Mary Cavagnaro were in the same grade and struck up a close friendship. There were the freaks and the jocks. Curtis and Mary hung around the stoner, hippie crowd. And Dennis, Curtis's older brother, was also part of the scene.

Mary eventually became like an older sister to many of the Mahoney boys — and to Dave Connick too. Once she and Mike got together, the boys from Mahoneyville routinely hung out at the Stedman house. Her fisherman husband was often offshore. Mary relished their company. She was always more than happy to set another place at the dinner table or whip up another batch of hash brownies.

It was the middle of January in 1978 when Dave Connick and Seamus Mahoney, the youngest Mahoney brother, made their way out to East Hampton for the weekend. Seamus was twenty; Dave was sixteen. Their four-year age difference was irrelevant. Though Pete Connick Jr. was technically his peer, Seamus had long since gravitated toward Dave, who possessed a preternatural degree of authenticity and sincerity.

They had grown up attending junior activities together at the Maidstone Club. Eventually, after Seamus and Dave hung up their tennis whites for good, Mahoneyville became their de facto meetup spot. When Seamus was first learning how to surf, his brother Dennis passed along a secondhand kneeboard (a cross between a boogie board and a mini-surfboard that you ride on your knees instead of your feet). The board wound up being too small for Seamus. So the following summer, maybe in 1973 or 1974, he passed it along to Dave. Stoker was off to the races.

But that winter in 1978, the boys stayed at Mahoneyville. It was freezing cold, and they warmed themselves by a roaring fire. One morning before going surfing, they dropped some acid together. With their minds altered, the sun shone even brighter than usual. Two-foot waves peeled off, one after another. Overhead, resident Canada geese, the ones that hadn't migrated south for the winter, flew in a perfectly coordinated V-shaped pattern in the stark winter sky.

"It was an amazing bonding experience," Seamus recalled.

By then, both boys were committed pescatarians. They subsisted on pots of lentils and rice. Other nights, they'd take a bag of freshly caught bluefish cheeks, cover them in flour, sauté them in butter, and devour them alongside a mountain of vegetables. That weekend, sleeping in the unheated Mahoney barn in unwashed sheets, surrounded by empty oceanfront mansions, it was Dave and Seamus against the world. Their nonconformity felt like freedom.

Dave was fearless. He'd travel the world — whether Hawaii, Mexico, or El Salvador — with little more than a few dollars in his pocket. After Dave returned from a trip to El Salvador, Morgan recalled that his friend claimed to have survived on a bananas-only diet. Seamus also remembered Dave's trademark daredevil sensibility. When they met up in the city, Dave headed out on his skateboard. Courting danger (or worse), he'd grab on to the rear of a city bus and ride his skateboard southbound, city blocks whizzing past. "Something was definitely wrong there," Seamus said of Dave's natural-born impulsiveness.

There's a photograph of Dave that hangs in Seamus's house in St. Paul, Minnesota. In the picture, Dave stands bare-chested, wearing a rubber fishing bib. Tilefish surround his feet. "He was radiant," Seamus told me. "He was in his prime."

By 1985, a year after Dave disappeared aboard the *Wind Blown,* Seamus realized that he was battling many of the same demons as his father and his brother Curtis, who in 1980 had died of the same disease. Seamus did a monthlong stint at Hazelden, an addiction treatment center in Minnesota. Sobriety transformed his life. He now works as a public defender.

Mahoneyville eventually came to an end. In 1980, in order to pay for college tuition, Barbara Mahoney sold the front lot for $250,000. The dilapidated Mahoneyville barn still stood toward the back of the property, but the real estate agent wouldn't let the sale go through unless Barbara agreed to tear it down. In 1981, she built a new home on the property and replaced the old barn with a new one. Two years later, in 1983, Barbara embarked upon a happy next chapter of her life. She married John Brooks, a *New Yorker* writer and novelist.

Near the end of her life, although she suffered from dementia, Barbara still came out to the house in East Hampton. Though her short-term memory had started to fail her, the interior of the house had become hard-wired into the deep recesses of her brain.

She made Dennis promise to take care of his brothers, and he is now the executor of the family's trust. The Mahoneyville property eventually went on the market. Its sale, in 2019, equipped Dennis with enough resources to help look after his brothers, his nieces, and his nephews.

Dennis is now in his late sixties. He spent his career as a psychiatric social worker working with veterans, and when I spoke with him, he shared with me a developmental psychology theory. Apparently, trauma can interfere with developmental growth and often freezes people at the emotional age they were when the trauma first occurred. The deaths of his own father, his brother Curtis, and Dave Connick formed Dennis's early foundation. Memories from childhood and adolescence imprint themselves on people differently than do memories in adulthood. One of the reasons that Dennis became a therapist was to help others process the darkest periods of their lives — and hopefully transcend them.

In late March of 1984, after the *Wind Blown* went down, Dennis drove around local beaches, searching for wreckage. He was high as a kite. From the comfort of his car, the violent storm was a tremendous sight to behold. The hurricane surf looked eerily apocalyptic.

All these years later, he can still transport himself back to when he was six or seven years old. It was in those moments as a boy, riding his bicycle around East Hampton, before anything bad happened, that Dennis felt the most carefree. And for a generation of boys who came of age there, Mahoneyville was the best definition of a misspent youth.

7.

CATHERINE

Catherine Cederquist in Minnesota in 1988.

"Have you spoken to Nana yet?" Seamus Mahoney asked me when I interviewed him on the telephone. Nana was Dave Connick's girlfriend at the time. It wasn't the first time I had heard her nickname. During our conversation, Thorson Rockwell had mentioned that she was the half sister of Chevy Chase, the actor. But to me, Nana was a mystery. At first, no one could recall her full name or current whereabouts. I worried that my arsenal of investigative tools had failed me. Nana seemed to be hiding in plain sight, almost as if she didn't want to be found.

But Seamus felt she was an essential piece of the puzzle, and after a bit of sleuthing, he e-mailed me two telephone numbers for a woman named Catherine Cederquist. Both landlines rang and rang. A few days later, I tried the numbers again. This time, Harry Matthews, Catherine's husband, picked up the phone on the second or third ring. Praying he wouldn't hang up on me, I explained, as succinctly as I could, who I was and why I had called to interrupt his afternoon.

A journalist himself, Harry took pity on me. For ten years, he jokingly said, he had been competing with a dead man. No one, it seemed, quite measured up to Catherine's first, true love. Despite the decades that had passed, Harry warned me, the sorrow of losing Dave Connick reverberated in Catherine still. Every March, the month the *Wind Blown* went down, she went through a dark period of mourning and remembrance. Harry thought the experience of talking about Dave might prove cathartic for Catherine. But he also warned me that she was somewhat fragile when it came to discussing him.

Until that point, I had come up with a rough sketch of who I thought Dave Connick had been. But Catherine held a key that unlocked an unknown door. During our three conversations, she filled me in on a side of Dave Connick no one else had or would convey. Her nickname came from Norse mythology: Nanna Nepsdóttir was the Nordic goddess who married Baldr, the god of light.

At fifteen, Catherine Cederquist felt awkward and invisible. Unlike her blond, blue-eyed contemporaries, she had dark hair and dark eyes. Although she became a ravishing beauty, Catherine was still growing into her unconventional looks. Once, a friend suggested she stop by the Ford Modeling Agency, but a scout said she appeared too exotic to book.

Catherine attended Nightingale-Bamford, the Upper East Side girls' school. Among her peers, the uniformed, preppy girls who wore pearl necklaces and diamond-stud earrings, she kept hearing Dave Connick's name. Catherine was part of a subset of rich girls who went to one of four schools: Brearley, Chapin, Nightingale-Bamford, or Spence. Though it wasn't obvious from outward appearances, Catherine's family lived well beyond their means, and she felt like an outsider.

Somewhat on a whim, Catherine applied to Friends Seminary, the private day school in Lower Manhattan. During an admissions interview, one of the deans at Friends asked whether Catherine knew anyone enrolled there. Though she had never met him before, one name came immediately to mind.

"Dave Connick," Catherine said.

On the first day of school at Friends in September of 1978, Catherine was sixteen and in eleventh grade; Dave was seventeen and in twelfth grade. For Catherine, Friends was a jarring transition. The school didn't require a uniform, and for the first time in her life, standing in front of her closet, Catherine had chosen what she wanted to wear on the first day of school. Odder still was having boys sitting beside her in the same classroom.

It was first-period geology class and the students sat huddled together at black Formica lab tables. In walked a young man attired in orange baggies (a type of surf wear), a red flannel shirt, and filthy white slip-on Vans with holes in the toes. He had shaggy brown hair, and his unbuttoned shirt revealed a beaded necklace and a tanned chest.

As the teacher took attendance, he called out: "Dave Connick."

Catherine nearly fell off her stool when the dashing young man whose movements she had just memorized nodded his head in response.

For Catherine, it was love at first sight.

At Friends, once school let out each day, Catherine followed Dave home. She lurked a half block or so behind. Rather than take the subway, they'd walk some seventy blocks — all the way from Sixteenth Street to their respective apartment buildings, which faced each other on opposite sides of Central Park — Catherine at the Eldorado, a twin-towered art deco apartment building at 300 Central Park West, and Dave at 1060 Fifth Avenue. Following Dave's lead, they walked the length of the Upper East Side. Catherine took the Eighty-Sixth Street crosstown bus home.

But Catherine wasn't as invisible as she felt. Later that fall, as it started getting colder, Dave turned around and asked her:

"Why don't you walk with me?" That afternoon, they took the long way home. Eventually they stopped at a park bench alongside the East River to talk.

"I was besotted," Catherine said. "He was my first love."

Around Christmastime, Catherine and Dave found themselves at Mahoneyville. Catherine lost her virginity to Dave that night, in the loft of the barn. Afterward, Dave fell fast asleep; the comforting weight of his wiry frame rested on top of her own. Looking out the barn's window, she watched the snowflakes spiral downward, as if trapped inside a snow globe. After a traumatic incident in her childhood, Catherine finally felt safe in the presence of a man other than her father. It was no small victory. Dave loved the natural female body in all of its forms. When Catherine had her period, Dave made love to her just as he always did. A little blood on the bedsheets was nothing to fear.

Both Dave's and Catherine's parents had separated around the same time, and both of them lived primarily with their fathers. At home, Catherine assumed the role of dutiful wife; she helped out with the laundry, ironing, and cooking. Every evening she listened as her father cried himself to sleep. Though Dave's parents had recently parted ways, their separation was still a trial one, and he lived primarily with Big Pete, his bear-of-a-man litigator father, in the penthouse apartment turned bachelor pad.

Alice, Dave's mother, was less beloved by her son — and that's putting it nicely. He apparently blamed his mother for walking out on his father (although Alice said the cheating was hardly one-sided), and had resorted to calling her "lady." In general, Dave avoided talking to Catherine about his feelings too much. Back then, it wasn't common for teenagers to be in therapy. Twelve-step speak had yet to enter the lexicon. Looking back, it's plain to see there was a lot of unprocessed anger toward his mother, but between the ages of eighteen and twenty-two, Dave rarely articulated things much beyond that.

Back when all four Connicks lived under one roof, Alice had allowed Dave to choose the paint color for his bedroom, which he still shared with his older brother when Little Pete was home from college. Because of Dave's obsession with the sea, he insisted on painting his walls a deep, bold shade of turquoise. Hanging out together in his bed, a coconut-scented bar of Mr. Zog's Sex Wax sitting on the nearby dresser, with records playing in the background, Catherine felt like they had catapulted themselves underwater.

Later that winter, the two conspired to sleep over at Dave's house on a school night. Her friend Kristen agreed to cover for her. Should Catherine's parents ask, Kristen had been directed to say that the girls were having a sleepover. Catherine and Dave were making out in his bed with the door closed, probably listening to Marvin Gaye's "Let's Get It On," when the phone rang. A panicked Kristen was on the other end. The ruse was up, she informed the young lovers: Catherine's father had discovered the truth and was on his way to Dave's apartment to bring his daughter home.

Dave and Catherine got dressed and raced down the back stairs, before the doorman buzzed her father upstairs. Running around the snow-packed Central Park reservoir at midnight — high on a heady mix of pheromones — they made it back to the Upper West Side a few moments too late. On another memorable evening, Catherine and Dave were sitting in her bedroom, drinking tallboys. Three times her father had knocked on the door, asking that Dave go home. Finally he reached his breaking point. "If you loved my daughter, you'd let her get the right amount of sleep on a school night!" he implored, before punching Dave in the face. His nose started to bleed. Catherine was mortified.

Eventually, all was forgiven. Theirs was way more than a passing fling. Nothing could separate the young lovers.

On school mornings, after taking the crosstown bus to the Upper East Side, Catherine met up with Dave on the number six train heading downtown. They'd wander between the subway cars until they found each other. Music was a frequent topic of conversation. Dave wrote his senior thesis on Bob Marley; Catherine had wanted to research Marley as well, but later settled on Bob Dylan. During twelfth grade, Dave traveled to Kauai for an extended beach observation as part of his senior project. For a month, content with living alone in a tent, he chronicled the rhythms of the sea, writing down his observations in a notebook. There was an innocent, purehearted quality about Dave — something about his Catholic upbringing and his deep reverence for carpenters and fishermen. A converted Buddhist and committed pescatarian who spoke fluent Spanish, Dave eschewed beef, milk, sugar — and, later, pornography.

College wasn't a high priority for either one of them. Once Dave became a commercial fisherman, Catherine helped out at the docks. The men there jokingly called her (as they did anyone who could bait a tub well) a *master baiter*. Before they switched from J-hooks to circle hooks, she'd sit for hours at a stretch, baiting tubs with cut-up pieces of squid and mackerel.

By then, Mike and Dave had become inseparable. From time to time, Catherine would accompany them aboard the *Marlin IV*. Mike was the captain, and Dave was his first mate. Catherine pitched in where she could, passing out cans of Pabst Blue Ribbon to seagoing passengers. Sometimes they caught fish, and sometimes they didn't. When the fishing was good, Dave and Catherine lived off of porgy sandwiches and little else.

Catherine, a fourteenth-generation Manhattanite (including her Mohawk lineage), split her time between Montauk and the city. "The city was a hard-core place," Catherine recalled. In the late seventies and early eighties, there were well over a thousand homicides each year. "Out in

Montauk, I was safe. Nobody could get to me." Years earlier, she had been a high-society, up-and-coming debutante. It was a role she adopted under duress, and only to appease her grandmother. At the invitation-only International Debutante Ball, held in the Waldorf Astoria's Grand Ballroom, Catherine wore a floor-length gown made of white satin, a copy of a Jean Harlow dress from the 1930s. Her naturally curly, chocolate-brown hair had been tamed into cascading, perfect waves.

One of the last times that Dave and Catherine were together was at his studio apartment off Second House Road. The hustle and bustle of Park Avenue and well-bred escorts felt light-years away from sleepy Montauk in the wintertime. She marveled at the icicles that formed inside Dave's shower. "He's a stoic little fuck," Catherine would mutter to herself, rinsing off as quickly as she could. She waited around for Dave to return, shivering like a lost puppy until he did.

After one of Dave's offshore fishing trips, he returned with flushed cheeks, carrying four just-caught lobsters. Though they had intended to eat them for dinner, Catherine and Dave wound up in bed together, content to forget about the lobsters until the

Catherine at the Waldorf Astoria in 1981.

next morning. After boiling them and eating them for breakfast, Dave broke out in an itchy, red rash. Despite his affinity for sea creatures, it turned out he was allergic to lobster.

Mike Stedman, freshly scrubbed and ready to begin another day of work, soon appeared at Dave's doorstep. The on-again, off-again intensity of a fisherman's schedule felt relentless. Catherine braced herself as she kissed Dave good-bye. The fish were biting. There was never enough time.

8.

ALICE

The first and only time I had the pleasure of interviewing Alice Connick-Ryan was at her home in Bridgehampton. It was March 28, 2018, when she and I sat down together. The next day marked the thirty-fourth anniversary of her son going missing.

One of the first things she shared with me was that losing her beloved Davey aboard the *Wind Blown* coincided with his becoming a Bonacker — the name given to members of the native-born East Hampton population who reside north of Route 27 in the wooded, hilly section called Springs. Some say that in order to be considered a true Bonacker, your bloodline has to stretch back three generations on both your mother's and your father's sides of the family. Though they're separated by only a few miles, an ocean may as well divide the locals and the seasonal visitors, since they rarely mix. "There were the Bonackers and the summer people," Alice explained. "We were considered summer people."

Woven deep within this story is the notion of *I told you so*. It's certainly the vantage point of Alice, and the source of the guilt that consumes her, all these decades later, for not forcing her son to get off that goddamn fishing boat.

At the time of our interview, Alice was in her mideighties. She sat indoors wearing green velour sweatpants, a gray down jacket, and a pair of maroon snakeskin flats. A fresh coat of shiny coral nail polish covered her fingertips. Parkinson's disease made her hands shake when she spoke. She looked like a frail bird, all one hundred pounds of her; cataracts had clouded her eyes, which shifted with the light from brown to green. Her mind, though, was still lucid. She spoke slowly and unhurriedly, as if we had all the time in the world.

Over the course of Alice's lifetime, she made hundreds of paintings, dozens of which now cover the walls of the Bridgehampton house she built with her second husband, Allan Ryan III, who she married in 1998. After a successful career in municipal finance, Allan had also turned his attention to his first love: making art. It was a passion they shared. Allan often drew in pencil; Alice painted in oil, watercolor, and pastels. When the couple designed the house, the architect made sure to include two separate artist studios, joined by a walkway.

The home's colorful interior was a beautiful, well-appointed feast for the senses. In every direction, objects had been perfectly curated and perfectly positioned at interesting angles to catch your eye. The floors, walls, exposed beams, and vaulted ceilings were made of solid pine. Ivory and blue were the predominant colors: blue patterned pillows, blue china vases, and blue coffee-table books; ivory couches, ivory lamps, and ivory wool rugs. Paintings, often multiple pieces hung together — of birds, of seascapes, of the natural world — covered all available wall space.

A placard reading ENTRÉE DES ARTISTES hung on the front door of Alice's studio. When walking through the atelier, which had sat unused since her Parkinson's diagnosis, she grew wistful. "To be a visual person and then to be stuck with this damn disease," Alice said, looking down at her hands. "Now I'm an old hag."

During my visit with her, a private nurse and a housekeeper took turns looking after her husband. He napped intermittently in the sunlit, majestic great room beneath soaring, twenty-five-foot ceilings.

About a year later, months after Allan's death at home, the couple's Bridgehampton house went on the market. Located on Day Lily Lane and hidden at the end of a long, winding driveway, the home, which had been featured in *Behind the Privets: Classic Hamptons Houses,* was once showcased as part of the East Hampton House and Garden Tour, an annual event that benefits the East Hampton Historical Society.

The listing advertised a nearly seven-acre, eight-thousand-square-foot compound with six bedrooms, seven and a half bathrooms, a heated gunite swimming pool, and a clay tennis court. The price started at $10,995,000, before it was reduced, in September of 2020, to $9,995,000.

But Davey never set foot in the house on Day Lily Lane, with its sprawling, mani-cured lawn and English-style garden. By the time his mother and father divorced, and Alice had married Allan Ryan, Davey was long gone.

Born Alice Lamm in New York City in 1932, she started her life, much like the two sons she later brought into the world, in a penthouse apartment on Fifth Avenue. Alice and her siblings grew up with a French governess. When she was ten, the Lamm family moved into Alice's grandparents' house in Greenwich, Connecticut.

Alice's father worked as a stockbroker. On weekends, to blow off steam, he retreated to the great outdoors — whether sailing or fishing or shooting animals. Steeped in Catholicism, he was a committed churchgoer and daily communicant. He was prone to angry outbursts; early on, Alice learned the delicate dance of walking on eggshells. Alice's mother, an elegant beauty, died while giving birth to Alice's youngest sibling. Her father eventually remarried.

She attended Sacred Heart Greenwich and the University of Arizona. But the desert proved no match for the familiarity of the East Coast. Her next stop, Manhattanville College, was all of fifteen miles from home. Greenwich was a company town, and many of its young men enrolled at Yale in nearby New Haven. In time, a handsome Yale Law School student named Pete Connick caught Alice's eye. He was witty and clever and, like her outdoorsman father, an avid athlete. Alice loved to watch Pete compete in tennis matches. But initially, despite her good looks, she had difficulty getting him to give her the time of day.

In her prime, with dark, shoulder-length hair and a slender, toned physique, Alice was sometimes compared to Jacqueline Kennedy Onassis. In later years, she became intensely fixated on preserving her appearance. Some recalled that in order to keep her weight down, Alice subsisted on boiled chicken breasts, which she'd carry around in her purse. In an effort to ward off hunger, she'd peel open a plastic baggie, sneaking little bites of microwaved chicken cutlets.

Pete's initial lack of interest became a bit of an obsession for Alice. But as with most things in her life, her willfulness prevailed. On March 17, 1955, the *East Hampton Star* ran their engagement announcement on its front page. Their fathers were both self-made men. Pete and Alice married at St. Catherine of Siena, a Roman Catholic church in nearby Riverside. The bride wore a silk gown, a veil of tulle and lace, and carried orchids and lilies of the valley. Though they certainly looked the part, Alice said the early difficulty in securing Pete's affections spelled trouble down the line: "The marriage was fraught with pain and suffering," she told me.

From the start, as Pete had done during his own childhood, he and Alice split their time between an apartment on the Upper

East Side of Manhattan and a summer house in East Hampton. And when Pete's mother, Mary, died, the newly married couple inherited the home she had purchased on The Crossways. It's a short, tree-lined street sandwiched between Georgica Road and Ocean Avenue. Dense, clipped hedges obscure most of the home. "It was great, and it was quite romantic," Alice said of early married life.

During the first few years of their marriage, Alice had trouble getting pregnant. Finally, a son, Peter, was born in 1959. Two years later, in 1961, their second son, David, evened things out. Starting when they were babies, Alice called her two boys Petey and Davey.

Come summertime, the Connick family lived in East Hampton. The Maidstone Club was the social glue that held together the Connicks and the close-knit group of summer families with whom they socialized. On Monday mornings, Pete commuted into Manhattan on the Long Island Rail Road, returning for supper on Friday evenings. Meanwhile, Alice and her two sons stayed at the beach. While their mother and her friends busied themselves playing games of doubles tennis, the Connick boys participated in junior activities at the Maidstone.

Fun was never the objective. Everything was broken down to its crudest form: *a competition.* There were winners, and there were losers.

Even as a young boy, Alice told me, Davey exerted his autonomy and his independence. Her son craved freedom. And once adolescence hit, surfing became a natural outlet for him. Out in the ocean, Davey could escape. He finally felt free. No one could reach him — least of all his mother.

Back then, surfers were part of the counterculture. They smoked weed. They weren't particularly ambitious. Unlike socially acceptable sports such as tennis and golf, surfing was an obsession Alice never understood, let alone condoned. To her, surfing marked the beginning of Davey's separation from his family. He was always in the ocean. Conveniently out of earshot, he would wait, set after set, to catch the perfect wave. "Davey alienated himself from us," Alice said. "And he was very upset about his father being a drinker."

But it wasn't just Big Pete and his drinking that was a problem. Davey viewed his mother as a coconspirator. He believed their privilege had shielded his parents from the real world, and he wanted no part of their

205

coddled existence.

His mother's love of skiing and tennis provoked ire, tennis in particular. When his older brother, Pete, started winning junior tournaments, Dave dismissively labeled it a "snob sport." Such pastimes — requiring uniforms and coaches and access to private facilities — were the provenance of entitled, rich people. Pete, wearing a pale-pink Lacoste shirt, looked like a classic, clean-cut, Upper East Side preppy. Dave, meanwhile, had started pushing the boundaries of social acceptability by wearing beaded necklaces and tribal prints, and growing his hair first to his chin and then to his shoulders.

Alice recalled showing up at Mahoneyville to claim her wayward son and bring him home, only to be met by a strong stench of marijuana smoke that she could smell from behind the wheel of her Ford LTD station wagon from a hundred yards away. "It was not a good era," Alice said. But her raised voice and idle threats fell on deaf ears. High-school-aged kids were drinking beer, smoking pot, and experimenting with psychedelic drugs. Young boys and their female companions were roaming around the Mahoneyville property in a dazed, altered state. Alice felt helpless.

"We were born to the people right before

the social awakening of the 1960s," Thorson Rockwell recalled. His father had similarly come of age during World War II. "Our parents didn't know what to do when their kids started going off the rails. Everyone was going loony tunes on drugs, and our parents had no coping mechanisms whatsoever."

During one of Alice's failed attempts to restore order at Mahoneyville, she came upon a local East Hampton fellow by the name of Michael Stedman, a commercial fisherman. He drove a green pickup truck. Or maybe it was red. What she does remember was that Mike was charming and handsome. Good looks are important to Alice, and Mike had that going for him, in spades. But despite Mike's good looks and easygoing charm, there was a darker side to him that Alice immediately regarded with some skepticism.

"He was a druggie, and behind the charm and the good looks, he was playing with fire," Alice said. "It's hard for me to talk about him." Mike's wife was also a provocative figure. "Mary was a mystic of some sort. She had some power, but the power was not good."

The Stedmans, as you can imagine, are a difficult topic for Alice to discuss. And the feeling goes both ways. Neither woman — the blue-blooded mother or the captain's widow — has very nice things to say about the other.

Looking back, the way Alice sees it, the trajectory was pretty clear: Surfing led Davey to Mahoneyville. Mahoneyville led Davey to Mike Stedman. And Captain Mike led Davey out to Montauk, where he taught him everything he knew. Davey felt a camaraderie with Mike and commercial fishermen that he never felt among his own kin. "He was going to be a fisherman, that much was clear. How was I going to stop him?" Alice asked.

Her youngest son never adjusted to the Connick way of life. Something about his privileged upbringing never sat right. The uniformed doormen, forever opening doors and pressing elevator buttons and delivering dry-cleaning, were a particular source of shame. Similarly, his parents couldn't understand their son's desire to make his livelihood from what he could harvest from the sea. "That's where his father could have stepped in and talked to him," Alice told me. She still blames her late husband for what she views as her son's avoidable death. By March of 1984, she said, Pete's drinking had taken a toll on the family; he had long since checked out of his fatherly duties. Lacking a reliable and trustworthy paternal figure, Davey went searching for one and found it in Mike Stedman.

The captain and his young mate soon became inseparable. Dave routinely showed up unannounced at the Stedman home — first on Newtown Lane and later on Stephen Hands Path — for one of Mary's famous home-cooked dinners. One summer Mary gave Dave, Chris, and Will identical bowl-shaped haircuts. Other summer nights, when it stayed light until nearly nine o'clock, Dave rode his bike around their neighborhood, smiling ear to ear, often with one of the young Stedman boys balanced atop the handlebars.

The warmth of the Stedman home was a welcome departure from the formality of Dave's own upbringing, where everyone dressed for dinner, often prepared by the family's housekeeper. Alice had even outsourced toast and scrambled eggs with pepper. In the Connick household, dinner was served at five-thirty sharp. Spontaneity, in the form of uninvited guests, was generally frowned upon. By 7:00 p.m., when the housekeeper left for the night, the kitchen was immaculate. Not a dish was out of place.

Dave Connick riding with Will Stedman on his handle-bars.

To Dave, home felt icy and remote. At the Stedmans', by contrast, rehashing the day over a six-pack of beer, Dave could finally let his guard down. There wasn't anyone he had to impress. He wasn't being inter-rogated with trivia questions or being asked what, exactly, it was he planned to do with his life.

The last time Alice saw her son, it was clear Davey was battling his demons. Out in Montauk, he had recently parted ways with his dark-green Buick Skylark from the early 1970s and had taken to riding around town, showing up at the docks, on a Harley-Davidson chopper. Davey was becoming

210

rougher around the edges. Inaccessible, really. His close friends remarked upon a similar, sudden shift. Davey seemed angry — about what, no one seemed to know. Mary and Dave were close confidants. Had she shared something with him during one of their many intimate conversations when her husband was away, or out of earshot? Or was he weighed down by something else?

What was clear was that aboard the *Wind Blown,* alongside Captain Mike, Davey was testing out his manhood. Alice respected her son's obvious need for space. But Davey was all of twenty-two. Surely in time, she figured, her youngest son would have a change of heart. In all likelihood, commercial fishing was merely a phase he'd eventually outgrow.

A few weeks later, Davey disappeared aboard the *Wind Blown.* During the ten-day search for wreckage, Alice genuinely believed her son was out there — still floating somewhere in the North Atlantic. All she had to do was find him and bring him home. "Of course, that was a fantasy," Alice told me, of her early conviction that he had survived. Big Pete thought the search, and the private plane their friends had loaned them to look for Davey, was a waste of everyone's time and resources. He never thought rescuers were going to find their son.

In a framed photograph that rests on her bedside table, Davey sits next to Mike Stedman on a party boat, presumably the *Marlin IV*. The top of the silver frame is inscribed with Alice and Pete's initials: A.M.L. — A.J.C. On the bottom of the frame is their wedding date: APRIL 16, 1955. In the photograph, neither man has a shirt on; both are wearing swim trunks. Mike, with a fishing pole in hand, looks out toward the horizon. Dave, wearing a red beaded necklace, sits by his side. The joy between the two men is palpable. They're having the time of their lives.

Looking at the photograph, Alice doesn't know how she survived a lifetime's worth of grief. Over the years, she has experienced more than her fair share of heartbreak. Her first marriage ended in divorce. Her two siblings — first her brother and then her sister — committed suicide. Her younger son was lost at sea.

"It was a killer. Even more killer was when we finally gave up and decided that we weren't going to find him," Alice said. After the search ended, Alice refused to set foot in the Connicks' summer cottage on Georgica Road ever again. It was as if the four walls of the house couldn't be scrubbed clean of the trauma — the inescapable, unending layers of grief.

"Davey was so attractive. He was so winning. He was so *young.*"

A long pause followed.

"It makes me feel like weeping," Alice said, reaching for a tissue.

Her hazel eyes again filled with tears.

Dave Connick aboard the Marlin IV.

9.

CATHY

Unlike the Stedmans, the Connick men didn't leave behind written records of their histories. A few weeks after interviewing Alice, I tracked down Cathy Pradié-Connick, Pete's second wife, hoping she might be willing to share with me her side of the story. Alas, I was too late to speak with Big Pete himself. He died of cancer in 2011.

I asked Cathy whether her husband had ever written down his life story. It had been on her late husband's to-do list, she told me. Big Pete was a scrupulous list-maker. Every morning he sat down at his desk and made a roster of people to call and things to do.

Come September, after leaving East Hampton and returning to their Upper East Side apartment, he sat down at his desk, armed with four sharpened number-two pencils and a yellow legal pad. As on Alice's bedside table, a framed eight-by-ten photo-

215

graph of Davey sat on a nearby window ledge, right beside Pete's desk. In the picture, which Cathy e-mailed me, Davey stands barefoot aboard a docked boat, wearing swim trunks, a T-shirt, and a backward baseball cap. Three fishing rods accompany him. Cathy keeps a copy of the photo in her wallet, beside a picture of her late husband.

But when it came time to write down his own story, Pete came up empty.

"Was it illness that stopped him? Was it sadness over the loss?" Cathy asked in a follow-up e-mail. "I don't have the answer. I do know the intention was there."

Cathy, now in her early sixties, works as the Spence School's associate director of admissions and financial aid. She never had the pleasure of meeting Davey. Pete and Cathy first crossed paths in March of 1992 — eight years after Davey was lost at sea.

"He went about his retirement in typical Pete fashion," Cathy explained. After leaving Milbank, Pete leapt into action and joined the board of directors for the Women's Prison Association, which works with women and families impacted by the criminal justice system. Cathy was already a board member. In 1993, after her first husband passed away following a brief illness, Cathy suddenly became a widow with two young children to raise all on her own. At the time, though Alice and Pete were technically still married, they had been living apart for quite a while. They divorced in 1997.

Timing was everything. Pete came to Cathy's salvation, and they married in June of 1998. It was a Thursday afternoon at the Church of St. Luke in the Fields, the third-oldest church in Manhattan — downtown, on Hudson Street — when Pete and Cathy vowed to spend the rest of their lives together. They made a handsome couple. In a photograph taken on their wedding day, Cathy held a bouquet of pastel flowers, the stems bound together by a long pale-pink ribbon. Pete wore a navy blazer with gold buttons, a white dress shirt, and a checkered bow tie, which matched the lilac hue of Cathy's knee-length dress and suit jacket.

It's one thing to lose a spouse. But grieving the loss of a child is another kind of heartbreak altogether. And Davey's death was clearly a catastrophic loss. Both Cathy and Pete had experienced grave sorrow, and despite their twenty-seven-year age difference, they made immediate sense to each other. "Our relationship had a lot to do with loss," she explained. The two of them routinely discussed their shared anguish.

Pete's coping mechanism, he explained to his wife, was that he eventually learned to compartmentalize his life. "It's always right there," Pete would say about his dead son. "But I can't allow it to be everything."

A piece of driftwood from Davey's Montauk apartment lived atop Pete's desk. Shaped like a boomerang, the well-worn fragment was maybe four or five inches long. It was a small way of making sure some piece of Davey was always nearby.

Cathy couldn't recall exactly when Pete started going to Episcopal services, but the church became a big part of their lives. A lapsed Catholic, he craved routine and generally went about his days in a methodical fashion. And the habits of his faith were hard to break. Every evening at six-thirty, before he turned on the CBS news broadcast, he crossed himself and said a quick prayer for Davey. Similarly, whenever he passed a Catholic church while traveling in a cab or a crosstown bus, he would cross himself. The ritual became a silent act of remembrance.

Like most Americans, Pete and Cathy considered Memorial Day to be the official start of summer. At the end of May every year, the couple ventured out to East Hampton, to their cottage on Georgica Road, for

Dave Connick's headstone.

the long weekend. Shortly after unpacking their things, Pete would ask Cathy: "I need to go see Davey. Will you come with me?" They'd pile into the car and drive over to the Most Holy Trinity Roman Catholic Cemetery on Cedar Street. It was an annual rite of passage, clearing from Davey's tombstone the debris that had accumulated during the wintertime. Every so often, Truman, one of Pete's nephews, still comes around and places a few rocks on Davey's gravestone. In the summer of 2020, Cathy met me there.

Standing over Davey's empty grave was the only time all year that Cathy saw her husband's eyes well up with tears. "I wish you had known him," Pete would say to

Cathy, as his outstretched hand reached for hers. "He would have loved you."

Ten years ago, Pete died at the age of eighty. Father and son are now memorialized side by side in the Connick family plot, joined in the mossy lawn by Louis and Mary Connick.

According to Cathy, Pete's opinion of his younger son's career path was very different from the version that his first wife maintained. She never heard about the so-called disapproval that Alice had described. Pete never wanted Davey to go off to a fancy New England boarding school, she told me. Whether it was surfing or fishing, his father could plainly see that Davey made sense in the water.

For Pete, the fact that Davey turned his back on the clear trajectory that had been painstakingly laid out for him became a quiet source of pride. In later years, Pete encouraged his two stepchildren to do the same. It was a hard-won victory, he told them, to blaze your own trail and eke out an independent life different from the one your parents had imagined for you.

At a cocktail party a few years back, Cathy got to talking with one of Pete's former Milbank colleagues, and Davey's name came up. Cathy mentioned how difficult it must have been for Pete to return to work after rescuers searching for the *Wind Blown*'s foursome came back empty-handed. The colleague, one of Pete's former partners, agreed. He shared with Cathy one thing about Pete that had changed — irrevocably.

Pete's penmanship was iconic. His elegant, cursive handwriting was unmistakable. But after Davey went missing in 1984, it took on a different shape, almost as if the grief of losing his son had changed its rhythm and its cadence.

His handwriting never went back to the way it was before.

■ ■ ■ ■

PART THREE:
MIKE STEDMAN

■ ■ ■ ■

10.
THE STEDMANS

Mike's story may seem as if it began in the fall of 1983, when he fell in love with the *Wind Blown* — sight unseen — while flipping through boat advertisements on an ordinary Sunday afternoon. But it actually started decades before that, far deeper into the Stedman lineage.

The Stedman men were all driven to achieve something. It was a pattern that repeated itself from one generation to the next. When Mike Stedman left Montauk the day after Christmas and journeyed down to Texas, betting his family's savings on a fishing boat that had surely seen better days, he was hell-bent on blazing his own path, like the father and grandfather who came before him. Seamen, all of them.

They were hearty outdoorsmen who gravitated toward water, not land. "As fishers of men, they had traits of leadership. They reared huge families. They were fruitful folks who married young and, if their spouses died, remarried. They buried their dead and went on," Alfred Stedman, Mike's grandfather, wrote in an unpublished memoir, "The Stedman Story," in 1964.

Mike's great-grandfather and great-great-grandfather trout-fished the brooks and bass-fished the lakes and rivers. "On the sparkling riffles, they tempted everything having fish and scales. They were bait fishermen. No flies or doodads for them!" Alfred wrote. "When they dropped a baited hook into deep, dark pools, they often knew exactly how far it would sink before being taken. I myself have seen my dad seining for minnows with a homemade seine, getting it so full of adult fish that it could barely be lifted to the top of the water."

Bruce Stedman, Mike's father, was born in 1920 in St. Paul, Minnesota, to Alfred and his wife, Hazel. They had met as students at nearby Hamline University. The young family soon relocated to the Washington, DC, area in 1929, driving there in their first automobile, a Ford Model T. The nation, which had just elected President Herbert Hoover, soon plunged into the worst depression it had ever known.

Alfred was a newspaperman. He became the one-man Washington bureau of the *St.*

Paul Pioneer Press and Dispatch. Keeping up with the *New York Times* and the *Washington Post* proved a round-the-clock job. "Washington meant incessant reading, painstaking writing, and long hours," he wrote. His long absences left Hazel to do the work of settling the couple's three young children into their new surroundings in Takoma Park, Maryland, pretty much all on her own. Bruce was nine. John was five. And Carol was two.

During summers, when their father went to St. Paul on business, the family tagged along. They rented cabins at Blue Bird Lodge or Belle Shores Resort on Lake Belle Taine in Nevis, Minnesota. The annual pilgrimages cemented their familial ties to the Midwest. The summer getaways became a beloved family tradition all three Stedman children shared with their own children in the decades to come.

"We picked blueberries and chokecherries and even some June berries. We had fish fries and grilled steaks and roasts. We watched the northern lights flare over the skies," Alfred wrote. After their children had grown, the summer vacations took on new meaning. "We were shown picture slides of Bruce's travels around the world. We had night bull sessions on the state of the world.

We fished bass in the newly opened Pine Lake. Through the years, all these things added up to a marvelous human adventure."

Water and fishing are recurrent themes in the Stedman story. It's almost as if the men in the family had a genetic aversion to becoming landlocked. Generation after generation, from Alfred to Bruce to Mike, the men all made their way to the water, whether a stream, a river, a lake, or the ocean.

Although he was born Richard Bruce Stedman, Mike's father only ever went by Bruce. Like his father, Bruce saw virtue in sitting down at a typewriter and recording his own history. In R. Bruce Stedman's memoir from 2003, he wrote that his father, Alfred, "loved to fish whenever he could find the time — fly-fishing was his method of choice. On one famous occasion, he had taken the car to the Cannon River on a solo fishing trip, and while he was wading, he evidently lost the car keys in the water. His return home was much delayed, to my mother's anxiety and irritation."

Throughout his career, Alfred toggled between journalism and government service. Under President Franklin D. Roosevelt, he worked as the assistant administrator for the Agricultural Adjustment

Administration, a program enacted under the New Deal to control crop yields. Though Alfred and Hazel attended occasional White House dinners and receptions, they didn't "go in deeply for the social opportunities Washington afforded." While the Stedmans did their best to assimilate, the social-climbing spectacle proved a bit much. They generally avoided the pomp and circumstance and remained true to their midwestern roots.

During the summer of 1936, in searing July heat, Alfred and Hazel drove their family across the country through the Great Plains. After days of being squeezed inside the car, the family arrived in Bozeman, Montana, where they met up with John Dexter, a fieldman working for the Agricultural Adjustment Administration. The Dexters lived nearby and had arranged for a cabin large enough to comfortably house the five Stedmans.

The crisp, clean Montana air stood in sharp contrast to the drought-stricken plains. For three weeks, the Stedmans occupied a little island in the middle of the Gallatin River. Different varieties of trout — brown trout, rainbow trout, brook trout — swam in nearby streams. Alfred had passed along the fishing gene to his eldest son. It was Alfred's and Bruce's idea of paradise.

In between fly-fishing excursions with his father, something besides fish soon caught Bruce's eye: Ruth Dexter, John's daughter. "She was an attractive Montanan, an outdoor girl, who teased me as an Easterner," Bruce wrote. "Ruth was a skier, horseback rider, camper, and all-around outdoor girl. She was a smoker, as was her father, and not a scholar. She had a lovely, musical laugh, and was good fun to be around. This was not a romance, but for me, at least, an affectionate casual relationship."

Years later, their early twenties coincided with the start of the Second World War, and the friendship between Bruce and Ruth slowly blossomed into more. Once the couple married, though they settled on Long Island, they'd make annual pilgrimages to Minnesota. Every other summer they spent a week or two in the same cabins Bruce had stayed in as a boy. It was a secluded, quiet spot, surrounded by Norway spruces and white pines. Deer tracks speckled its back roads. Their Minnesota vacations were when each Stedman grandchild learned to fish.

By then, Alfred and Hazel's descendants had more than multiplied. Boys ran in the

The Stedman brothers (from left to right): Jim, John, Matt, and Mike.

Stedman family. In Bruce and Ruth's family, two-year gaps neatly separated their sons: John, Mike, Jim, and Matt. Bruce's brother, John, also had four boys; his sister, Carol, had two sons and one daughter. As the eleven grandchildren entered their teenage years, Alfred marked their coming of age by bestowing upon each one a brand-new fly rod — indoctrinating them into the water-loving Stedman lineage once and for all.

Carol's family rented one of the log cabins nearby. Far outnumbered in a sea of wild Stedman boys, Carol's daughter, Sue, was the only girl. Sue and Mike were born a year apart but shared the same early January birthday. The families congregated on the beach during the day and played shuffle-board and card games at night. Sue remem-bered Mike as a happy, good-looking, athletic guy. As he grew older, his obses-sions alternated between fishing and surf-ing.

Even as a young girl, Sue observed that the family vacations weren't exactly relaxing getaways for Mike's mother. Ruth may as well have stayed back home in East Willis-ton, New York, since her domestic chores seemingly quadrupled while on vacation. Each day, while the men went off fishing, Ruth was in constant motion: laundering clothes, shopping for groceries, doing the dishes, and making dinner. Ruth's only bit of solace was sitting by the lake most afternoons, where she'd smoke cigarettes and knit.

Bruce spent his days on the water in a motorboat that came with the cabin, with a pipe in his mouth and a fishing rod in his hand. As evening cocktail hour approached, he prepared the nightly appetizers. His specialty was a homemade clam dip he'd serve in a bowl alongside rectangular club crackers. Before dinner, Bruce and Ruth downed two martinis apiece. His was a generous pour; each drink contained two or three shots of gin.

"Bruce was a very strong personality. He was definitely in charge," Sue said. He dictated both the cocktail and the dinner hours — making sure the families never deviated from the schedule he had set. "Everybody was a little afraid of him."

His softer side, according to Matt Stedman, the youngest and last surviving of the four brothers, only became evident well into his eighties — and even then, it was a rare occurrence. "Attaboys" were as uncommon as pats on the back. "We never expected it, so we didn't miss it," Matt said to me. "When the chairman of the board was speaking, we all shut up and listened." Over the years, Bruce shared with his sons the three things that had made him successful: "First, work hard. Second, learn to speak well. And third, be kind."

True to his Depression-era upbringing, Bruce was also a dedicated penny-pincher. Nothing pleased him quite like saving money. For Bruce's sons, borrowing money from their father always came with strings attached. So many strings, they eventually learned, that it was better not to ask for help in the first place. Which was why, rather than risk the humiliation of asking his father to bail him out, Mike relied on a stable of close friends to come up with the down payment he needed to buy the *Wind Blown.*

He must have been remembering the experience of John, his older brother, who once called his father to ask for a loan to open up a dog kennel in Wisconsin. The only problem: he was $40,000 short. On the phone, after hemming and hawing, Bruce finally agreed to lend John the money. A few days later, a check arrived in the mail. John tore open the envelope, drove to the bank, signed his name and account number on the back of the check, and stuck it inside a plastic pneumatic tube for the drive-thru teller to deposit into his checking account.

A few moments later, the bank teller spoke over the intercom. "John, did you take a look at this check?"

"It's good," John said. "It's from my dad."

"Look at where he signed it," the teller said, pushing the check back through the tube for him to examine.

Puzzled, John looked down at the signature line. The amount was correct — "FORTY-THOUSAND AND 0/100 DOLLARS" — but his father's signature was missing. In its place, Bruce had written in all-caps: "OVER MY DEAD BODY."

As with his four sons, Bruce proved a tough act for his two younger siblings to follow.

During high school in Maryland, he earned more or less straight As and, somewhat on a whim, applied to Harvard College. Excellent grades and letters of recommendation persuaded Harvard to give the Montgomery Blair High School senior a shot. His acceptance there altered the trajectory of his life.

Bruce arrived in Cambridge, Massachusetts, in September of 1938. His train itinerary took him from Washington's Union Station through New York's Pennsylvania Station to Boston — or that was his plan, at least. A late-summer hurricane interfered with his travels. Already running a day behind schedule, he ultimately abandoned the train in favor of a Greyhound bus bound for Boston, carrying with him his portable typewriter and violin, and finally arriving with two days' worth of stubble and soiled, wrinkled clothes.

Having attended a public high school, where everyone was more or less on equal footing, Bruce soon learned to navigate New England's elite social strata. He and his freshman-year roommate, J. Malcolm Barter, a conservative New England Yankee, didn't initially seem like a great fit, but in time, they forged a lifelong friendship.

Back home in Maryland, starting in the

sixth grade, Bruce had earned extra pocket change by delivering copies of the *Washington Post* around his neighborhood before the school bell rang. In Cambridge, he duplicated his childhood enterprise by delivering the *Boston Globe.* He awoke at the crack of dawn each morning to drop off copies to individual student subscribers and fill metal stands around campus with fresh stacks of newspapers. An hour a day of work netted him $25 by week's end. Determined to pay his own way through school, Bruce also washed dishes at eating clubs, worked as an assistant librarian, and received small scholarships during his junior and senior years. "The bottom line, I am proud to say, is that after freshman year, my college costs to the family were minimal, tuition and not much more," Bruce wrote. "In other words, Dad paid $400 and I paid twice that toward my total college costs."

Bruce's innate frugality suited his austere temperament. His drive for self-sufficiency was something he later instilled in his own sons. Curiously, for a Harvard graduate who went on to become a civil servant, Bruce's ego wasn't wedded to what his sons accomplished in their professional lives. Quite the opposite. Bruce's only sticking point was that each of them learn how to pay his own way. If his sons never learned how to stand on their own two feet, Bruce felt he had fundamentally failed them as a father.

"Are you disappointed that no one followed in your footsteps?" Matt, his youngest son, once asked him.

"No. I couldn't care less," Bruce told him. "I just want you to be happy and be able to support yourself."

Matt now lives in Bear Lake, Michigan, where he runs a successful plumbing and heating business. His backyard overlooks Lake Michigan, which looks less like a lake and more like an ocean.

Bruce's freshman year at Harvard was a formidable challenge. Many of his classmates had attended the best boarding schools money could buy, and he had a lot of catching up to do. Though he started to hit his stride by sophomore year, he might have fared better in the classroom that first year if a serious romance had not distracted him.

Joan Todd, a Radcliffe student jokingly nicknamed Hot Toddy, was a radiant, flirtatious beauty, sought after by upperclassmen and junior faculty alike. Bruce soon fell under Joan's spell. The two started spending a great deal of time together. Headed on a premarital track, Bruce even paid a visit to Joan's parents' New Jersey home. It didn't last, though. The decision to split was, apparently, mutual. "She made it clear that she required a rich man and she thought rightly that I would never qualify," Bruce wrote.

Putting the anguish of young heartbreak aside, Bruce became president of the Harvard Glee Club and devoted more time to studying anthropology. Bruce's new life of "no dates, no outside interests except Glee Club — just study, study, study" instilled lifelong habits that served him well.

One Sunday — December 7, 1941 — he and his roommate were studying, with the radio tuned to the New York Philharmonic, when an announcer interrupted the concert. What followed became embedded in his generation's memory bank: "We interrupt this broadcast with the following news bulletin. The White House has announced that the Japanese have bombed Pearl Harbor." All studying ceased. The young men sat transfixed. Until that moment, Bruce and his classmates had been self-described peaceniks. But the bombing of Pearl Harbor provoked an instant shift.

The United States declared war on Japan and Germany. All men of military age registered for the compulsory national draft.

Those who were already in college could finish their studies before being called to serve. "We assumed (how little we knew!) that the American response to the Japanese would be quick and devastating; the war would probably be over before we could get into it!" Bruce wrote.

Six months later, in the late spring of 1942, he graduated magna cum laude from Harvard. By then, World War II was in full swing, and the fighting was far from over. Late in his senior year, he'd received the Sheldon Traveling Fellowship, a prestigious honor bestowed upon one graduating senior each year. The list of previous winners included Theodore H. White, who became a political journalist and historian. Bruce was desperate to seize the opportunity. The scholarship covered a year's worth of expenses for a student who couldn't otherwise afford to travel abroad.

Bruce had set his hopes on spending the year traveling through Mexico, but first his draft board in Maryland had to approve his deferment. Bruce pleaded for four to six months of leeway. Even a letter from Vice President Henry Wallace, stating it was in the best interest of the country to allow Bruce to take up the scholarship, was apparently met with laughter.

"I want to be sure that I understand you, Mr. Stedman," the chairman of the draft board told him. "You are saying to this board that you are perfectly prepared for your friends, classmates, neighbors, to go off and fight and perhaps die for their country, so long as you can go swanning around the world on some traveling fellowship, right?"

"No, sir!" Bruce responded. "I want to fight for my country. But first, I want four months to take advantage of this great honor which has been offered to me."

In the end, the draft board gave Bruce a four-month deferment, with the strict proviso that he not extend his travels by one additional day. He packed his bags and headed to Mexico, where Harvard's anthropology department helped arrange his itinerary. It was Bruce's first time stepping foot outside the United States, and those four months in Mexico not only proved a grand, carefree adventure but sowed seeds for future exploration abroad and his eventual career as an international civil servant.

Officer training school, an elite program that admitted the generation's best and brightest intent on becoming naval officers, was next. Based in Chicago, each of its classes comprised 1,500 men. It was a brutal indoctrination. The men awakened before sunrise each morning for a series of punishing physical exercises specifically designed to humiliate them. The trainees learned to march to and fro, to the exacting beat of a snare drum. Training lasted 120 days. The commanders had their work cut out for them: in four months' time, they had to transform smart-ass college boys into proper sailors.

Bruce Stedman, with his Harvard pedigree, proved an easy target. He was a whiz in the classroom, but a miserable failure when it came to learning how to march. Invariably, his rifle landed on the wrong shoulder, no matter how many times he tried to get it right.

Ensign Zirkle, the company commander, took particular delight in singling out Bruce. "What's your name, mister?" he would shout.

"Stedman!" Bruce hollered back, already familiar with the torturous back-and-forth.

"What?"

"Midshipman Stedman!"

"WHAT?"

"Midshipman Stedman, sir!"

"Stedman, did you actually go to college?"

"Yes, sir!"

"What *college* could have possibly graduated *you?*"

"Harvard, sir!"

"Haarvaard? A Haarvaard man! Who doesn't know his left from his right, soldier? Is that right, Stedman?"

The United States Navy worked its magic on Bruce Stedman. In a few months' time, the military transformed him into "an officer and a gentleman." Before going off to war, he headed home to Maryland for a two-week leave to tidy up his domestic affairs.

During Bruce's time at Harvard, the Dexter family, whom the Stedmans had met in Montana several summers prior, had moved to Maryland, where John Dexter took a job alongside Alfred Stedman at the Department of Agriculture. John's daughter, Ruth, enrolled at the University of Maryland. After the attack on Pearl Harbor, she quit school, like many young women of her generation, and supported the war effort by working as a secretary for the American Red Cross.

Bruce and Ruth started spending more time together. Granted, it wasn't the red-hot romance he had shared with Hot Toddy, but Ruth had a steady, reliable temperament that slowly grew on him. As Bruce and

Ruth's relationship developed, Hazel kept a watchful eye from the sidelines. "I don't know what your intentions are regarding Ruth Dexter, but I think she's a wonderful girl," Hazel told her son, taking him aside one afternoon. "And if your intentions are not serious — and I suspect they are not — you had better tell her, because I think she's been sort of waiting around for you."

Bruce assured his mother that while he had grown quite fond of Ruth, matrimony was not in the cards for him, what with the uncertainty of the war and all. Besides, Bruce and Ruth had already discussed the matter. Theirs was a friendship, plain and simple.

However, the isolation he experienced while on his first assignments — first at Little Creek, a naval base in Virginia, and then at sea on a World War I submarine chaser with a nineteen-man crew — led him to rethink the foolishness of his self-imposed "no marriage" rule. He and Ruth struck up a friendly courtship — mainly by correspondence, but interspersed with occasional visits to Maryland. And in May of 1943, during a telephone call, he worked up the courage to ask for her hand in marriage. At first, she flat-out refused. But Bruce kept asking, not one to take no for an answer, and she finally agreed.

On July 17, 1943, during one of his three-day leaves, they married at the Grace Episcopal Church in Silver Spring, Maryland. Her family's Episcopal rector and his family's Presbyterian minister shared ceremonial duties. White and pink gladioli decorated the church. Ruth wore a white marquisette gown and a fingertip-length veil; ribbon streamers decorated a white Bible. It was a Saturday afternoon, and Bruce walked the five or six blocks to the church in the hot July sun, sweat soaking through his dress whites. Ruth departed from the reception at her parents' house wearing a blue linen suit. Their honeymoon was brief, just a one-night stay at a run-of-the-mill motel in nearby Petersburg, Virginia.

Practicality reigned supreme. While Bruce was out navigating the world at large, Ruth kept watch over the home front. She ran a tight, orderly ship. Though her husband would break some of their wedding vows over the course of their nearly fifty-year marriage, Bruce and Ruth were a team. They looked out for each other.

Once Bruce finished his stateside training, an overseas tour loomed on the horizon. He met his ship, the USS *Robert F. Keller,* which was being built at a Houston shipyard. By late summer 1944, she was ready to go to war. From Houston, she sailed to nearby Galveston, the same Gulf Coast port where, thirty-nine years later, Bruce's son, Mike, purchased the *Wind Blown.*

The next port of call was the Philadelphia Navy Yard, where the *Robert F. Keller* received a camouflage paint job. Before she sailed away, Bruce and Ruth bid each other a teary farewell. They parted ways, not knowing when or where or even *if* their paths would cross again. The couple split their remaining cash: Ruth kept $30 and Bruce took $15. It was all the money they had. Ruth returned home to Maryland, moved back in with her parents, and went to work.

Because they rarely made port, the *Robert F. Keller,* a 315-foot vessel, took on fuel, supplies, and mail while at sea; ships pulled up alongside her periodically to restock. The mail arrived in batches, maybe one delivery every couple of weeks. Alfred subscribed to the *New Yorker* on his son's behalf and mailed Bruce copies. Besides letters from Ruth, the magazine's periodic arrival was his only reliable connection to what was happening in the outside world. The "orgy of reading" lifted his spirits immeasurably.

One of the articles left such an impression that it altered the course of Bruce's life.

E. B. White reported from San Francisco on a conference discussing the formation of a newfangled organization: the United Nations. "The speeches were subdued, lofty, and long. The atmosphere was that of a cathedral. . . . There was a feeling in the room (or at any rate it appeared so to me) that an old order was dead and a new one was about to begin," White wrote. "And here, beautifully situated upon a hill, were a handful of architectural apprentices whose drawing board contained a neat and precise blueprint labeled the Future."

The scene White described in San Francisco was a balm to Bruce's war-weary soul. Mussolini and Hitler were dead. It was time to start imagining a new world order that combined justice, law, and human rights.

Besides, life at sea felt lonely and monotonous to Bruce. He had grown tired of the rolling deep. When the war ended, he made his way back to the States. Ruth, eager to begin the next phase of their lives as husband and wife, had scrupulously saved her weekly paychecks for a place to call their own. She proudly showed off her checkbook, with its "healthy balance," to her husband.

But the couple's economic stability hinged on Bruce finding a decent-paying job. Alongside hundreds of thousands of other well-qualified veterans, he entered a frenzied job market.

Alfred described his postwar son as "a most determined young man." Upon being reunited with his father, who was by then serving on President Harry Truman's Famine Emergency Committee, Bruce pounded his right fist into his left palm to drive home his earnestness. "I've got to have a job!" he exclaimed. Alfred referred his son to friends in the Civil Aeronautics Administration and the State Department, but Bruce had a different plan in mind.

In January of 1946, the United Nations existed in London, England, but only in embryonic form. The organization hadn't yet moved its headquarters to New York City. By the time March rolled around, Bruce had set up interviews with several senior UN officials who had established temporary offices at Hunter College, which was then an all-women's school, in the Bronx. Bruce wore his navy uniform, complete with combat ribbons, to his interview with David Vaughan, the UN director of general services. Because Bruce outranked him in the military, Vaughan kept saluting

Bruce and calling him "sir." It made Bruce uncomfortable. He would have happily shined Vaughan's shoes if it meant securing a job — even a temporary one — with the United Nations.

Though the UN initially offered Bruce a job for one year and one year only, it became the only place he ever worked. For the next thirty-three years, he slowly ascended its labyrinthine ranks. A career civil servant, he served on three political missions in the Middle East and eventually became the United Nations Development Programme's resident representative in Kenya and Ethiopia. In 1977, while helping run the United Nations Environment Programme, the first agency headquartered in Africa, Bruce retired with the rank of United Nations assistant secretary general.

Bruce's ambition seemed to skip a generation. When it came time for one of his four sons to grab the mantle and run with it, an heir apparent never quite stepped forth. But whatever Mike, the second-eldest son, lacked in book smarts, he made up for in likability and hard work. He was a natural-born leader. You were rooting for him. Like his father, you'd follow him into battle.

11.
UP-ISLAND

Bruce and Ruth Stedman.

Early in their marriage, Bruce and Ruth bought a three-bedroom house, built in 1928, on William Street in East Williston, Long Island. Besides its proximity to the city, East Williston was a well-appointed Nassau County suburb with tree-lined streets, single-family homes, and, perhaps its best selling point, high-ranking public schools.

249

Sons soon outnumbered available bedrooms. John, the eldest, slept in the attic. Mike had his own bedroom. Jim and Matt, the two youngest brothers, shared a room.

Each morning, Bruce commuted thirty miles by Long Island Rail Road into New York City. Five days a week, he was gone from 7:00 a.m. to 7:00 p.m. — and that's when he wasn't traveling overseas. In 1952, the United Nations moved to its current location in midtown Manhattan, overlooking the East River. A born conformist, Bruce set his sights on climbing the mammoth bureaucratic ladder. Standing over six feet tall and wearing a pressed suit and a bow tie, he cut a striking figure.

It didn't hurt that Bruce was charming, witty, and clever. But he was also a masterful delegator. His subordinates soon learned that their boss didn't miss a trick. His management style was clear and direct: if you didn't cut the mustard, he told you as much.

By the mid-1960s, when it was time to get the United Nations Development Programme up and running, Bruce worked with a particular brand of intensity. He had high expectations and gave minimal instructions. Underlings quaked when they heard his heavy shoes pounding through the long corridors, headed in their direction. Unusual for a senior man, Bruce worked without his jacket and smoked a heavy, dark pipe that billowed blue smoke. As one of his colleagues described him: "Bruce Stedman led by personal example, demonstrating the best of what an international civil servant should and could be. He was an American of the world, and had the depth, strength, and commitment of Dag Hammarskjöld." Much like his son Mike, Bruce had an unmistakable presence. When he entered a room, everyone stood up a little taller.

Both he and his wife were children of the Great Depression. *Credit* was a dirty word. If the couple couldn't pay for something in cash, they didn't indulge. They never bought things simply because they wanted them. They only made purchases based on legitimate needs. Bruce didn't even approve of his sons getting braces on their teeth; such luxuries were status symbols, and the last thing he wanted for his sons was to reflect any kind of privilege. Cadillacs were far too showy. Ruth drove around town in a wood-paneled Chrysler station wagon. And as her own mother-in-law had done, she stayed home, looking after the children. Ruth was a resourceful, devoted homemaker. She took seriously the task of whipping four young boys into shape.

Mike didn't make casual acquaintances. By and large, the friends he made, he kept for life.

Starting in the seventh grade, he attended the Wheatley School, a prestigious public school in Old Westbury that went up to the twelfth grade. It functioned as a great suburban equalizer. Students filtered into Wheatley from surrounding neighborhoods: Albertson, East Williston, Mineola, Old Westbury, and Roslyn Heights. Mineola was blue-collar; East Williston was white-collar. Protestants and Catholics constituted half the student body; Jews made up the other half. The Stedmans, who were Protestant, attended the Community Church of East Williston. Catholics went to the Church of St. Aidan in Williston Park. And Jews worshiped at Temple Sinai in Roslyn Heights. The Wheatley School was also racially segregated. In the 1968 Wheatley yearbook, its custodial staff was all-Black and its teaching staff was all-white.

In junior high school, Mike fell in with a group of young boys who called themselves the Choppess (rhymes with *shops*) — a play on the term *bust your chops.* The fifteen

252

boys, all athletes, were inseparable. They became familiar faces in after-school detention and soon earned reputations as pranksters.

On Halloween, armed with cartons full of eggs, the Choppess rampaged through the neighborhood. Come wintertime, they threw snowballs at the windshields of passing cars, running through backyards and over fences to avoid being caught. Wherever they went, the Choppess loved to trespass and make mischief. They didn't commit felonies, exactly, but they racked up more than a few misdemeanors along the way. "There were no other such groups at Wheatley and as I recall, the school administration was, at best, slightly opposed to our existence," Dave Berwald, one of the original fifteen Choppess, wrote in a chapter of his self-published memoir, *Chinese Buffet: A Journal of My Life and Career.*

This was, of course, decades before middle-school students started carrying cell phones. If their parents needed to reach them, the Choppess could typically be found at one of two local intersections, in Roslyn Heights or East Williston, respectively. The former was where the girls hung out. The latter, adjacent to the baseball field at North Side Elementary School, where

Mike had gone, was where the boys passed around a can of beer wrapped in a brown-paper bag after a pickup ball game.

The Choppess had a reputation for being quite competitive with one another, especially when it came to attracting members of the opposite sex. And pound for pound, Mike was one of the strongest among the pack of virile boys. Choppess member Steve Rosen described him to me as a young Brad Pitt. Mike loved girls, and the feelings went both ways. Even older girls took notice of him. Gary Fuschillo, another Wheatley classmate, remembered attending Cub Scouts alongside Mike at the age of six or seven. Early on, Gary said, the two boys established a friendly rivalry and competed for the affections of the "best-looking Jewish girls." By high school, Mike had become a full-fledged ladies' man. "Mike was an extremely persuasive person," Gary said. "He was the golden boy."

Mike was no wallflower. And by high school, he had hit his stride. In the 1968 yearbook, he appeared on half a dozen pages. In one photograph, of the tenth-grade class council, he holds court at the very center of the picture. Wearing a beret, he makes direct eye contact with the camera and radiates self-assured contentment.

But Mike wasn't only popular. He was also a versatile athlete. During his sophomore year, he was a member of Wheatley's varsity football and wrestling teams.

His grades, however, posed a constant source of frustration.

During their sophomore year, a few of the Choppess somehow discovered a stack of exams, xeroxed them, and circulated them among themselves. "The Syndicate" became the nickname for their top-secret, grade-inflating operation. Suddenly Choppess who had been squeaking by with Cs were now scoring solid As on their final exams. Apparently, Wheatley's teachers never did pinpoint the source of the underground scheme.

In middle school and high school, something else started capturing more and more of Mike's attention. Surfing, then a relatively new sport on Long Island, combined Mike's athletic prowess with his love of the water. But there were only so many hours in the weekend, and as winter turned to spring and the days grew longer, Mike found himself gravitating toward another group of boys who, unlike the Choppess, had similarly caught the surfing bug.

These boys called themselves the Mene-

The East Williston gang hanging out in front of He'e Nalu, one of Montauk's first surf shops.

hunes. In Hawaiian mythology, the Menehune were an ancient, dwarf-like race of people who occupied the Hawaiian Islands before Polynesian settlers displaced them.

A close-knit circle of four East Williston families, made up of all boys, formed the core of the Long Island Menehunes: the Stedmans, the DePasquales, the Geerys, and the Stuarts. In each family, there were tiers of older brothers, middle brothers, and younger brothers. They grew up together, joining the Boy Scouts, playing Little League, and riding the subway to the Bronx to see Yankee games.

Once they formed the Menehunes, their

families paid a few dollars in monthly club dues to cover gas money. Jeb Stuart and Bruce DePasquale, the eldest members of the tribe, presided over the feral group. One of the fathers designed the club's black-and-white circular logo. Its yin-yang symbol resembled a crashing wave.

For the Menehunes, East Williston was home base. But living in a landlocked Long Island suburb twenty miles from the ocean meant that transportation posed a constant problem. Most Saturday mornings, their parents took turns dropping the boys off at local beaches — usually Gilgo Beach or Long Beach — until they were finally old enough to drive themselves.

Mrs. Geery often played the role of designated driver. She would take the boys' gas money and fill up her Ford Falcon station wagon. As many as eight boys crowded in, with eight surfboards spilling out the rear windows and hatchback. It was a miracle the car never broke down. Once the boys arrived at the beach and the salty, humid air filled their lungs, they couldn't wipe the smiles off their faces. In the 1960s, the Long Island surf scene had just started to kick in. It looked like a scene right out of *Gidget.*

The Menehunes documented their excursions on a Super 8 movie camera. After catching a wave and standing up, they'd prance across their boards. In the video footage, the boys rode slow, rolling waves that peeled off, one after another. This was years before the invention of Velcro leashes, which wrap around your ankle and attach the surfboard to your body. In the videos, after wiping out, each boy swam toward shore, retrieved his board, and paddled back out into the surf. Falling down and getting back up again, each boy developed a distinctive style.

The Menehunes called Mike Crusher.

The DePasquales were a family of surfers. And during Mike's adolescence, they played a critical role in not only his maturation but also his introduction to Montauk.

Gene DePasquale owned a concrete plant; his wife, Jean, was a homemaker. They gave their sons — Bruce, Jamie, and Eugene — Hannon surfboards and O'Neill wetsuits as Christmas and birthday presents. As a teenager, Gene, who carried himself with the self-assurance of a young John Wayne (others described him to me as a cross between Burt Lancaster and Charlton Heston), had worked as a lifeguard at Jones Beach. He learned to surf and soon befriended John "Jack" Hannon, who had started making surfboards. Hannon Surfboards later became one of Long Island's biggest surfboard manufacturers.

Among the boys, Gene possessed demigod status. He was the only father who surfed. Bruce Stedman, forever in a suit and tie, might venture out to Montauk once a year (say, every Easter Sunday) to go fishing with his friends at sunrise, but Gene lived in swim trunks, and on Saturday mornings, he strapped a stack of surfboards on the roof of the family's green Buick station wagon and drove to Gilgo Beach. No one wore seat belts.

As the weather started getting chillier, skateboarding became a new outlet for the boys. Conveniently, it was also a hobby they could pursue closer to home. On their driveways in East Williston, wearing canvas high-top sneakers, blue jeans, and wool turtlenecks, the Menehunes rode skateboards before being called in for dinner. At first they tried skating down their asphalt driveways on homemade boards. But once Hobie began to manufacture fiberglass skateboards, they shimmied across the pavement and defied gravity — the sensation was not unlike catching a wave. Surfboards were changing too; they were getting shorter and shorter.

When his eldest son was thirteen or fourteen years old, Gene DePasquale took the family on a summer camping trip out to Montauk, the first of many. At first, they stayed in pop-up campers at Ditch Plains Beach, and eventually splurged on a small cottage rental for the entire summer. Shortly thereafter, the DePasquales purchased a summer home on Surfside Avenue in Montauk. At 1,100 square feet, with three bedrooms and one bathroom, its best asset was the location: you could walk to the beach. Gene and Jean DePasquale, who later retired there, fell in love with Montauk. It felt like a largely undiscovered slice of heaven on earth.

Once the Wheatley School let out for the summer, the DePasquales' new driveway overflowed with cars from up-island. The boys slept on their floor, on the lawn, or parked in their vans. The Menehunes of East Williston befriended some of the local kids in Montauk. The tribe roamed free. When the surf was breaking (and the Menehunes weren't exactly picky), they'd head to Atlantic Terrace or Ditch Plains for the day. Back then, there were never more than a dozen guys in the water at one time. The scent of weed and patchouli wafted through the air. At lunchtime, the boys went cooler-diving for sandwiches, subsisted on leftover hot dogs, and stopped into town for day-old rolls and pastries from Wayd's Bakery and Konditorei, where some of the boys had part-time summer jobs.

Eugene DePasquale Jr., the youngest of the three DePasquale brothers, recalled Mike Stedman with particular fondness. Unlike many of his older brothers' friends, when Mike stopped by the house, he didn't chase scrawny Eugene out of the basement or play pranks on him. He was gentle and kind. When he came over to play a game of catch, he took the time to look Eugene in the eye and ask him how he was doing. And his sincerity left an impression. Mike always wore a smile on his face.

In 1968, Eugene's parents paid either $23,000 or $32,000 (Eugene couldn't recall) for their summer house. In 2016, the family sold it for a seven-figure profit. Montauk used to be a workingman's vacation destination. Surfing was a subculture. Surfers weren't coming out on the weekends and booking $800 hotel rooms at the Surf Lodge. Many of them made ends meet by working as busboys or waiters in Amagansett and Montauk restaurants. They opposed the Vietnam War and smoked a lot of pot. "Now it's clean-cut soccer moms and surf schools," Jamie DePasquale, Eugene's older brother, said. "Older surfers like me are horrified by the whole thing. We'd much rather have it be like it was back then."

Jamie is a modern painter who lives in Bridgehampton. Among the Menehunes, he was the artist of the group. From the 1970s to the 1990s, he worked as Roy Lichtenstein's studio assistant. Roy's son was also an avid surfer, and whenever a hurricane hit the East End and the surf picked up, Roy gladly extended to Jamie the courtesy of an afternoon off.

As a teenager, Jamie shot most of the video footage that showcases the Menehunes learning how to surf and skateboard. Once they were back home in East Williston, they rode their bikes to the local camera store to drop off the Super 8 negatives. A few days later, Jamie would pick up the film, which had since been converted, like magic, into a moving picture. When the Menehunes gathered in someone's basement to watch the footage, there wasn't an agenda. No one took minutes. The boys met up, between wrestling matches, when they could.

The Super 8 footage appears grainy, and in the compilation Jamie mailed to me, classical music plays in the background. It's a

The Choppess' tenth anniversary camping trip to the Catskills circa summer of 1980.

difficult video for Jamie to watch. It fills him with nostalgia. Many of the Menehunes — not just Michael Stedman — died young.

The Menehunes lacked the organization of the Choppess, who, all these decades later, still stay in touch. Among their members are an atomic physicist, a nuclear physicist, an accountant, a chef, and a commercial fisherman. They still meet up for reunions every now and again, and sign their group e-mails "Choppess are Toppess."

But Mike Stedman never sent an e-mail. In 1984, e-mail didn't exist. He was the first of the fifteen original Choppess to die. His shoulders never grew hunched. His belly never sagged. His full head of sun-kissed hair never thinned or turned gray. He never got divorced. Among the Choppess, Mike will forever remain the bare-chested, athletic young man who was taken down in the prime of life.

All of the Choppess I was able to track down remembered exactly where they were when they got the call that Mike Stedman was lost at sea. On March 29, 1984, Steve Rosen was sitting at his desk in Manhattan at E.F. Hutton & Company, the brokerage firm, where he worked as a bond analyst, when Walter Vogt, a member of the Choppess and one of Mike's closest childhood friends, called to tell him the news. The two men sat in stunned silence on the drive out to Montauk, where they soon linked up with search crews looking for the missing foursome.

Mark Vedder, who died of heart disease in the spring of 2018, was the second of the Choppess to go. He and his three brothers grew up alongside the Stedmans. Mark was one of Mike's closest childhood friends, dating back to their days at North Side Elementary School. The pair called themselves the M&M's. "He was knock-your-socks-off California surfer-dude material," Cathy

Vedder, Mark's widow, said of Mike. "He was sweet, nice, kind, adorable, and hunky."

Some of the Choppess made an early pact not to leave Long Island. Mark Vedder was among the first to test his wings. Shortly after high school graduation, he left the island for college and eventually received a PhD in physics. Mark could take anything apart and put it back together again. As a wedding present for Mike and Mary — Mike was the first among the band of brothers to get married — Mark found a broken washer and dryer, repaired both units, strapped them to the top of a friend's van, and drove them out to the couple's first apartment in Montauk.

In all their years together, Cathy saw her husband cry on just three occasions. The first was when Mike vanished in 1984. Cathy and Mark had been together for about a decade by then, and Cathy was on tenterhooks, not knowing how he would ever make peace with the sudden death of his closest childhood friend.

Mark stayed silent. He never said a word. A few days after getting the news, he went out to the back of their house in Manalapan, New Jersey, and, using a rototiller, dug up a half acre of land. He transformed half of it into a rose garden, and the other half into a vegetable garden. Cathy described it as "a silent act of pure male physical strength."

Cathy and Mark named their second child, a son, Michael. When the movie version of *The Perfect Storm* came out, it provided them with some measure of relief. The film offered Mark a visual representation of what may have happened to his childhood friend. Looking back, Cathy thinks that watching it marked the end of her husband's bereavement.

In late March of 1984, shortly after the *Wind Blown* went down, Jamie DePasquale walked from Ditch Plains to Montauk Point searching for flotsam and jetsam, which soon washed up on southward-facing beaches: a four-man life raft with WIND BLOWN stenciled on it, pieces of maroon-colored wood, part of the wooden pilothouse.

After the crew vanished without a trace, East End residents held a benefit called Art for Rescue at what was formerly the Laundry Restaurant on Race Lane in East Hampton. James Brooks, Willem de Kooning, Elaine de Kooning, Roy Lichtenstein, and Saul Steinberg were among some two dozen local artists who donated artwork that was raffled off to a large crowd of community members. Alice Connick donated a pastel drawing; Jamie DePasquale offered an oil painting on wood titled *Aquatic Resonance.* Tickets were $5 apiece. Several attendees wrote MARY STEDMAN on their raffle tickets instead of their own; she took home a charcoal drawing by Esteban Vincente of Bridgehampton. Proceeds from the fundraiser, some $30,000 in all, went directly to the Stedman family. The donations helped provide Mary and her three sons with an added layer of financial security during those chaotic first months.

Though the money helped the Stedmans, the community didn't extend financial support to the families of the other missing crew members. On May 18, 1984, Donna Llewellyn, Scott's mother, sent a letter to Hans Hokanson, a local sculptor, who, along with Anne Sherry, spearheaded the Art for Rescue benefit. In the letter, Donna objected that a picture of her son, which she had allowed the *Star* to use, was used for promotional purposes to help advertise the benefit. "As you pointed out, the Art for Rescue was to raise monies for my son as well as for the Stedman family," Donna wrote. "If this is true, you may send my son's share of the proceeds to my home address, above."

Later that year, shortly before Christmas, Jamie delivered a wreath he had fashioned out of tree branches to Mary's house in East Hampton. DEAR MARY, he inscribed on a small card. HAVE COURAGE. Mary hung the wreath next to her front door. "The wreath was an important reminder for me," Mary said. "I was so young, and every time I would get really despairing, I would read Jamie's words."

Jamie is still an avid surfer, though frustratingly less agile the older he gets. Now in his midsixties, he has less tolerance for the freezing water than he once did. Sometimes, in between sets at Turtle Cove, a rocky point southwest of the Montauk Lighthouse, or nearby breaks, he thinks about the Menehunes.

Surfing is technically prohibited for most of the year at Montauk Point State Park, an area local surfers call North Bar, but it's a ban the town of East Hampton rarely enforces. The lighthouse erected there sits atop Turtle Hill. In 1796, when President George Washington commissioned the all-white tower (eventually a reddish-brown band was added), it sat about three hundred feet from the edge of the cliffs. In the centuries since, erosion and the volatile Atlantic Ocean have slowly eaten away at it.

Conservationists estimate about a foot of land disappears into the sea each year. Nowadays, a mere seventy feet separates the lighthouse from the bluff.

None of the Menehunes were native sons of Montauk, yet all made their way to the easternmost tip of Long Island in search of a particular way of life. Most stayed on the East End and built their lives around it. Over the years, the ashes of some of the Menehunes (including Jamie and Eugene's brother, Bruce DePasquale) have been scattered nearby. Their father's ashes were released into the ocean too. Jamie likes to think that some part of Mike is still nearby. He can't imagine Mike — or anyone, for that matter — ending up in a coffin, buried six feet underground.

John Geery died while surfing in Puerto Rico. Mike Stedman died while fishing off the coast of Montauk. Jamie figures it's as honest a way to go as any — doing the thing you love most until you can't do it anymore.

Christmas of 1980: Will, Mike, and Chris.

12.
FATHERS AND SONS

In the late summer of 1968, just before Mike's junior year of high school, the United Nations reassigned Bruce Stedman from its headquarters in New York City to Nairobi, Kenya. For Bruce, the relocation to Africa was a lateral move, though it came with a fancy new job title: the United Nations Development Programme's resident representative in Kenya. Several years later, he assumed the same post in Ethiopia.

Articulate and sociable, Bruce was the ideal man for the job. Between 1968 and 1977, he and Ruth split their time between Kenya and Ethiopia. During the sixties and seventies, as more countries gained independence, the United Nations expanded its reach by opening field offices throughout the world. Bruce was an idealist at heart, and his work in Africa felt like a calling of the highest order. He took pride in belonging to a team that spoke truth to power.

When he approached foreign heads of state, his sons were a particular source of delight. The paternal bond was a surefire way to bridge any cultural or racial divide. "I'd like you to meet my boy," Bruce would say, his right arm outstretched and his left arm wrapped around one of his sons.

In Nairobi, whether with his sons or visiting dignitaries, Bruce shared his passion for the great outdoors in general — fly-fishing, in particular. The nearby Aberdare Mountains, a national park with soaring, 13,000-foot peaks in western Kenya, became a new source of delight. Like a good Stedman, Bruce headed straight for its streams, which teemed with brown trout. "Bruce and I spent many happy hours fishing those streams," a United Nations colleague later wrote. "Of course, there were a lot of renegade lions and buffalos in the same area, but somehow we never noticed them, we were so wrapped up in our quest for trout."

Shortly after celebrating their fiftieth wedding anniversary, Alfred and Hazel paid a visit to Nairobi in 1969. They stayed for most of the winter. In a three-page addendum to his memoir, the last thing he shared with his family, Alfred wrote that the early glimpses of Kenya, Uganda, and

Tanzania becoming independent, autonomous nations filled him with hope for a more democratic future. But traveling through Africa and seeing Mount Kilimanjaro and Mount Kenya, the rhinos, the elephants, and the flamingos, paled in comparison to seeing his descendants blaze a path that would outlast him and Hazel: "We have seen our children and grandchildren grow and develop into a cause for deep and boundless pride."

Alfred and Hazel eventually abandoned Washington, DC, and returned to Minnesota. The familiar pull of the Midwest proved too strong to resist. After working at *US News & World Report,* Alfred had grown frustrated with its lack of bylines and individual recognition. "Perhaps the idea of being a big frog in a small pool rather than a small frog in a big pool was a factor in my future planning," Alfred wrote. The couple packed up their belongings and moved back to St. Paul, where Alfred returned to the *St. Paul Pioneer Press and Dispatch.*

All the time Alfred and Hazel were away, the state's backcountry called to them. "A big motivation for me was a wish to get back to the land and waters where I had grown up. I imagined them as they were when I was a boy," Alfred wrote. "I thought of the waters as being clean and sweet as contrasted with the polluted Potomac, the Susquehanna, the Delaware, and the Hudson, where a fish couldn't live in the filth except in times of flood or high water."

Alfred is writing about the Midwest, but his yearning for fresh water and clean air is the same thing that led his grandson Mike Stedman to the eastern end of Long Island in the early seventies. "There is still fresh air to breathe and clean waters to swim in, even though we have to go farther and farther to find them," Alfred wrote. "The scenic places, the forests, the lakes and rivers and the wild creatures of woods and waters make life pleasanter."

Meanwhile, the school the Stedman boys attended in Nairobi, the Prince of Wales School, which later became the Nairobi School, felt light-years away from sleepy, suburban East Williston. The brothers were the only Americans in a school run by the British. Instead of wrestling and playing football, Mike joined the swim and rugby teams. The school had a strict headmaster. He caned students who misbehaved. The dress code required navy-blue blazers and khaki shorts. First names were frowned upon. During morning assembly, when the headmaster called out the last names of students to be caned, he simply announced: "Will Stedman come to my office." Across the auditorium, the Stedman brothers exchanged worried glances. They never knew which of them was about to get beaten for his misdeeds.

Back in East Williston, Earl Ewing had been Mike's ninth-grade math teacher. It was his first year on the job, and at twenty-three, he wasn't much older than his teen-age students. While teaching at the Wheatley School, Earl became friendly with Bruce and Ruth Stedman. And once the Stedmans settled in Nairobi, they invited Earl to stay with them during his summer vacation.

By then, Mike was nineteen and Earl was twenty-nine. During the trip, Mike and Earl solidified what later became a close friendship. Using Bruce's UN visa and passport, the group took a trip through Uganda (where Americans were prohibited from traveling at the time) and northern Kenya, until they arrived at Lake Turkana, the world's fourth-largest salt-filled lake, rich in fish. During the trip, Mike took charge, escorting everyone around the foreign, volcanic terrain. He never once complained about pitching tents and checking shoes for scorpions. Nile crocodiles and carpet vipers also lurked nearby.

During the two-week trip, Earl had a front-row seat to the dynamics between father and son. Mike's older brother was already away at Wesleyan University. And, much to his father's frustration, Mike was far more concerned about being free than about following in his brother's footsteps.

From Earl's vantage point, it was plain to see that father and son shared little in the way of common ground. With Bruce, there was always an agenda. Over a friendly game of bridge, he'd relentlessly pepper his partner with questions. Bruce was always keeping score. Even on vacation in Africa, he presided over the five o'clock cocktail hour with exacting precision. He had trouble letting loose. Like a dictator commandeering his troops, Bruce raised his martini glass to toast the giraffes milling around in the distance, maybe a few hundred yards from their campsite.

By 1970, the Vietnam War was still five years away from being over; any young man born between January 1, 1944, and December 31, 1950, was at risk of being drafted. Although Mike's birthday fell on January 4, 1952 (and the draft ended before his number came up), it was a time of tremendous generational upheaval and uncertainty. His older brother, John, was a conscientious objector. For the Stedman brothers, Vietnam was their generation's war and everyone in their peer group knew someone who was sacrificing his future in service to his country. Some of these men — those who returned — came back having experienced unspeakable horrors. Many in their generation never recovered.

After graduating from high school in Nairobi, Mike enrolled at the State University of New York at Oneonta. But college wasn't the right fit and he left after a few semesters. Dropping out of college in the seventies wasn't exactly a breaking-news story. Still, Bruce hadn't raised his sons to be quitters. "Bruce must have been irate," Gary Fuschillo explained. "If you're going to hitch your horse to a wagon, Mike ain't the horse."

But Mike was on a vision quest of sorts. He was searching for a place where he felt like he fit in, just as he was. Now sporting long hair, a pierced ear, and flip-flops, he eventually paid a visit back home to Long Island. In East Williston, the Choppess barely recognized him. "He was way out there," Dave Berwald wrote.

"He looked like he had just stepped out of a Mozambique tailor shop," Gary recalled, when Mike showed up to his dorm room at CW Post, part of Long Island University. Records of the Grateful Dead, Neil Young, Fleetwood Mac, and Joan Baez played on repeat. Mike was wearing a paisley-printed V-neck shirt, white pants, beaded necklaces, and a bracelet made of elephant hair. Sitting on Gary's bed, he opened up a leather satchel and pulled out a huge brick of African hash. "We need to sell some of this," Mike said to Gary. And they did — for $60 an ounce (a lot of money in those days).

Mike eventually returned to Nairobi to regroup. Bruce, who believed you never got a second chance to make a first impression, was apoplectic. Mike's decision to drop out of college was one thing; his son's new hippie lifestyle was something else altogether. Gary wondered: *Had Bruce passed along none of his persistence, none of his grit?* Father and son were worlds apart. Members of two different generations, they had difficulty finding common ground.

Although Bruce drank two martinis before dinner and a beer after dinner, he was firmly against anything that altered your consciousness. Drugs were out of the question. Long hair was another nonnegotiable.

One night, Bruce couldn't let Mike's shaggy hair go.

"Listen, Dad," Mike argued. "It's hair. It's not heroin. And it's not anywhere near as bad as yours and Mom's smoking. The day you quit cigarettes, I'll cut my hair off."

Even Bruce had to admit, his son had a point.

A few weeks later, Bruce and Ruth finally quit smoking. That evening, after Ruth had gone to bed, she felt a lump beneath her pillow. She pulled out a brown-paper bag. Inside, she found large clumps of Mike's hair.

Her son, much like his father, was true to his word.

For the past thirty-five years, Greg Donohue has had a photograph of Mike tacked to his bulletin board. Greg and Mike overlapped at SUNY Oneonta before both men dropped out. In the picture, Mike has a light-brown mustache and a few days' worth of stubble. A white cotton headband wraps around his forehead. Greg thought that Peter Beard, the legendary Montauk photographer, was responsible for the photo, but it was actually taken by Mary Stedman.

After Greg and I spoke on the telephone, he mailed me the photograph, on yellow-tinged newsprint. "This pic tells a tale of our generational migration to Montauk in

279

the early '70s. It was the perfect time to get acquainted with Mother Earth and live the way we wanted to live," Greg wrote in the note that accompanied the picture. "Somehow it's a special expression of our collective life experience. It was a good time."

The Beach Boys had planted the seed. If you were a surfer on the East Coast and you couldn't make it all the way to Malibu, California, then Montauk, New York, was the next best thing. After a childhood divided between East Williston and Africa, and a few semesters at college, Mike happily shed his up-island roots. Out in Montauk, Mike soon fell in with a burgeoning surfing tribe. His elders welcomed him with open arms. Moving there felt like coming home. He had found his people.

"The beauty of surfing was one way to drop out of the worldwide anger and confusion of the time," Russell Drumm wrote in an anthology about Montauk. Russell, who went by Rusty, worked at the *East Hampton Star* for thirty-plus years.

A natural-born storyteller, Rusty was a beautiful, elegant writer. His love of the natural world transferred easily onto the page. And he was the resident expert on all manner of things related to the town: the environment, surfing, commercial and recreational fishing. But this book started taking shape a few years too late; he died of cancer in 2016 at the age of sixty-eight.

Like Mike Stedman, Rusty was an East End transplant from up-island. In 1973, right around the time that Mike and Mary Stedman first became an item, Rusty moved from Amityville to Montauk and never left.

In *Ice Cream Headaches: Surf Culture in New York and New Jersey,* Rusty explained the pull that drew a generation of like-minded contemporaries to Montauk. Though the surf had lured them there, the scene quickly became about more than just catching waves.

"Things really started here in Montauk because the surf was so much better than anywhere else on Long Island. We started coming out here on the weekends. Back then, Montauk was empty. It was a really small fishing village. So we raised hell, you know," Rusty wrote in an essay for the book. "Then came the summer of '67, which was the summer of love, right. And that summer, the place was awash in very good drugs, lots of acid, lots of pot. So the word got out that Montauk was the place to come. By 1967 and 1968 all hell was breaking loose in the country. You were either going to Vietnam or you were going surfing.

That was the start of Montauk as a surf town."

By 1969, John F. Kennedy, Robert F. Kennedy, and Martin Luther King Jr. had all been assassinated. Eighteen-year-old men attended anti-war rallies and prayed they wouldn't get drafted. As the Menehunes of East Williston came of age, many of them joined a growing tribe of antiestablishment surfers out east. Some were dodging the Vietnam War. Others wanted to surf, smoke weed, and experiment with drugs. In Montauk, you could meet a beautiful girl at the Shagwong Tavern and have sex on the beach without using a condom. Promiscuity aside, for a lot of the young men, it was about leading more unconventional lives than the ones their more straitlaced fathers had lived. And surfing was an undeniable part of the draw.

Montauk is heaven on earth for surfers. Unlike the straight, sandy beaches from Florida to New Jersey, Montauk's unique topography — with its jagged edges, rocky reefs, and dense fog — sculpts incoming swells (whether late-summer hurricanes or springtime nor'easters) into some of the best waves on the Eastern Seaboard.

"Being a surfer is like being in the mob. Once you're in, you can never get out," Lee

Beiler said to me. "In those days, Montauk was a cowboy town. It was a special time that will never be duplicated again." Lee fondly recalled seeing Mike and Mary Stedman around town. "Those two would be clinging to each other twenty-four/seven," he told me. "I never saw two people hanging on each other like that." Lee also remembered the way Mary wrangled her young sons like a litter of wild cats. "Mama Mary was the matriarch. She symbolized the maternal order of motherhood."

In 1971, Beiler and Tony Caramanico, both Amityville transplants, opened a surf shop and restaurant called the Albatross on South Elmwood Avenue (it later became Bird on the Roof). Lee got his first surfboard and wetsuit the weekend that President John F. Kennedy was assassinated. Coming out to Montauk and discovering Ditch Plains was like embarking on a surf safari. As young twentysomethings, they were explorers, charting new ground. Years ahead of its time, the Albatross served gourmet omelets, fresh-squeezed orange juice, and French press coffee. "We hired a decorator to do the place," Tony recalled. "It was hippie-dippy, free and easy. Everybody was really friendly." In 2020, at seventy, Caramanico, who is still sponsored by surfing companies, was finally inducted into the East Coast Surfing Hall of Fame.

Back then, most of the local surfers had found jobs as waiters, fishermen, or construction workers, and everyone had Sundays off. And since you couldn't buy beer until noon, the Albatross became the de facto meetup spot. They didn't have smartphones. Text messages didn't exist. Everyone just showed up. Hung over from the night before, Thom Fleming would stumble into the Albatross, order eggs Hussarde, and drink two or three pots of mocha java before heading off to surf with however many knuckleheads he could round up. "We are the bones of Montauk. The muscle and fat comes and goes, but the bones stay behind," Thom explained to me. "You could surf and go get laid, look at the stars, walk on the beach, get a six-pack and some hot dogs and go to Shagwong Point and have the time of your life." When the Albatross closed down in 1980, it marked the end of an era.

Thom, formerly a model and now a carpenter, hadn't thought about Mike Stedman for quite some time. He told me our conversation gave him "chicken skin." Mike, after all, was one of the first among their young tribe to die. For years after the *Wind Blown* went down, Thom halfway expected

Transformation of surfers to waiters.

to see him pull back through the jetties —
as if the whole thing had been some cruel,
twisted joke. "We were lost boys in the Peter Pan sense. We were finding our way,"
Thom explained. "Mike Stedman was a
huge part of that. He played a leading role."

By 1980, Mike and Mary Stedman were living in East Hampton on Newtown Lane
near the Long Island Rail Road station
when Bruce paid the family a visit. They
were all on their best behavior. Still, though
Mike couldn't have cared less, Bruce and
Ruth disapproved of Mary. They thought
their son had married too young. Or maybe
they thought he could have done better.

Mary at the Stedman house on Newtown Lane.

During cocktail hour, Bruce took out his leather travel case, which contained vodka and crystal goblets. With cocktail in hand, he walked up to his son, the commercial fisherman. He slapped him on the back and asked: "When are you going to get a real job, Mike?"

Mary, who was pregnant with Shane at

the time, watched as her husband's face fell. She tried to change the subject. No matter what Michael Stedman did with his life, he was never going to get the stamp of approval from his old man.

She could more than relate.

As a young girl growing up in East Hampton, she had always felt different from her father and her three younger siblings, whose dark eyes and olive complexions stood in stark contrast to her green eyes and pale skin. She felt like an alien. Every summer, no matter how much Coppertone sunscreen she applied, a fresh constellation of freckles appeared across the bridge of her nose.

"Mary Ellen Cavagnaro," the nuns would say to her when she was a young girl at the Academy of the Sacred Heart of Mary in Sag Harbor. "You don't look Italian."

On August 15, 1968, when Mary was thirteen, she had just come out of an early-evening mass celebrating the Assumption of Mary at the Most Holy Trinity Church, where her family worshipped, on Buell Lane in East Hampton. Her parents were lapsed Catholics who never went to church themselves; they sent their children to atone for their sins. Mary's mother, Cletus Cavagnaro, was a blackout drinker. Her father, Albert Cavagnaro, was physically violent.

When she got home after mass, Mary wrote her mother a note explaining that she was going over to a friend's house nearby. She promised to be back by nine o'clock, when it started getting dark. Determined not to get stuck babysitting her three younger siblings while her parents and their friends smoked Salems and drank scotch into oblivion, Mary scooted down the driveway. Moments later, Cletus stormed out of the house. Running after Mary, she grabbed a fistful of the long, brown hair that cascaded down her daughter's back. It stopped Mary in her tracks.

"Please, come help me!" Mary yelled to her father, Al, who stood idly by. "Momma's drunk and she's going insane! Dad, please help me!"

"Don't yell for him!" Cletus shouted. "He's not your father."

Cletus Duggan was twenty-seven and living in Queens when she discovered she was pregnant. It was 1954, and the birth control pill hadn't been invented yet. The accidental pregnancy would ricochet through her life in ways she couldn't yet imagine. Cletus never lived with Mary's biological father. The two got married in a New York City courthouse and departed in separate cars after the brief ceremony. The marriage was a stipulation their Catholic families had required to help lessen the blow of their children's sins. Shortly thereafter, the Roman Catholic Church annulled the marriage.

Cletus took twelve-week-old Mary Ellen, born in 1955 during an early January snowstorm, to live with her sister and brother-in-law out in East Hampton, on the opposite end of Long Island. As a condition of the annulment, Cletus requested neither visitation nor child support from Mary's biological father. When Mary was two years old, Cletus married Albert Cavagnaro and became a homemaker. Three children, one son and two daughters, followed.

Unlike Cletus, Al Cavagnaro had long-standing ties to the East End. During the Great Depression, his family had moved from Brooklyn to East Hampton. Al grew up downtown, in a building on Newtown Lane. His family ran two businesses: Cavagnaro Deli and Cavagnaro Bar and Grill. (Mary's Marvelous now occupies the ground floor of the former local bar, adjacent to the train station, which Al's cousin, Albie, ran, sitting at his familiar perch right where customers walked in.) After graduating as salutatorian from East Hampton

High School, Al served in the military during World War II before graduating from Harvard College in 1948 — six years after Bruce Stedman.

During summers, Al worked as a lifeguard at Main Beach and at the Maidstone Club. One summer, he apparently rescued Sarah Churchill, Winston Churchill's daughter, from the rough Atlantic Ocean. It's possible that Louis and Mary Connick, Dave's grandparents, were sunbathing on the same beach that very season, alongside the other summer people.

Al eventually went to work as a Suffolk County detective; Suffolk County later appointed him its commissioner of jurors. Meanwhile, Cletus joined the Ladies' Village Improvement Society of East Hampton and volunteered at the East End Hospice and Meals on Wheels. "She looked like a million dollars, but she was always sick," Mary recalled. "She was always very thin." No doubt because she suppressed her appetite with cigarettes and alcohol.

Like her three daughters — Mary, Rosemary, and Marguerite — Cletus never left the East End. When she died in 2007 at the age of seventy-nine, a funeral mass was held at the Most Holy Trinity Church, followed by a burial at the Most Holy Trinity Cemetery. Then as now, East Hampton was a small town, and if you're Catholic, it's still the only game in town.

The truth of Mary's parentage was a secret that Cletus shielded not only from her daughter. Mary eventually passed along a telephone number for her half brother, Albert Cavagnaro Jr., known as Albie (the nickname runs in the Cavagnaro family). He explained to me that he didn't hear about Mary's biological father until he was well into his thirties. Now a lawyer living in North Carolina, Albie left East Hampton as a teenager to attend a military high school in Florida. He later went to Duke University on a Navy ROTC scholarship. His sisters, meanwhile, stayed behind on the East End. And Mary wasn't the only sister who married a commercial fisherman. Margie did too.

In the spring of 1973, shortly before Mike and Mary got married, Albie attended Mike's bachelor party in Montauk at a friend's apartment near Fort Pond Bay. He liked his soon-to-be brother-in-law right away. Surfers and fishermen surrounded Mike on all sides. During the raucous bachelor party, a topless young woman jumped out of a cake. Albie was fourteen; the half-naked woman left an impression.

291

Uncle Freddy (far right) with Mike and his sons eating ice cream.

Nineteen eighty-four was a watershed year for the Cavagnaro family. Fred Echevarria — Uncle Freddy, a seminal, stabilizing figure during Mary's childhood — passed away shortly before the *Wind Blown* was lost at sea. And later that same year, Cletus and Al called it quits.

After Albie and I hung up the phone, he e-mailed me a series of photographs. In one, Mike is eating ice cream with his three sons and Uncle Freddy after a celebratory event at the Most Holy Trinity Church, where Freddy was an usher. Chris sits between the two men. Mike and Chris wear jackets, button-down shirts, khaki pants, and matching boat shoes. Uncle Freddy wears a checkered jacket with a pocket square and penny loafers. Mike's left hand, the one with his gold wedding band, holds his ice cream cone, maybe vanilla or mint chocolate chip. A wisp of light-brown hair falls across his face. Mike balances Shane between his legs. Still a baby, Shane is wearing red pants, a cable-knit fisherman's sweater, and white leather shoes.

The photograph captured Mike in his element. To someone passing by, it must have looked like an ordinary family trip to get ice cream. But for Mike, it was another opportunity to be a different kind of father than his own father had been — a hands-on father. His sons would stumble and fall. And Mike would be there to catch them when they did.

On March 19, 1984, ten days before her world fell apart, Mary wrote a letter to the *East Hampton Star,* thanking the community for the outpouring of support following Uncle Freddy's death. More than a hundred sympathy cards covered her aunt's kitchen table.

"The beauty of this pile is the essence of what love and friendship is all about," Mary wrote. The night of Freddy's passing, there had been a snowstorm, and she came across an old *Saturday Evening Post* from 1951. In it, Mary found a poem, "The Fragile Day" by Esther Wood, which she shared with the *Star*'s readers. The poem eerily foreshadowed what was to come. It read:

The world is made of glass this winter
   day.
Even a breath might shatter it away. . . .
. . . . Oh, if a wind should blow!
Mortal, beware, go secretly and go
Only on shoes of cloud and feather quill
Into a day so fragile and still.

"The snow has melted and spring begins this week. I would like to take this opportunity to thank everyone for their love and prayers," Mary wrote. "It is a real comfort to my aunt and family to know so many people care."

It was this same close-knit East Hampton community — from family to friends to casual acquaintances — that came to her salvation in the weeks and months and years to come.

13.
SUSIE

After raising their sons in East Williston, Bruce and Ruth Stedman spent more than a decade in East Africa. In 1979, two years after Bruce retired from international civil service, the couple moved to Hayward, Wisconsin. Two of their grown sons settled nearby. Despite having spent the bulk of his childhood in suburban Maryland, the Midwest always felt like home to Bruce, as it had to his father. All his life, he followed Minnesota politics and rooted for Minnesota sports teams. And retiring in Wisconsin felt like an undeniable homecoming.

In April of 1984, neither Bruce nor Ruth stuck around for Mike's memorial service. A week or so into the search for survivors, they departed East Hampton with some excuse about needing to repair the kitchen cabinets back in Wisconsin. In time, Bruce and Ruth would learn the inescapable quality of their grief. Some days, it felt sharp and sudden. Other days, it was softer and more remote. But it never went away. Bruce later confided to his grandson Chris that he thought of Mike every single day of his life.

Ruth took the loss of her son particularly hard. After Mike died, no one could recall a single photograph in which Ruth smiled at the camera. The family carried on. No one brought it up. It became kind of the Stedman way — that whenever anyone asked Ruth how she was doing, a response of "I'm fine" would silence further questions.

A year after the *Wind Blown* went down, Mary and her three boys traveled to Minnesota and Wisconsin to see the rest of the extended Stedman clan. Cocktail hour was well underway one evening, and Ruth was already a few drinks in. "There we were. Mike is dead. Ruth turns around to me and says there's no such thing as grief for a husband," Mary recalled. "There's only grief for a dead child."

During the last several years of their marriage, Ruth and Bruce slept in separate bedrooms — not because they had grown estranged, but because they both snored. The couple never divorced. They went the distance.

For years, Ruth had been bedridden from illness, and her husband had helped take care of her. In 1991, she suffered a fatal stroke. Bruce waited a full week to inform their youngest son, Matt, that his mother had died.

Matt made the twelve-hour drive, and he and his father went out and grabbed a pizza together. A few days later, after Ruth's memorial service, the whole family went back to the house, which overlooked Spider Lake. Bruce laid out his late wife's belongings across her bed.

He told his three sons: "Take what you want."

Memories are curious things, as are the memoirs that chronicle them. The parts that are omitted, whether purposefully or not, are often as revealing as the parts that are included. The anxieties and depressions that go unchronicled. The affairs of the heart that never make it onto the page. The years that bleed together, indistinguishable, one after another. Obituaries, while a useful catalog of life's outward accomplishments and highlights, rarely, if ever, tell the whole story.

In the 2003 memoir that Bruce Stedman mailed to various family members, he apparently intended to write a complement to a previous draft that had exclusively highlighted his United Nations career. The first draft left out any trace of his personal life. It was almost as if he had been leading a double life.

"I have finished a memoir about my UN career from beginning to end, but it is single-dimensional. It does not tell the story of my non-UN life. So I have decided to try to give my family and loved ones an account of my personal life, or at least elements of it that I can remember at this late date," he wrote on the first page of "Book II: The Bruce Stedman Story (A Personal History)."

When you're telling a story, it's often easier to smooth out the rough, incongruous edges. Everyone wants a happy ending. You certainly don't want to leave your reader in a state of shock.

But even Bruce's second, supposedly more personal, memoir leaves out any mention of 1984 and the son he lost at sea. It ends abruptly, with his retirement from the United Nations. And while he wrote in respectful and loving terms of his marriage to Ruth, he neglected to mention the passionate love affair he had with Susan Goodwillie. It turns out that Bruce wasn't only a distant father, he was also a master at emotional compartmentalization. What you

Bruce Stedman and Susan Goodwillie on their wedding day.

saw wasn't really what you got.

In December, 1993, two years after Ruth died, Bruce married Susan Goodwillie, whom he affectionately called Susie. At their wedding ceremony, Susie joined Bruce and two of his sons, John and Jim, singing a Swahili love song called "Malaika" that had become a family anthem. Matt did not attend.

For Bruce and Susie, it was a chance to start again. He and Susie, who had circled each other clandestinely for the better part of their lives, were finally free to conduct their love affair in public. For Bruce, it must have been a huge relief. He no longer had to lurk, a dangling man, in the shadows.

Susie and Bruce first met in January of 1967, while working at the United Nations Development Programme. She was twenty-seven; he was forty-eight.

"It was a most inappropriate, very complicated, difficult situation for me," Susie explained to me over the telephone. She was forthcoming and direct. Though she later disagreed with my characterization of our conversation, it seemed to me like she wanted, once and for all, to set the record straight.

Besides a physical attraction, the two shared a passion for civil rights and international diplomacy. What started with platonic lunch dates soon crossed over into more intimate territory.

Shortly before the Stedmans relocated to Kenya, Bruce confided to Susie: "I never imagined that I could love anyone as much as I love you. But I made a promise, and I'm going to keep it." Bruce was a man of his word. Though the confession broke her heart, it only made Susie love Bruce even more. Once the Stedman family moved to East Africa, Bruce used a private mailbox in Nairobi to correspond with Susie. It wasn't a double life, exactly, but it was close enough. Bruce and Susie were twin flames. Electricity ignited whenever their itineraries overlapped on the same continent.

The two eventually agreed that Susie should get on with her life, and she did. In 1971, she married another man, eventually left the UNDP, and started a new career with the Ford Foundation in West Africa. Bruce even paid a visit to Susie and her husband at their new home in Lagos, Nigeria. Susie and her first husband separated in 1978 and divorced a decade later.

In 1982, after years of supposedly keeping their love affair under wraps, Ruth learned of their relationship when she intercepted a letter that Susie had mailed to Bruce. For years Bruce had instilled in his sons one virtue above all else — *to be men of their word* — while, behind the scenes, the civil servant wasn't exactly leading by example.

Bruce mailed Susie a typewritten letter saying: "Do not ever write to me again." He signed it "R. B. Stedman."

Even from far away, Susie could see the gun pointed in Bruce's direction. She respected the boundary Ruth had established; Bruce and Susie fell out of touch for some years thereafter.

In late March of 1984, when Susie was

working in Geneva for the UN High Commissioner for Refugees, Bruce left an urgent message with her home secretary at her office in Boston about his son being lost at sea. By the time Susie returned from her assignment abroad, the message had been lost.

And three years after that, when her father was murdered, Susie reached out to Bruce. John Morley Goodwillie, a retired advertising executive, was found dead inside his Park Avenue apartment in late December of 1987, after he and his son-in-law had been arguing about the ownership of an extensive rare-book collection. An autopsy confirmed the cause of death was strangulation and blunt-force trauma. A grand jury indicted his son-in-law, Jonathan de Sola Mendes, for manslaughter and first-degree murder. In an e-mail, Susie explained to me that "with the aid of some very expensive lawyers, he got the first-degree murder charge dropped before the trial began. He was not totally acquitted, but charged only with something like assault and battery." Mendes ultimately served a brief sentence.

In the wake of the murder, Susie and Bruce connected by phone and Bruce suggested they resume their correspondence, so long as Susie wrote nothing but casual, chatty letters, addressed to Mr. and Mrs. R. B. Stedman. The point was to share what was happening in their lives, without getting too personal.

After Ruth died, Susie helped Bruce with the arduous task of cleaning out the contents of her bedroom. Susie came across an essay Ruth had written for her high school's fiftieth reunion. In it, Ruth shared with her classmates the story of Bruce and his illustrious international career, his exotic travels around the world, the fancy dinners where Bruce was the guest of honor. "It would have impressed her classmates, but where was Ruth?" Susie wondered.

Long after his sons had become adults, Bruce described them to Susie: John was the intellectual, often-aloof public servant; Mike was the nature boy and adventurer; Jim was the romantic poet and songwriter; and Matt, who became a master plumber, was the most practical, most financially successful son, who was sure to look after his father in his old age.

Bruce's assessment rang eerily true.

"My brothers did not call or show any interest, as far as I know," Matt explained, of staying in closer touch with their father after their mother died. "I went out to Maine every year after Thanksgiving to help set up the Christmas decorations."

In 1994, Susie and Bruce had moved to Maine, settling in Westport Island. Bruce became an active member of the community, joining the United Nations Association of Maine and the Lincoln County Democrats, in addition to serving on the local planning board and volunteering as an adult literacy tutor. He and Susie donated leftover produce from their vegetable garden to nearby food pantries.

Bruce died in February of 2013 at the age of ninety-two, in the comfort of his bedroom, which overlooked the Sheepscot River.

Hours prior, Susie had called Matt to inform him that if he wanted to see his father one last time, he should come right away. But his father was gone before he could get there.

A few hours before he died, Susie sat by his side. By 2013, the couple had shared forty-five years of history. For twenty of those years, they had been husband and wife. Dozens of family photographs surrounded them. In one, Mike, Matt, and John are standing before a lake as little kids; each boy has a fishing rod. Susie glanced over and picked up a black-and-white photograph of another young boy, with closely cropped hair, holding a fish. She asked Bruce if he knew who the boy in the picture was.

"It's me," Bruce said.

"Did you catch that fish?" Susie asked.

"Yes," Bruce replied.

"Was that your first catch?" she wanted to know.

"No, Ruthie was my first catch," Bruce said. His blue eyes had lost none of their mischievous sparkle. "And you were my second."

Susie bent down and gave Bruce a kiss.

The downing of the *Wind Blown* was like the still point of the turning world. The four men were dead. It was the survivors who were left to grapple with what came afterward — not only the loss of their loved ones, but the life that continues being lived, both the wonderful and the not-so-wonderful parts. Mike Stedman, in all likelihood, never knew about Susie Goodwillie, apart from the fact that she was his father's work colleague. And Dave Connick certainly never met Cathy Pradié-Connick, the lovely, warm woman who would have become his stepmother.

Long after five of the six original Stedmans

were dead, the burden was left to Matt, and Matt alone.

■ ■ ■ ■

PART FOUR:
MONTAUK THE END

■ ■ ■ ■

An advertisement for the Viking *on Montauk High-way.*

14.

THE FISHERMAN'S SPECIAL

Commercial fishing in Montauk would never have become a big business were it not for two bold, risk-taking entrepreneurs: Austin Corbin and Carl Fisher. Not unlike fishermen intent on striking it hot, Corbin and Fisher saw in sleepy, rural Montauk a small, remote town ripe for the picking. Over a fifty-year period, although the two men never overlapped in real time, they worked in tandem. What one man started, the other finished. Together, Corbin and Fisher reimagined the East End by transforming miles of quaint farming and fishing villages into a seaside, summertime resort destination.

Back in the nineteenth century, Montauk had an isolated, largely uninhabited beauty. Some have likened its rolling hills to the moors of Scotland and the South Downs of England. Although Montauk more than equals Manhattan in area, and lies within easy striking distance of the city (Montauk Point is 125 miles from New York), its remoteness, especially in winter, when deer outnumber people, has drawn comparisons to Mongolia.

In 1881, Austin Corbin, a wealthy and influential New York banker, became president of the Long Island Rail Road. At the time, the utility was bankrupt, burdened by debt, and hemorrhaging money. Corbin was a take-charge go-getter; in eight months' time, he transformed the LIRR into a revenue-generating operation. He conceived of a series of high-speed trains that whisked passengers from New York City to the eastern end of Long Island. When Corbin looked at Montauk, he didn't see pastoral hills dotted with cattle, sheep, and horses. The businessman in him saw Montauk's Fort Pond Bay as a future transatlantic port of entry for ships traveling to and from Europe.

But transportation proved a challenge. Unless you had a horse and buggy at your disposal, Montauk was inaccessible. One of Corbin's more daring plans was a twenty-mile-long railroad extension. It connected Bridgehampton to Montauk, where Fort Pond Bay was deep enough to accommodate massive ocean liners. Corbin's radical idea was that travelers could avoid the inconvenience and hassle of landing in New York Harbor altogether. Instead, they would travel by high-speed train between Montauk and New York City.

On December 17, 1895, the first train pulled into Montauk's new railroad station. Although many of Corbin's dreams died with him (following an untimely carriage accident in 1896), the newly expanded Long Island Rail Road outlived him. It fueled Montauk's economy into the next century. Vacationers soon traveled by express trains to previously unreachable destinations. In the 1870s, wealthy New York families started colonizing Southampton. And by the mid-1880s, moneyed families had crept farther east, building summer houses in East Hampton and eventually forming the Maidstone Club.

Before the invention of the automobile, it took six solid hours to drive a horse and wagon from East Hampton to Montauk Point — a distance of twenty miles. A century ago, it was a big deal to travel between Springs and East Hampton. Venturing as far west as Sag Harbor required an overnight stay.

Starting in the 1920s, Montauk became a

commercial and recreational fishing hotbed, drawing fishermen from New York City and up-island to mine its fertile waters. Before access to a railroad that stretched the entire length of Long Island, commercial fishermen in Montauk could only ship salted or smoked fish, which didn't require refrigeration.

In 1925, when a resident of East Hampton wanted to spend the day in New York City, he or she boarded a train the LIRR advertised as the Cannon Ball (a name Corbin had coined). The train ran daily, except for Sundays and holidays, leaving East Hampton at 6:48 a.m. and arriving in Manhattan at 9:42 a.m. — two hours and fifty-four minutes later. By 1935, the same East Hamptonites had carved twenty-five to thirty-five minutes from their commute, whether heading into the city or returning home.

A story from October 24, 1935, that ran on the front page of the *East Hampton Star* explained this time savings as the work of fastidious schedule-makers, who shaved valuable minutes along the route whenever possible. Besides the addition of air-conditioned buffet cars, which served breakfast and lunch, and passenger cars constructed of steel, the investment in ten-wheel, steam-powered locomotives altered the experience for passengers and crew alike. The new locomotives came equipped with eleven-thousand-gallon tenders, making it possible for the trains to run straight from Queens to Montauk without stopping in Speonk for additional water.

The LIRR Cannonball train still exists, by the way; but despite technological advancements, the travel time remains, frustratingly, about the same. On summer Fridays, when office buildings in Manhattan clear out by lunchtime, workers get a jump start on their weekends. Once aboard the 4:06 p.m. Cannonball at Pennsylvania Station, happy hour has already begun. Young men grab giant cans of beer wrapped in brown-paper bags; young women pull out chilled rosé and plastic cups, discreetly passing the bottle back and forth across the aisle. By the time everyone disembarks out east, between 6:03 p.m. (Southampton) and 6:48 p.m. (Montauk), they've all got a decent buzz going.

In the 1930s, largely because of the Long Island Rail Road, Montauk began solidifying its reputation as the only big-game fishing grounds on the North Atlantic coast. George Le Boutillier, vice president of the LIRR and ardent sports fisherman, helped make the connection. Le Boutillier arranged for the operation of special trains ferrying city fishermen every Saturday and Sunday in the fall and the spring, with five-day-a-week service come summertime. Advertised as the Fisherman's Special, the trains originated at Pennsylvania Station and whisked urban fishermen door-to-door in two and a half hours, give or take. In 1935, a round-trip ticket cost $1.50.

Out in Montauk, the railroad company smartly invested in the construction of a new dock. Come summertime, party boat captains greeted the morning arrival of incoming trains and the corresponding rush of seasonal revenue. In 1935, a full day of fishing (including bait) ran $2.00. By October of that year, thirty thousand anglers had bought tickets aboard the railroad. Everyone steamed east, headed for the promised land.

Fishermen returned to the city hauling their catch (a combination of sea bass, porgies, flounder, pollock, and codfish, depending on the season and what was running), which traveled in special refrigerator cars to accommodate the needs of the seagoing passengers. Back home, their families ate like kings; for days afterward, they feasted off the bounty. And it wasn't only men who journeyed to Montauk for the day. Their wives and children sometimes came along for the ride. If seasickness was a concern, they spent the day at nearby Fort Pond Beach, where a restaurant and freshly painted bathhouses provided food and shelter until their husbands and fathers set foot on dry land. Content to have spent the day in the sunshine, everyone returned home with fine grains of sand between their toes and a sticky layer of salt covering their sun-kissed skin.

In 1926, Carl Fisher, a charming, powerful real estate developer with a Midas touch, landed in Montauk. Fisher intended to transform Montauk in much the way he had developed Miami Beach — converting marshy Florida swampland into miles of hotels, nightclubs, restaurants, and boutiques. In fact, Fisher's slogan was: "Miami Beach in Winter; Montauk in Summer." In Miami, land had to be manufactured and trees hauled in from afar. But in Montauk, Mother Nature supplied all the landscaping necessary, and then some.

Although Carl Fisher missed Austin Corbin by some thirty years, he took the skeleton of Corbin's vision, added layers of grandeur, and made it his own. Taken together, the two visionaries helped lay the foundation for modern Montauk. The Montauk Beach Development Corporation, Fisher's company, bought ten thousand acres of Montauk for about $3 million. His plans were said to have been made in a single afternoon, sitting aboard his yacht, the *Shadow,* map in hand. Fisher built Montauk's first churches, library, school, golf course, resorts, and yacht club. He used dynamite to blow up the sandbar dividing Lake Montauk from the Long Island Sound. Commercial fishing boats (the *Wind Blown* included) eventually docked there, in proximity to three thousand miles of ocean. Much of Fisher's legacy still stands: Montauk Manor, Montauk Yacht Club, and Montauk Downs Golf Course, among several other landmarks.

Even though Fisher eventually lost a good deal of his fortune in the stock market crash of 1929, his transformation of Montauk helped stratify the two economic classes that continue to dominate the East End well into the twenty-first century: the summer people and the working-class inhabitants who farm its lands, fish its waters, and care for the lavish mansions that sit shuttered for much of the year.

The cliffs circa 1970.

15.
SELLING A DREAM

In the 1960s, Macy's department store sold about two hundred fully furnished Leisurama homes built in Montauk's Culloden Shores subdivision, about a block from Ditch Plains, to middle-class homeowners for $13,000 apiece. It was a Levittown-like development with two specific things in mind: *rest and relaxation.* At the 1964 New York World's Fair at Flushing Meadows Park in Queens, the angular, ranch-style houses played a starring role. They were a prime example of American ingenuity.

The houses themselves were the brainchild of Andrew Geller, the so-called architect of happiness; Herbert Sadkin, a developer; and Macy's, which featured a full-scale model with all its contents on the ninth floor of its Herald Square flagship department store. But the builders weren't looking to lure old money out east — not by a long shot. By making each Leisurama home relatively affordable (for as little as $590 down and $73 a month, or somewhat more, if you wanted to splurge), they put the dream of second-home ownership within the grasp of the middle class. Suddenly, you didn't have to be rich to live near the ocean.

Each tract home came fully equipped with everything a family needed for its leisure time at the beach — from modern appliances to sofa beds, from drop-leaf dining tables to color-coordinated toothbrushes. In a clever attempt to get the buy-in of discriminating housewives, each house also featured a five-piece dinette set, eight plastic place mats, and a fifty-piece set of stainless flatware. Every Leisurama home had cathedral ceilings and compact bathrooms with hidden storage compartments, which made for perfect childhood hiding places. New Yorkers, who constituted a majority of the Leisurama homeowners, personalized their individual homes by choosing among various models and color schemes.

Despite their charm, the houses themselves weren't really the main attraction. It was all about the beach. You could hear it. You could smell it. You could walk to it, on a clear-skied night, guided by the light of the moon.

These days, a vacant dirt lot costs upwards

of $1 million. The old Montauk, once a workingman's vacation destination, worlds away from the standoffish old money of Southampton, Bridgehampton, East Hampton, and Amagansett, no longer exists. To stay at Gurney's Resort in Montauk over the July Fourth holiday in 2020, a standard ocean-facing room ran about $1,000 a night (excluding taxes and fees). A two-bedroom cottage booked for the same holiday costs around $2,700 each night.

Summertime insanity aside, house after house has changed hands — a predictable pattern from year-round old-timer to seasonal, wealthy newcomer. Many of the original Leisurama houses have been either remodeled beyond recognition or torn down and replaced. Over the years, some locals say, they've watched Montauk wither and die. Much how the ocean has eaten away at the cliffs beneath the Montauk Lighthouse, it's been a slow and steady deterioration. Please don't get them started on the drunken parade of hipsters who arrive via helicopter wearing wide-brimmed fedoras and crowd into illegal share houses, or the same millennials who pay homage to the Memory Motel, where the Rolling Stones used to stay, by posting selfies with clever hashtags to Instagram as if they were the ones who first reveled in its run-down, seedy splendor.

Long Island, about 125 miles from east to west, is the largest island on all of the East Coast. From Manhattan, as you drive east, the island splits into two arms. The North Fork, bordered by the Long Island Sound, is known for its rows of vineyards and quaint villages. The Atlantic-facing South Fork is home to "the Hamptons," which are divided into two main townships (Southampton and East Hampton) and several independently governed incorporated villages within those towns (including, somewhat confusingly, Southampton Village and East Hampton Village).

On the South Fork, from September to May, once the wealthy vacationers and summer people depart, it's largely members of the working-class community who stay behind, many struggling to make ends meet. They make the bulk of their money in June, July, and August and figure out the delicate balancing act of making this seasonal paycheck stretch the other nine months of the year. Lacking affordable housing, landscapers and house-cleaners have made makeshift apartments out of motel rooms. They are the largely unseen, behind-the-scenes part

321

of "the Hamptons," light-years away from part-time celebrity residents like Alec Baldwin, Gwyneth Paltrow, and Jerry Seinfeld.

Even the phrase "the Hamptons" makes many locals cringe. In an essay Biddle Duke wrote for *EAST* magazine, he explained that H. P. Hedges, a local historian, used the term in print as far back as 1897. And by the 1920s, it had started popping up in real estate advertisements in New York City newspapers, around the same time that summer colonies in Quogue, Southampton, and East Hampton increased in popularity. Another story goes that "the Hamptons" was a clever name conjured up by Allan Schneider, a successful real estate agent, in the go-go eighties or thereabouts. The slogan apparently helped Schneider and other real estate brokers lure wealthy Manhattanites in search of second homes to the eastern tip of Long Island.

No matter its precise origin, "the Hamptons" was always about selling a dream — a place where frazzled, frenzied New Yorkers could escape at a moment's notice. A hundred years ago, it was impossible to imagine that start-up companies would deploy private helicopters to transport some of Manhattan's heaviest hitters. These days, for $795 per passenger, you can travel from West Thirtieth Street in Manhattan to East Hampton Airport in thirty-nine minutes.

"The Hamptons" first appeared in the *New York Times* in a story on July 29, 1973: "Why are the Hamptons — that series of South Shore communities on Long Island that stretch 30-odd miles along Route 27 on the way to Montauk Point — preferred as beach resorts by discriminating New Yorkers? Some say it's because the Hamptons have always had a reputation for being chic."

Neal Ashby, a New York City–based freelance reporter, researched portions of that story while stretched out in the sand. It was a plum assignment. Ashby wrote: "To my way of thinking the Hamptons are 'in,' and deserve to be so, because the shoreline along which they are situated is a place of natural perfection that has fallen into the hands of thinking people who have left the good things alone and kept the neon and concrete to a minimum." The sunbathers at East Hampton's Main Beach (frequently ranked among the best beaches in the country) caught his eye: "They are attractive, trim, up-to-date and look as if they are doing things that matter, or require talent. Sketch pads, armfuls of paperbacks, stapled manuscripts identify, for instance, artists, educators, editors and writers. It seems good company to be in."

Helen Rattray, the publisher of the *East Hampton Star,* forbids the use of "the Hamptons" in her weekly newspaper. The newspaper's stylebook has all but banned the phrase, unless it appears in quotes or other extenuating, unforeseen circumstances. Helen encourages her reporters to substitute "South Fork" or "East End" in its place. Or, better yet, the actual names of the small towns, from west to east, each with its own distinct personality: Southampton, Water Mill, Bridgehampton, Sagaponack, Sag Harbor, Wainscott, East Hampton, Springs, Amagansett, and Montauk.

Everett Rattray, Helen's late husband and the *Star*'s former publisher, wrote in the foreword of his book about the South Fork that "the Hamptons" is a term deployed by "glitzy summer tourists and gossip columnists — rarely, if ever, used by the area's natives." He made another important geographic distinction I hadn't before considered: the South Fork is technically an island within an island, since the Shinnecock Canal in Hampton Bays separates the South Fork from the rest of Long Island.

For the native-born population, some of

whose families have resided on the South Fork for hundreds of years, the thirty-mile strip of hills and dunes and woods that starts in Southampton and stretches east has never belonged to the summer people. Such interlopers, like myself, are frowned upon. The South Fork belongs to the generations of families who call it home. It certainly doesn't belong to the fancy newcomers who call it "the Hamptons" and who only visit on summer weekends, renting homes for tens of thousands of dollars from Memorial Day to Labor Day.

Tumbleweed Tuesday, which occurs the Tuesday after Labor Day, is a sacred local tradition. It's the day when the city slickers have departed and everyone who remains can finally breathe a huge sigh of relief. Ask anyone who actually lives here: September is hands-down the South Fork's most glorious month. The crowds are gone. The ocean is the ideal temperature for a swim. And you can actually find a place to park.

Montauk's blue-collar origins separate it from the rest of the historically more affluent South Fork. The twenty-minute drive east — past the manicured hedgerows, gated estates, and luxury boutiques that line East Hampton's Main Street — makes Montauk feel a little rougher around the edges. But over the past decade, as celebrities have scooped up ocean-front real estate at mind-boggling prices, Montauk has started to shed its working-class roots. The worry is that it is fast becoming the most Hamptons-like destination of them all. Unless they were grandfathered in, the sons and daughters of commercial fishermen can't afford to live there anymore.

The origins of the South Fork date back to the 1600s. Southampton historians have long argued their town is the oldest in all of what eventually became New York State. In 1639, the story goes, Lion Gardiner left Old Saybrook, Connecticut, and sailed across the Long Island Sound to take possession of a private island (cleverly named Gardiner's Island), which he had recently purchased from Chief Wyandanch, sachem of the Montaukett Indians. The Gardiner descendants still own the island, some four miles from Montauk. The close friendship between Gardiner and Wyandanch helped pave the way for the first white settlers of East Hampton, a group of Englishmen from Maidstone, Kent, who, in 1648, went on a buying spree, scooping up land from Southampton to Napeague. A delegation of Long Island sachems complained to Francis

Lovelace, the second English governor of New York: "They take our lands away everyday, a little and a little." How, they wondered, can you claim ownership of the deer, the trees, the fish?

Shortly after settling in East Hampton, a group of men wanted to pasture cattle in Montauk, a wild expanse of land occupied by grazing cows, sheep, and horses. Chief Wyandanch apparently gave them the right of pasturage with an option to buy. By 1660, Wyandanch was dead and his widow and son sold most of Montauk to the East Hampton men for the equivalent of £100. It was the bargain of the century and thus continued a centuries-long pattern of privileged white newcomers displacing prior inhabitants. It didn't stop there. In 1879, Brooklynite Arthur W. Benson bought most of Montauk at a partition sale for $151,000. At first, wealthy sportsmen envisioned the largely uninhabited land as a rich man's game preserve. It was a gunner's paradise, at a time when men went hunting for days to weeks at a time and lived off the bounty of the land, with little to accompany it besides coffee, hardtack, and potatoes. But Austin Corbin eventually swooped in, seeing to it that Montauk would become a seaside city of pleasure rather than Long

Island's Wild West.

As far back as the seventeenth century, Quakers fleeing Puritan persecution sought refuge on nearby Shelter Island, which sits sandwiched between the North and South Forks. By 1687, Southampton was home to some two dozen whaling companies that produced more than two thousand barrels of whale oil that year. And by 1790, Sag Harbor had become New York State's first customs port, with Long Wharf the main point of commerce for two valuable commodities: sperm whale oil, which fueled lamps, and salt cod. Centuries before artists and writers flooded into town, Sag Harbor was a prosperous whaling port.

Like much of the United States, the South Fork of Long Island has an unfortunate history of settlers displacing its native-born population, from the Shinnecocks in Southampton to the Montauketts in Montauk. In 1897, the Montauketts filed a suit to try to get their land back. In a 1910 New York State Supreme Court decision, Judge Abel Blackmar ruled against them, saying the tribe was extinct, and as such, they had no claim to the land their ancestors once called home.

And the displacement, though of different populations, continues unabated. Starting in the eighties, Wall Street bankers scooped up family farms and a different sort of affluence slowly trickled east. It was no longer old family money that stormed into town, appropriating oceanfront summer estates, but new money looking to leave an indelible mark. America was changing too. By 1984, technology had brought the CD player, the camcorder, and the Apple computer into the American home — all in a span of three years.

Among the year-round population on the South Fork, class distinctions have remained stubbornly fixed. Like the upstairs-downstairs dichotomy that still pervades much of Great Britain, the divide between these two East End worlds is difficult to traverse. Weekenders take heed: no matter how much time you spend on the South Fork, if your mother didn't give birth to you at Southampton Hospital, it's best not to say you're from there.

Freshly caught golden tilefish.

16.
GOLDEN TILEFISH

"It was the most satisfying work I ever did on the water," Rick Etzel said of his years as a longline fisherman. Though Etzel mostly caught cod, nearly every Long Island tilefisherman I interviewed recalled the mid-1980s with undeniable nostalgia. Every baited hook held a thirty- to fifty-pound golden tilefish. Bottom-feeders swarmed the North Atlantic. In the first half of that decade, quotas and federal fishing regulations were practically nonexistent. For commercial fishermen, only three things stood in their way: their ambition, their stamina, and their strength.

"Back then, you got a boat and you went fishing," Lance Hallock, the former commercial tilefisherman, explained to me. "Tilefishing was the Wild West." Forty years ago, from October to May, a half dozen Montauk-based fishermen converted party boats and steamed offshore to go longlining for tilefish. Now, nearly all are draggers. In the whole of Montauk Harbor, only two longliners — the *Seacapture* and the *Kimberly* — have survived. Montauk is still the uncontested tilefishing capital of the world: these two powerhouses are responsible for nearly 75 percent of the entire federal quota for golden tilefish. In 2019, 1.4 million pounds of freshly caught tilefish (at $3.81 per pound) equaled a $5.4 million payday.

In the fall of 2018, Morgan McGivern and I paid a visit to the Liar's Saloon, a local watering hole on West Lake Drive. In all of Montauk, Liar's is one of the few places that still feels like it belongs to the people who actually live and work there. A young deckhand and his girlfriend sat at the bar; they each nursed a $2 pint of Budweiser. His navy-blue hoodie with "F/V Kimberly" embroidered on its back was a dead give-away. Ever since he was nineteen, the deckhand explained, he had tilefished year-round aboard the *Kimberly* alongside Captain David Tuma.

Weighing from two to seven pounds, the tilefish their crew catches are generally smaller than the ones their predecessors aboard the *Wind Blown* caught a generation ago. The foursome aboard the *Kimberly* makes seventeen trips per year, ten days on and five days off; each trip averages twenty thousand pounds of tilefish. When the fish are biting, the crew works around the clock — from first light until two or three the next morning. Though the longline tilefishing gear has changed since 1984, Tuma explained, his crew traverses the same canyons, hundreds of miles offshore, that the *Wind Blown* fished forty years ago.

"Close your eyes and you think you are eating lobster," read a story in the *New York Times* from May of 1980 titled "Outdoors: Going for Tilefish Is a Far-Out Experience." Prepared and served cold, as you would tuna salad, it is a "dining delight," as one fisherman quoted in the story described it. The sweet, succulent flesh resembles the taste and texture of northern grouper; its flavor is thought to come from the tilefish's epicurean diet of lobster and red crabs, way down deep on the bottom of the ocean floor.

Scientists first described the modern-day tilefish as early as 1879. Captain Kirby, a Gloucester trawler, was out fishing for cod about 150 fathoms south of Nantucket when he pulled up a never-before-seen species. Nobody could identify what Kirby, and subsequently several of his peers, had caught. They were brightly colored — "a distinct iridescence was noticeable on the scaly trunk" — and at twenty to thirty pounds apiece, nothing to sneeze at. When cooked, the foreign fish tasted so delightful that the United States Bureau of Fisheries (later folded into the US Fish and Wildlife Service) sent someone from its headquarters in Washington, DC, to investigate. The scientist returned from Massachusetts with promising news: an important new fishery had been discovered, and quite by accident.

Alas, initial hopes that the great northern tilefish would become a major source of food were premature; in 1882, vessels traveling from Europe to Boston and New York sailed through a seventy-mile-wide band of billions of dead, floating tilefish. It was an inexplicable marine cataclysm scientists later blamed on a series of unusually cold winters that had damaged their fragile habitat. Tilefish are finicky creatures. They thrive in water that's warm, but not too warm. For the next decade, apparently, not a single one was caught. By 1892, however, the hearty species had started to repopulate, to the delight of seafood lovers everywhere.

In 1915, North Atlantic fishermen caught ten million pounds of tilefish. At the start of the First World War, the Bureau of Fisheries launched a campaign to introduce the bottom-feeders to the American dinner table. In a *New York Times* story from 1929 titled "Bright and Tasty Tilefish Never Attained Popularity," it described them as "good boiled or baked or delicious as a fish chowder." The federal government had incentivized fishermen to start catching them and also disseminated recipes and informational pamphlets. Although tilefish became quite popular in Boston and New York City–area markets, the restricted waters in which they could be found soon forced fishermen to return to their habitual standbys: cod, haddock, and hake. The 1970s saw a huge resurgence of tilefish, most of which was processed (and still is) at the Fulton Fish Market in the Bronx before it's sautéed in butter and happily devoured by restaurant patrons and home cooks alike.

Golden tilefish are a slow-growing, deep-dwelling species that thrive near the ocean floor. You're never going to find them while snorkeling in the tropics, in sight of land. They live along the outer and upper continental slope of the East Coast — from Veatch Canyon (about 140 miles southeast of Montauk Point) to Hudson Canyon (about 100 miles southeast of New York City). Besides the North Atlantic coast, they can also be found throughout the Gulf of Mexico.

Known as "the clowns of the sea," with large heads and stout bodies, golden tilefish seem — if you want to anthropomorphize a fish — to possess a sense of humor. Generally speaking, their backs are an iridescent blue-green, interspersed with patches of yellow and gold, and their bellies are silvery white. Their heads are a rosy shade of pink, with a blue stripe beneath each circular eye. The dorsal and pectoral fins are sepia-hued, while the caudal fin is the color of a ripe eggplant.

As slow, steady growers, tilefish generally reach around twenty-five inches, though they can reach upwards of three feet. Relative to other fish their size, they have a decent life-span. Radiometric dating techniques indicate that if they don't find themselves attached to the end of a baited hook, tilefish may live as long as fifty years. In the Atlantic, they spawn from March to November; female tilefish release some two to eight million eggs each year.

They come in different varieties. For instance, when Montauk tilefishermen pull in blueline tilefish, they consider them a bycatch, and not the target species. The heads of these dull, olive-gray fish are a completely different shape from golden tilefish; a narrow gold stripe, underlined in fluorescent blue, runs from the tip of the eye to the snout. And buyer beware: blueline tilefish are on the Food and Drug Administration's "Do Not Eat" list because of their high mercury content.

Tilefish are unusually sensitive to cold and prefer deep water — some four hundred to nine hundred feet below the surface — that measures between forty-eight and fifty-seven degrees. When they aren't roaming around in search of their next meal, many live head-down, burrowed deep inside wide, funnel-shaped holes that obscure their entire bodies. Some scientists have speculated that such coverings provide protection by camouflaging their brightly colored bodies from lurking predators such as hammerhead sharks.

In a *New York Times* story from 1986, scientists postulated that burrowing tilefish had fundamentally altered the shape and texture of the seafloor. Following a series of submarine dives from Cape Cod to North Carolina, divers reported a startling new topographical discovery: the ocean floor, rather than being a relatively smooth accumulation of sediment, had been radically altered by tilefish that had used their mouths to create deep burrows and grottos. Some of the gigantic, cone-shaped burrows measured seven feet deep by fifteen feet wide.

And not just any burrow will do. "The fish seem strongly attached to their burrows," the *Times* story reported. Scientists also discovered that the enterprising tilefish had created makeshift pueblos by using canyon walls, made of clay, to carve out hidden grottos. "Some fish proved so loyal to their pueblos in Lydonia Canyon that the same ones were recognized when researchers returned a year later." Divers found the pattern the most extreme along the continental shelf, where steep canyons formed during previous ice ages. Their preferred habitat is literally prehistoric: "The canyon was formed 10,000 to 13,000 years ago by intense discharge of water when the last ice sheet was melting and low sea level exposed the continental shelf."

Nearly all of the golden tilefish caught and consumed on the East Coast of the United States originates in one of two ports: Montauk, New York, or Barnegat Light, New Jersey. In 1975, two New Jersey fishermen, Lou Puskas and Marty Cassidy, pioneered commercial tilefishing in the region. Two hundred miles away, Montauk was right in lockstep.

Montauk is the largest commercial harbor in New York State. It's home to some of the greatest sport fishing on all of the East Coast — species such as shark, tuna, and marlin. While longliners steam hundreds of miles offshore, depending on the season and what's running, party boats stick closer to the Montauk Point Lighthouse to hunt flounder, fluke, porgies, bluefish, and striped bass. When you're out fishing, location is everything, and Montauk's unique access point became its best-selling feature — near deep-water ledges and fast-moving rips, not to mention the Gulf Stream conveniently positioned some forty to seventy miles south.

The time-tested approach to catching tilefish involves the use of a longline. Typically located at the stern of a commercial fishing boat, the longline drum spools out dozens of miles of fishing cable (crews eventually switched from tarred nylon twine to galvanized steel cable), with thousands of baited hooks attached. The weighted cable soon sinks hundreds of feet below the ocean's surface.

Longlining has a rich, storied history. Scandinavians in the nineteenth century initially viewed it as undemocratic because it required enormous quantities of bait to gear up. Such economic restrictions prohibited many fishermen from joining in. And in the United States in the twentieth century, off the Massachusetts coastline, as the Grand Banks grew increasingly crowded, fishermen feared that if everyone started longlining in such proximity, their miles of fishing lines would become entangled and impossible to separate. Talk of conservation and fears of overfishing hadn't yet entered the discussion. Over the next century, improved fishing techniques yielded bigger and better catches, as line went from being made of hemp to nylon to microfilament; meanwhile, motorized vessels replaced those powered by oar and sail. As a result, depleted fish stocks became an issue that future generations of fishermen would soon confront.

The *Wind Blown* crew were right in the sweet spot, when tilefish stocks were still ascendant. In the late 1980s, Montauk's tilefishery began to contract. Depending on whom you ask, that outcome could be blamed on one of two culprits (and most likely a combination of the two): overfishing and burdensome government regulations. In the same *New York Times* story from 1986 that reported on the tilefish's hidden underwater burrows, submarine explorers also described a preponderance of abandoned burrows. The researchers believed it hinted at what was to come: a decline in the once-abundant population, with overfishing believed to have reduced the native population by a third to a half.

According to Kelly Anderson, a commercial fisherman who formerly worked aboard Lance Hallock's *Provider III* offshore in the late 1970s, catching tilefish was a no-brainer. You could dunk a washcloth in the water and catch one, he joked. But nothing lasts forever. The Wild West of tilefishing eventually came to a screeching halt. "We were fishing them out," Anderson freely admitted. "There also weren't the regulations that there are now."

By 1994, the National Marine Fisheries Service tabulated fish stocks and concluded that fishing fleets were about twice as large as the populations could sustain. In *Cod*, Mark Kurlansky wrote about rapidly diminishing cod stock along Georges Bank, a stretch of the seafloor between Cape Cod and Nova Scotia. During a four-year span, cod stock plummeted some 40 percent. Scientists had never before measured such a steep decline. It prompted tougher regulations and stricter measures that favored small boats over large trawlers. The changes reverberated farther south too. With their hands tied by stricter federal regulations, many commercial fishermen in Montauk were put out of business once and for all.

Remember that tilefishing, before ever-dwindling fish stocks, was lucrative, steady work. In Montauk, longliners routinely came back from offshore trips hauling fifteen thousand to thirty thousand pounds. The downside? Longlining is also danger-ous work. Because of the fast-moving, razor-sharp hooks (able to quickly slice off fingers and hands — or worse), commercial fishing consistently ranks among the nation's deadliest professions. One reason for the high rate of accidents is the lack of sleep. Nearly every fisherman I interviewed had terrifying stories of near-misses. Going back to the 1800s, 4 percent of the population of Gloucester, Massachusetts, was lost to the sea each year — whether the result of vessel casualties, rogue waves, or fishermen going overboard.

In 1995, Daniel Pauly, a Canadian fisher-ies biologist, coined a helpful new term: *shifting baseline syndrome.* Pauly wrote: "Es-sentially, this syndrome has arisen because each generation of fisheries scientists ac-cepts as a baseline the stock size and species composition that occurred at the beginning of their careers, and uses this to evaluate changes. When the next generation starts its career, the stocks have further declined, but it is the stocks at that time that serve as the new baseline."

Pauly was attempting to explain generational blindness to environmental destruction. Although he was writing about scientists wearing white lab coats, the same can be said of fishermen on the front lines. Whether they were netting, trapping, dragging, or longlining, the natural environment revealed a series of troubling changes that eventually became impossible to ignore. Or, to put it more plainly, Pauly made clear how a Montauk fisherman in 2021 is content with catching a five-pound tilefish when, in the 1980s, his peers fishing the same waters routinely hauled in tilefish ten times that size.

"Smaller fish, fewer of them, shorter fishing windows, holes in the annual itineraries of arrivals and departures, fewer species to catch," Paul Greenberg wrote in *Four Fish*, a delightful book about the proliferation of bass, cod, salmon, and tuna. And yet, for as long as scientists have tracked fish populations, they've increased and decreased. Marine life isn't linear. Much like the

343

ocean's current, sea life flows in cycles. Decades of scarcity follow decades of plenty. On Long Island, bluefish, butterfish, sea bass, striped bass, fluke, and scallops have declined — or all but disappeared — for years at a stretch. Some commercial fishermen believe that limiting the size of what they can catch is beside the point. Climate change and global warming aside, they argue that changes in marine life are part of the natural order of things. Mother Nature, in all of her inherent wisdom, sees to it that stocks are eventually replenished.

But tilefish are hardly the only species of fish that has grown smaller over the past half century. In a startling series of photographs from Key West, Florida, photos from the 1950s captured fishermen with groupers longer than the men were tall. By the 1970s, the fishermen stood far taller than the largest fish they could pull from the sea. And by the 2000s, the average catch was rarely longer than a foot.

So maybe Mother Nature's infinite wisdom doesn't have all that much to do with it, after all. Maybe, one hundred years from now, as glaciers melt and sea levels rise, the oceans will all have been fished out. In such a worst-case scenario, like the American whaling industry that largely collapsed

344

because whalers had hunted the ocean's most profitable creatures nearly to extinction, commercial fishermen would become a thing of the past — a long-ago relic, from back when sea life was still robust and plentiful, and before human beings decimated the planet.

■ ■ ■ ■

PART FIVE:
MICHAEL VIGILANT

■ ■ ■ ■

Michael Vigilant at the docks with tilefish.

17.
THE DOCK RATS

Like many commercial fishermen working in Montauk today, Paul Forsberg Jr. and Michael Vigilant were the sons of fishermen. Like nineteenth-century New England whalers, who toiled in the waters of the Atlantic when it comprised the American frontier, Paul and Michael were born into the work. Fishing was in their blood.

Paul, seven years older, grew up alongside Michael and considered him a younger brother. He called Michael's father, Richard Vigilant, Dickie and thought of him as an uncle.

For both of them, becoming fishermen was less of a choice than a way of life. The boys routinely cut school to go fishing. They were dock rats, eager to someday join their fathers' ranks — determined to work their way up from lowly crew member to first mate to captain. The dock rats were a wild, rambunctious group. If you were still a virgin by the time you turned thirteen, you were an anomaly.

Paul nearly failed the sixth grade because of his chronic absences from school. At dawn, he'd down a glass of orange juice and head not for the classroom, but to the docks. Wednesdays were generally busy days, and the next day he'd return to the Montauk School, which went up to the eighth grade, carrying a handwritten note from his mother. In the note, Mrs. Forsberg explained to his teacher that her son had been out of town. It wasn't technically a lie; just the day before, he had steamed dozens of miles offshore. To help make nice, Paul would slip his teacher a little plastic baggie filled with fresh fish. By his twelfth birthday, Paul was making $100 to $300 a day. It was more than his teacher, equipped with a college degree, earned all week.

His grandfather, Captain Carl Forsberg, founded the *Viking* fleet out of Freeport on western Long Island. The year was 1936. The operation eventually relocated to Montauk. "All the Fish You Can Catch" was the *Viking* slogan, with its crews running half-day and full-day fishing trips. Once Mike Stedman made his way to Montauk as a young twentysomething, he needed to find a job. Though he had fished as a hobby growing up, Mike had no idea how men actually made a *living* catching fish. Mike soon enrolled in Forsberg's "Viking College of Fishing Knowledge," as the fishermen around the docks called it. It was essentially an apprenticeship; Mike cut his teeth aboard the *Viking* boats. In time, he earned a reputation as a seasoned fisherman and an accomplished captain.

It was this celebrated fleet — the *Viking Star,* the *Viking Starlight,* and the *Viking Starship* — that lured Mike Stedman away from East Williston and into the subculture of commercial fishermen, and here that Mike first connected with a young mate who shared his first name. Michael Vigilant worked as an eager crew member aboard the *Viking* vessels. And Captain Mike liked what he saw. In much the same way that his friend Dave Connick rode a surfboard, Michael Vigilant was a natural. Seawater ran through his veins. He was, after all, the son of Wild Dick Vigilant, a commercial fisherman who had died six years earlier in a fishing accident. Captain Mike became a father figure to many of the young, fatherless men who crossed his path, and once he had a boat of his own, and a vacancy opened up, Mike extended to Michael Vigilant an invitation to work aboard the *Wind Blown.*

351

Before he died, Richard Vigilant had been after his son to keep his grades up. Michael graduated from East Hampton High School — six months early, in fact, eager as he was to begin his career as a commercial fisherman. And higher education was never in the cards. To the Vigilants, college seemed like a monumental waste of time and money. Those people wearing cable-knit cashmere sweaters in the ivory tower didn't even know how to fillet a damn fish.

Paul was heartbroken when Michael decided to fill in on the *Wind Blown* while Tom McGivern was away, instead of continuing to work aboard the Forsberg family's *Viking Star.* Shortly thereafter, the *Viking Star* and the *Wind Blown* struck up a friendly competition. Each offshore trip became a race to see which four-man crew could outcatch the other. But it was only Michael's second or third trip aboard the *Wind Blown.* In no time, Paul figured, when Tom returned, Michael would be back aboard the *Viking Star* where he belonged. The dock rats stuck together.

When Michael was a little kid, his parents, Richard and Maude Vigilant, bought a small place on West Lake Drive, near the former Seawind Motel. It was right around the corner from Christman's Restaurant and Bar, where the *Wind Blown* eventually docked from January to March of 1984. It was an unwritten rule that the families of fishermen lived within a mile of the docks. It was more affordable — and someone could easily come over and wake you up if you overslept. Or, if a big storm came through and the roads weren't passable, the docks were but a short walk away.

In between offshore fishing trips, Richard Vigilant's crew would stop by the house. Before snap-on gear became popular, tile-fishermen used tub gear (fishing line coiled inside galvanized tubs, with baited hooks separated two fathoms apart). The five members of the Vigilant family would sit together in the garage, baiting hooks with cut-up pieces of mackerel. The neighborhood kids got in on the fun too, baiting hooks for $10 a tub.

Drinking helped to while away the time between trips. "There's fishermen who drink and drunks who go fishing" is one local saying. Another describes Montauk as "a drinking town with a fishing problem." Once the workday is done and the weather cools, there's not a whole lot else to do. In Montauk, within a two-hundred-yard radius of the docks, you can stumble into half a dozen bars. Drinking was — and still is — a huge part of the subculture.

Before he sobered up, Richard Vigilant could drink anyone under the table. He was generally an outgoing, likable guy. But once he had a few drinks in him, it was best to keep your distance. If you crossed him, you were likely to get your ass kicked. Paul used to worry for the physical safety of Richard's wife, Maude. She was as shy and reserved as Richard was gregarious. And as with his own mother, he sometimes imagined the worst after a long night of drinking in the Vigilant household. "My household was abusive," he told me. "I don't imagine theirs was any different."

Had Michael lived, Paul knows he would have become a legendary captain at the helm of his own boat. It was only a matter of time. "He was going to be something, no doubt," Paul said. "Michael had his father in him in that way." His friends nicknamed him Millionaire. At seventeen, Michael started making between $3,000 and $5,000 per trip. He always had a wallet full of hundred-dollar bills. The joke was that, with Michael's dogged work ethic, he would be the first of his peers to earn a seven-figure salary.

Like many of the dock rats, Paul recalled

the 1984 storm as if it happened last week. It was the first and last time he could remember Montauk Harbor being impassable. Once the skies cleared, the entire *Viking* fleet searched for the *Wind Blown* in a grid pattern. The men found plenty of identifiable wreckage — a cooler, a refrigerator door, the mirror from the medicine cabinet — but no trace of their lost brothers. Paul's father, Paul Forsberg Sr., now well into his eighties, remembered seeing the *Wind Blown* with its wooden pilothouse for the first time shortly after Mike brought her home and thinking it really wasn't the right boat to go tilefishing on in the middle of the winter. "Winter weather is not the best for stuff like that. I feel badly that we didn't get after those guys to change it," he said. Paul Sr. accompanied the fleet to search for wreckage. As they endlessly crisscrossed the water, he kept coming back to one thought: *If we find a body, there will be closure.*

After the 1984 storm, Paul Jr. finally invested in a weather-fax machine so he could *see* the twice-daily printouts and examine the shifting weather patterns up close, rather than risk missing the broadcast version, which required that he stay tethered to his wheelhouse during two specific times of day, before dawn and close to midnight. The $35 rolls of replacement paper were a small cost to bear.

As a party boat captain, he eventually grew sick of taking people fishing. He wanted to go fishing — not to earn a living, necessarily, but for the sheer pleasure of going out on the water to catch fish.

"A person dies twice," Paul explained to me. "The first time they die is when their body stops moving. The second time they die is when the last person stops talking about them."

So long as people keep talking about Michael Vigilant, he's not dead yet.

Captain Richard Vigilant.

18.
THE VIGILANTS

Michael Vigilant wasn't the first man in his family to die at sea. On November 12, 1978, his father met the same fate.

"Mayday! Mayday! Mayday!" Richard Vigilant, the captain of the *Joni Renee,* screamed into his VHF radio, from inside his wooden wheelhouse. "This is the *Joni Renee.* We just got hit by a Japanese tanker. I'm sinking. Get the Coast Guard, please. Please stop the tanker."

It was five o'clock in the morning. Three of the five crew members had been fast asleep. One of them, Peanuts, heard a screeching noise — the unmistakable sound of steel grinding against steel — and was promptly thrown from his bunk. He ran over to the galley and saw a big wall of steel dragging alongside the boat. Richard was already on the radio, calling for help. Peanuts, meanwhile, brought up life jackets from the engine room.

Water filled — and quickly sank — the *Joni Renee*.

Chaos ensued, with every man responsible for saving his own life. Richard, the captain, couldn't swim and wasn't wearing a life jacket. He pulled himself onto a hatch cover, an eight-inch-thick piece of foam. The other four, all wearing life jackets, split up. Some swam in the direction of the nearest visible oil rig, about five miles from the point of impact.

The *Joni Renee* was a seventy-eight-foot, Montauk-based wooden shrimping boat. Her five crew members had departed eastern Long Island only weeks prior, venturing south on an exploratory trip to hunt bottom-feeding tilefish in the Gulf of Mexico. Far from home, they hoped to strike it rich. At the time, they were at Southwest Pass, a busy shipping lane about twenty miles off the New Orleans coastline.

Seventeen hours after the initial Mayday alert, a Russian oil tanker picked up George Hadjipopov, a thirty-four-year-old crew member. George treaded water to stay warm, reportedly losing twenty-five pounds during the seventeen hours he managed to stay afloat.

Peanuts similarly treaded water. Unbeknownst to him, he was stuck in the outflow of the Mississippi River. Currents pushed him into acres of jellyfish. Day turned to night, and night back to day. Thirty-six hours after the *Joni Renee*'s captain first signaled for help, a US Coast Guard helicopter finally swooped low enough to see a bright-orange life jacket bobbing up and down in the water. Rescuers scooped twenty-five-year-old Peanuts from the shark-infested waters.

Once Peanuts made his way inside the helicopter, the pilot gave him his thermos of hot coffee to drink. He explained that he was on his last pass, when something implored him to "turn around and go low." The pilot informed Peanuts that the search had been called off and he was returning to the base when he saw a tiny orange object out of the corner of his eye. Peanuts owed the man his life: "I wouldn't have survived another night."

While floating out there all those hours — exhausted, thirsty, and on the verge of hypothermia — Peanuts realized how inconsequential human beings are when compared to the vast ocean: "I'd get lifted up onto a wave and there would be nothing. Nothing at all."

Three of the *Joni Renee*'s crew weren't so lucky. Richard Vigilant, the forty-two-year-old captain, and two other young mates — Claude Maillet and Raymond Banks — all drowned. George Hadjipopov died in 2014. Peanuts is the last survivor.

When I tracked him down — his real name is Walter Galcik — he had recently moved from Montauk to rural Maine. In the early 1990s, he pivoted away from being a commercial fisherman after a back injury made the physicality of the work all but impossible. Now in his sixties, Peanuts works as a machinist, welder, and fabricator. Maine, where working people can still afford to buy a house and a few acres of land, reminds him of Montauk in the 1960s and 1970s — decades before hedge fund and private-equity money invaded town.

Peanuts acquired his nickname as a baby. Shortly after he was born, doctors diagnosed him with a collapsed lung. Awaiting further test results, his father went downstairs to the hospital's vending machines to find something to eat. Dry-roasted peanuts were all they had left. The nickname stuck.

Although Peanuts tries not to dwell on it, his memories of the *Joni Renee* are always there. It's like a bad dream he can't shake. The trauma of almost dying at sea will torment him until his last breath.

And as the years go on, he worries that people will forget about fishermen who've been lost at sea. It's not the summer people Peanuts gives two shits about, but the locals. "No one ever thinks of us," Peanuts said. "I'm not saying that everyone should go out and become a commercial fisherman, but the men who died just need to be remembered. It's as simple as that."

On March 29, 2020, Peanuts posted an update on Facebook, reminding his friends about the thirty-sixth anniversary of the *Wind Blown*'s downing: "Please take a moment to remember these four men, and all the rest who have been taken from us over the years."

"Behind every fisherman is a good wife," a retired Montauk fisherman said to me. Nothing truer could be said of Maude Vigilant. She not only fell in love with a fisherman, she gave birth to one.

Maude and Richard both grew up in Brooklyn. When she visited his family for the first time and walked into his childhood bedroom, with nautical charts plastered on the walls, the sight foretold her destiny: she would marry a fisherman. Richard's own father didn't much care for fishing, though he'd take his son down to Sheepshead Bay so he could catch a few fish and watch the boats come in. But Richard eventually befriended the local fishermen, and when he was old enough, they hired him to work as a mate on their boats.

In 1961, shortly after marrying in Sag Harbor, Richard and Maude made their way out to Montauk, intent on making a new life together. Richard soon invested in his first charter boat, the *Triton I.* In 1965, after four years of renting and with two young children underfoot (Linda was three; Richard Michael — who was named after his father but only ever used his middle name — was one), the couple poured every penny they had into a three-bedroom, single-story ranch-style home. A third child, Gary, made five. As the family grew and required additional square footage, they slowly added onto the modest house, room by room, with a sandbox and a tire swing out back.

Maude lacked seagoing experience, but she worked as her husband's mate, helping out in any way she could. And once she became a mother, she contributed to the family-run business in other capacities. After every trip, with three kids in tow, Maude helped clean up and restock the boat for the next day. No work was beneath

363

her. She answered the telephone, cooked and cleaned, filled her husband's calendar with half-day and full-day charter trips.

The Vigilant kids grew up, quite literally, at the docks. When they were old enough, they would head down on their own, hanging out at the jetties or meeting the boats as they came in. Other times, they'd bring nets to catch killies, a type of minnow used as bait, and sell them to the Marine Basin to make a quick buck. Cash in hand, they'd head for the Four Oaks General Store on Flamingo Avenue, buying up fistfuls of candy and snacks. The Vigilant family dog, a German shepherd named Maxie, was always hovering nearby, instinctively keeping watch. Among the dock rats, he was known as Beer Can Max, because whenever the party boats came in, he made a beeline for the docks to make his rounds. Captains would hand him a full beer can and passengers would watch in disbelief as Maxie crushed the can with his paws and his teeth and drank the beer. Then he'd trot over to another party boat, eager to replicate the trick.

Richard was a natural-born entrepreneur, a trait he passed along to his enterprising children. When they were teenagers, he started making his own fishing lures by buying raw lead, melting it, and pouring it into the appropriate molds. His daughter, Linda, got in on the fun, and created a little side business making homemade lures and selling them, at a slight profit, to local charter captains.

By 1968, business was going well and the Vigilants invested in a second, larger boat, the *Triton II,* built in Virginia. Though the three Vigilant children grew up with salt air in their lungs, only Michael inherited the sea-leg gene. Whenever Linda or Gary stepped on a boat, seasickness ensued.

Wild Dick Vigilant, who spent two years at State University of New York Maritime College in the Bronx and four years in the US Navy, was an experienced seaman. He owned and operated Montauk charter boats for nearly twenty years, with hundreds of offshore trips under his belt. Like the *Wind Blown,* the *Joni Renee* was a new business venture, prompted by rumors that the Flower Garden Banks (vast underwater mountain ranges about a hundred miles off the Texas and Louisiana coastline) teemed with historic numbers of tilefish, just waiting to be poached.

But Richard had more at stake than the other young, unmarried crew members aboard the *Joni Renee.* When he drowned in 1978, he left behind thirty-eight-year-old Maude and the couple's three children. Linda was sixteen, Michael fourteen, and Gary thirteen.

The Vigilants never recovered from his death.

"You have to remember, this was before the days of the Internet, GoFundMes," Linda Vigilant-Holdeman explained to me via e-mail. "Our tight-knit community was very helpful with support, but in the long run, my mother was still left a widow with three teenagers."

Money was tight. Maude worked in a pharmacy. She worked in a restaurant. All three kids took after-school and summer jobs to help make ends meet.

And every year, on November 12, Linda Vigilant-Holdeman, who now lives in Naples, Florida, posts something on Facebook to commemorate the anniversary of her father's drowning aboard the *Joni Renee.*

One thing still haunts her: the last conversation she had with her father. At the time, she was dating her first boyfriend. Richard disapproved of the match and repeatedly told his daughter she could do better. But Linda was sixteen and newly in love. Hours before Richard left Montauk to go fishing for several months in the Gulf, father and

The Joni Renee.

daughter had an explosive argument.

"I had no clue I would never see him again," Linda wrote. All these years later, she can't help but think of her father, clutching the floating hatch cover for dear life, having just lost his brand-new boat, worrying about the four crew members for whom he was responsible, and rehashing the last conversation he would ever have with his only daughter.

More than anything, Linda didn't mean the unforgivable things she had said to her father. Their argument tormented her for years. At the time, she was a typical sixteen-year-old girl, who thought she knew what was best for her. Only years later, when her own son became a teenager, did she come to appreciate how, in the heat of the moment, we don't necessarily mean the awful things we say to the ones we love most.

On March 29, 1984, Linda was working as a server in a Fort Lauderdale restaurant when her supervisor motioned for her to come to the phone. The voice on the other end of the line told her that Michael's boat was missing.

She figured it had to be some kind of cruel joke. After all, April Fool's Day was right around the corner.

Late March was still the height of the winter tourist season in Florida, when snowbirds from the Northeast flocked south to escape the cold and snow. Linda's supervisor was skeptical when she explained she needed to head home to Montauk once her lunch shift was over. It wasn't until the *Wind Blown* and her brother's name made the national news that her boss finally believed that, all along, Linda had been telling the truth.

Back in Montauk, the moment the *Wind Blown* went missing, friends and fellow fishermen's wives flocked to Maude's side. For her, it was eerily familiar territory. Only six years before, search crews had gone looking for her husband in the Gulf of Mexico.

"I've been this route before and I know it doesn't look promising," Maude Vigilant told a *Newsday* reporter on March 31, 1984, two days after Michael and the *Wind Blown* crew vanished. "I know that the sea takes what it wants." The loss of his father at sea had only driven Michael harder to follow in his footsteps. Maude cried and she cursed. "It made him determined to do a job, and that job was at sea. I hated it. I tried to make him see why I hated the water and why he should hate it," she said. "But he always wanted to be a boat captain, to finish what his father was doing when he died. I'm going insane, but I'm trying to keep the faith."

Only weeks earlier, Maude had sat Michael down and had a heart-to-heart, expressing her concerns about the *Wind Blown*. She wasn't a nautical engineer, she conceded, not by any stretch of the imagination. But her late husband had taught her enough about height-to-width design for her to see in the *Wind Blown*'s shoddy construction a fatal design error. Something about the draft of the boat, the roll of the boat. She worried that it didn't seem sturdy enough to survive offshore during the winter, when storms come seemingly out of nowhere. The conversation with her son wasn't an easy one to have. Every offshore trip meant a great deal of money. Five thousand dollars was a lot of cash to leave on the table. But Michael supposedly heard his mother's concerns and promised her that once Tom McGivern returned from his surfing trip, he would be back alongside Paul Forsberg, working aboard the *Viking Star.* As much as Maude hated the notion of her son at sea and desperately wished he'd find another line of work, there was a sense of comfort and safety in the familiar.

Maude was never the same woman after Michael died. "I'm not sure how any mother can come back completely from the loss of a child, especially so soon after losing a husband," Linda wrote. Although she eventually remarried, Richard Vigilant remained Maude's first, true love. And the loss of her son only magnified that pain. Maude's only solace is that she may return to them in the afterlife.

Shortly after the *Wind Blown* went down, Peanuts and Maude walked the local beaches together for hours at a stretch, searching for any clues they could find. Maude was afraid to be alone. The grief and pain felt all-consuming. She wanted someone by her side day and night.

Linda didn't go to Michael's memorial service. It's a decision she now regrets, but at the time, she simply couldn't wrap her head around the fact that she'd never see her brother again. Michael would eventually come home; Linda was sure of it. Although traumatic, the loss of her father was easier in some ways to process. There was a body, albeit a remnant of one, ravaged by sharks. There was proof that he was gone. But with Michael? Nothing.

There are often a surprising number of loose ends to tie up when someone dies — especially when the death is unexpected. For the family members of fishermen lost at sea, the legal process is particularly burdensome. Lacking a body, New York State law requires that family members must prove their loved one is, in fact, dead, and not just missing.

Maude had familiarized herself with the cumbersome legalities in 1978, shortly after her husband died. Because Richard Vigilant hadn't left a will, Maude applied to the Surrogate's Court in Suffolk County to administer what was left of his estate. All told, Richard left $65,000 in personal property.

In 1985, a year after the *Wind Blown* went down, Maude's grief led her down a warpath of sorts. Lacking a body, Maude wanted answers. Suing for damages felt like the closest she would ever come to closure. At sea as on land, when there's been a loss of life, litigation frequently follows. Admiralty or maritime law governs such matters. Specifically, Maude wanted to know whether the *Wind Blown* had proper lifesaving devices aboard. Having done the bookkeeping for her husband's business for so many years, Maude knew there would be documentation, in the form of receipts or certificates.

This time, she lawyered up; she hired Kenneth Nolan, an attorney with Speiser Krause, a Park Avenue–based law firm that specialized in wrongful death lawsuits. She felt she could trust the fellow Brooklynite to represent her.

"We work on contingency fees," Ken, who still recalled the details of the case, said to me. "If they recover, we recover." Once the Vigilant case got underway, though, it became clear there was little left behind in the way of monetary value. "There wasn't much to go after," he recalled. "It wasn't heavily litigated."

Still, Maude figured, it was worth a shot. In sworn testimony, Maude said that as the captain of the *Wind Blown,* Michael Stedman's negligence had caused her son's death. The Surrogate's Court case briefly mentioned a $50,000 wrongful death action against the estate of Michael Stedman, but little else. In the years since, some have described it as an attempt by the townies to finally get even with the Stedmans — widely considered part of an elevated social and economic class (though light-years away from the privileged Connicks).

But before Maude could begin a wrongful-death lawsuit, she first had to prove that her son was dead. Around the same time, Mary Stedman hired an East Hampton–based attorney to prove the same for her husband. In New York, under admiralty and maritime case law that originated in the 1930s, a presumption of death is generally made following a person's five-year absence. However, an earlier finding can be granted if the facts clearly establish that a vessel, aboard which the missing person was established to have been, collided with a specific hazard.

In a May 15, 1985, decision, Ernest Signorelli, a judge affiliated with the New York State Surrogate Court in Suffolk County, summarized Michael Vigilant's short life in four pages. Born on June 10, 1964, court documents explained, Michael was a commercial fisherman by occupation who was employed as a crew member of the *Wind Blown*. On March 22, 1984, the year Michael would turn twenty, he informed his mother he was leaving that evening to go on a fishing trip aboard the *Wind Blown*. As was Maude's custom, she helped Michael prepare his clothing and ready his gear. Both Gary Vigilant, his brother, and Frank Dext, a friend, testified they last saw Michael in the marina parking lot, carrying his gear and bags aboard the *Wind Blown*.

"Michael was a happy young man who had a good relationship with his family and friends. They have neither seen nor heard from him since the evening of March 22, 1984," Judge Signorelli wrote. "All of his personal belongings, including his vehicle parked in the marina parking lot, have never been claimed nor disturbed since his disappearance." Signorelli concluded by writing: "Michael Vigilant has never been seen or heard from since his departure on the *Wind Blown* and there has been presented no satisfactory explanation for his disappearance other than the fact that he is deceased."

The vanishing aspect of this story cannot

be overstated. When you don't have a body, there's something definitive about a judge's declaration. Mary Stedman sought similar black-and-white proof. But Mike Stedman's legal case was a bit more convoluted. Like Richard Vigilant, Mike hadn't left a will. Besides their home on Stephen Hands Path, Mike possessed little of value; his personal property didn't exceed $7,500. Still, in order to proceed with administering what there was of his estate, Mary applied to the court for a formal declaration that, as a result of a shipwreck, her husband was lost at sea.

To ensure impartiality, even the deceased get attorneys. In Mike's case, the state appointed Richard Stettine as guardian ad litem. Stettine wrote: "The storm was more severe than originally predicted and Mr. Stedman acted prudently in returning on Thursday evening, March 29. The accident that occurred must have been sudden and so swift that Mr. Stedman nor any members of his crew were able to give an SOS with regard to their peril or their location."

Stettine continued: "Mr. Stedman had a happy married life, and no known debts, other than normal bills. The business was successful and operating at a profit. There is nothing in the petition or the supporting papers, to support any suspicion that Mr. Stedman did not die as a result of the alleged accident." Buttressed by overwhelming evidence, Stettine concluded that Mike Stedman died as a result of injuries or drowning and should be considered deceased.

On July 18, 1985, Judge Signorelli wrote a three-page assessment that mirrored what he had concluded in the Vigilant case. He wrote: "A finding of death may be made by the court when a person has been absent for a continuous five-year period and cannot be located after a diligent search where there can be no other satisfactory explanation for their disappearance. However, a finding of death may also be made before the expiration of this five-year period where the facts clearly establish that the alleged decedent met his death by exposure to a specific peril. It has been established that a shipwreck, such as the fate that befell the *Wind Blown,* is a catastrophic peril. Michael Stedman is declared to have died on March 29, 1984."

Amid the bland, cumbersome legal language, the description of *catastrophic peril* felt about right to the survivors left to pick up the pieces. Still, more questions than answers remained. One sentence rang out like a shot across the bow: "Rights of Action may exist against those whose actions brought about the death of Michael Stedman."

As we know, weather was certainly to blame. The boat's construction was probably at fault too. Stedman's judgment as captain is a knottier matter altogether. But it's water under the bridge, since the statute of limitations (two to three years in New York State) has long since passed. In future years, the Vigilant and Clarke families filed no additional litigation; following the loss of their sons, neither family received a settlement. Granted, nothing could bring their children back from the dead; but the lack of acknowledgment in the form of even a meager settlement felt, to their families, like a final slap in the face.

Maude had had enough. Shortly thereafter, she picked up and moved to Pennsylvania. She refused to live near the ocean — and its constant reminder of her dead husband and dead son. Gary, meanwhile, stayed in Montauk.

These days, Maude, Linda, and Gary Vigilant all live in Florida. Gary was thirteen when he lost his father and seventeen when his brother died. Like many of the survivors in this story, he processed his grief by numbing his pain. He got into drugs and did some jail time. "I'm the fuckup in the family," he said.

Had Michael lived, Linda thinks he would have stayed in Montauk. He would have eventually become the captain of his own charter boat. He would have fought for the right to continue to fish, even as the industry imposed ever-harsher restrictions and regulations on fishermen trying to earn an honest wage.

19.
KIM

Michael.

Kim Bowman made it to the docks on Thursday, March 22, 1984, just in the nick of time. The *Wind Blown* crew was busy readying supplies for a routine weeklong trip offshore. Friends and loved ones rarely showed up at the docks to bid the men farewell. These weren't Nantucket whalemen from a prior century who were gone for two to three years at a time. The *Wind Blown* crew would pull back into Montauk within a week.

Still, all day long, Kim's stomach had felt queasy. She and Michael had been arguing for the past few days. About what, exactly, she doesn't remember. She promised Michael she would try to make it to the docks before he boarded the *Wind Blown.* The night before, he had asked her to come and say good-bye before they left.

Kim was finishing her senior year at East Hampton High School. During class, in the margins of her spiral-bound notebooks, she'd write KIMBERLY VIGILANT in cursive script. She liked the symmetry of how the six syllables sounded. Over the lowercase *i*'s, hearts replaced dots. Once school was over that afternoon, Kim took the bus home to her family's three-bedroom house on Duryea Avenue, four blocks away from the docks. She dropped off her backpack and grabbed Frankie, her fourteen-year-old brother, for moral support. Her heart soared when she saw the rust-colored *Wind Blown* still sitting in its berth. Her stomach fluttered with butterflies. Michael walked toward Kim, pulling a bouquet of two dozen long-stemmed red roses from behind his back.

"I'm sorry," Michael said. "I love you."

And then: "When I get in, I'm going to marry you."

He didn't bend down on one knee.

He didn't have a ring.

Kim looked at the gorgeous young man standing in front of her — his brown hair, dark eyes, and stubbly, unshaven face. They kissed and hugged, over and over. Whatever they had been arguing about instantly dissipated into the cold March afternoon. Kim clenched her bouquet of red roses, wrapped in cellophane. She told Michael they'd talk more about getting married in a week's time, when he got back. It was young love, and even five or six days felt like an interminable separation.

Before boarding the *Wind Blown,* Michael turned around and asked if she would wait for him.

"I can't even put that into words," Kim told me.

Bad boys had always been Kim Bowman's thing.

The Bowmans were a relatively new family in Montauk. A decade before, in 1974, they had moved from Westchester County, plunking down $45,000 for a simple cottage less than a mile away from the Vigilants.

It was July of 1983 when Kim first laid eyes on eighteen-year-old Michael. She was seventeen, and two months away from starting her senior year of high school.

Kim's father, a mechanic who ran B & B Auto Service in Montauk, didn't approve of the young romance. He thought they were too young. Behind his back, Kim started sneaking over to Michael's studio apartment near Liar's any chance she could get.

"You tell me not to do something and I'll do it because you tell me not to," Kim explained of their love affair. "The forbidden part was the biggest thrill of it."

After high school, Michael started working on party boats during the summer and taking offshore fishing trips in winter. When he wasn't fishing, he studied for his captain's license. On weekends, to let off some steam, he was a familiar face on the local party circuit.

Whenever he came back from five to seven days offshore, Kim used to tell him he needed to shower before coming near her. Peeling off his denim jacket and blue jeans, which reeked of rancid fish guts, Michael laughed.

"I don't smell like fish," he would say to her, a sly smile spreading across his face. "I smell like money."

Like his father, Michael Vigilant loved being on the water. Out there, he made sense. When back on dry land, he always seemed slightly out of place. Despite growing up within a few miles of some of the best surf breaks on all of the East Coast, surfing held zero appeal for him. And even though his father had drowned at sea, Michael refused to learn how to swim. His obsession with the water consisted of one thing and one thing only: catching fish.

One night, Michael told Kim about his father. After describing the drowning incident, he looked her straight in the eye and told her that when it was his time to go, he wanted to die just as his dad had died — at sea.

"His smell, his eyes, his touch, I remember it all," Kim said. She can still smell his Aqua Velva aftershave. "When he didn't come home, it was like someone had ripped my guts out. The whole town went crazy."

Like the old version of Montauk, Michael Vigilant was here and then he wasn't. Kim fell apart shortly thereafter.

"My sister took it hard. She spiraled out of control when she was younger," Frankie Bowman told me. "Not everyone is built to come back from something like that." Kim never did graduate from high school. The month after the *Wind Blown* went down, administrators expelled her after discovering two ounces of marijuana in her locker.

She worked as a cook in Montauk's restaurants for several years, numbing her pain with alcohol and opiates. She later smoked crack and freebased so much cocaine that a hole formed in her nose. When we sat down together, it was plain to see that her newfound sobriety was a daily, sometimes hourly, struggle. Now in her midfifties, Kim rents a bedroom in Shirley, a working-class hamlet about an hour up-island. She lost her license due to drinking and now works in a nearby laundromat. It was the only job she could find within walking distance of her house.

Besides her younger brother, who witnessed the proposal, Kim apparently never shared the news with anyone else. It was a *secret,* the last one she and Michael ever shared.

"I didn't think it was anybody's business," Frankie told me. At his sister's urging, he kept any news of the proposal to himself.

"The whole town was devastated," he added, referring to the disappearance of the *Wind Blown*. "And after it happened, nobody talked about it."

Kim's mind still churns with unanswerable questions. Michael never came back. They never found his black rubber boots. They never found a body to bury. The mystery surrounding his disappearance torments her still.

In the fall of 2017, when Mary Stedman and I were first becoming acquainted, I casually asked her if any of the other fishermen who died aboard the *Wind Blown* had left girlfriends behind.

Maybe ten years earlier, she and Frankie Bowman had attended the same East Hampton wedding. The two got to talking, and Frankie shared with her the story of Kim and Michael's secret proposal. It was the first time Mary had heard anything of the sort.

In time, I looped back around with Michael's sister, Linda Vigilant-Holdeman. She wrote: "They did date, I do not deny that. It's not just the engagement, but the whole timeline I am struggling with. At nineteen, he would not have been ready to settle down." It was inconceivable, she claimed, that her kid brother had proposed marriage. And he certainly wouldn't have proposed without a ring. That didn't sound like him at all.

Before he died, Michael routinely discussed deeply personal things with his mother. Maude wanted to know: "Where would he have gotten two dozen roses in the middle of winter in Montauk in 1984? It just sounds off."

According to Linda, their brother, Gary, also found the proposal hard to believe. And both Michael's former girlfriend, Diane Duca, and Donnie Briand, one of his closest childhood friends, shared similar doubts with me.

Linda and I continued to go back and forth. "If you are running with the fact of an engagement in your book and you have no other source but the Bowmans to back this up, I do not feel you are doing Michael justice," she wrote to me. "If you truly are trying to tell the best story of the lives of the men of the *Wind Blown* and the history, I would ask that you leave out the part of any engagement, unless you have other verifiable proof outside of the Bowmans. Like I said, those closest that I know disagree on this account."

Looking to corroborate stories, I again

reached out to Rick Etzel, who suggested that I contact Vincent Damm. A commercial fisherman, Vinny owns two red boats: the *Lady K* and the *Jolly Roger*. Like Michael, Vinny was a dock rat, and in mid-March of 1984, when he heard about the temporary opening aboard Captain Mike's new boat, the *Wind Blown,* he jumped at the chance. Vinny was a year younger than Michael and already an expert at playing hooky to go fishing. He and Kim were in the same class at East Hampton High School. But this time his mother, who was generally permissive, forbade him to skip school. "It was her birthday on March twenty-seventh, and she wouldn't let me go," Vinny explained.

I shared with Vinny the discrepancy at the heart of Michael Vigilant's story. Montauk is a small town, and everyone who grew up there knows one another. At first, Vinny also didn't believe Kim's claim. Once we got off the phone, he went down to the docks, where he knew one of the Bowman cousins could be found. A few hours later, his telephone number again flashed across my caller ID. "I can't believe it," Vinny said, "but it's actually *true.*" The cousin had telephoned Frankie Bowman. After hearing Frankie relay the exact same story of Michael's proposal to Kim in real time, Vinny came away a believer.

Perhaps the marriage proposal was another instance in the narrative where people's memories didn't exactly line up. It was, after all, a *secret,* shared between Kim and Michael, moments before the *Wind Blown* steamed offshore for her final voyage. Besides Kim's brother, who witnessed the proposal, the only other person who could substantiate her account was Michael Vigilant himself.

But I believe Kim. Her tears and her grief felt undeniably real to me. While it's possible the so-called truth resides somewhere in the gray areas, as it often does, we'll never know for sure.

■ ■ ■ ■

PART SIX:
AFTER

■ ■ ■ ■

The 1984 storm.

20.
AT SEA

"There was a horrible lot of wind. It was a bad, bad situation. It had to be a horror show," Captain Richard Stern told the *National Fisherman* in June of 1984. "Whatever happened, it happened quickly."

On March 29, 1984, no one heard a distress call from the *Wind Blown*. No one received a call on a satellite phone because such technology didn't exist in 1984. Whatever transpired in those last minutes was likely so sudden and so swift that Captain Mike didn't have time to send out a Mayday alert, conveying either the boat's exact location or the dire peril that he and his crew were up against. It's unlikely the four men had sufficient time to even zip up their survival suits — or reach for the Givens life raft they hoped never to have an occasion to inflate.

Once seawater hit the batteries located in the *Wind Blown*'s engine room, communication with the outside world became impossible. Had the four men been wearing survival suits, cumbersome and buoyant as they are, the force of the water would have likely plunged them straight down, making it impossible to reach the surface before their lungs ran out of oxygen. The weight of thousands of pounds of freshly caught tilefish, stored inside wooden boxes cemented onto the *Wind Blown*'s deck, also hurt their chances of survival.

Some have surmised that a freak sea or a rogue wave — a vertical wall of water that comes out of nowhere and breaks from the pattern of waves both before it and after it — took the *Wind Blown* down sometime between 7:30 and 8:30 a.m. on March 29, possibly pitchpoling or cartwheeling the vessel, end over end, in one heart-stopping instant. But no one really knows. Her last minutes remain a mystery.

"Ocean waves develop when wind blows over a body of water," Bill Patzert, a retired climatologist and oceanographer, explained in a *Los Angeles Times* story about a record-breaking seventy-five-foot wave that broke off the California coastline in 2019. "During large storms, winds transfer energy to the water, creating both waves and surface currents." Patzert said that three things determine the size of waves: "Wind speed, duration of the storm, and fetch — the size of the area of water over which the wind blows. The longer the fetch and the faster the wind, the larger and stronger the wave." Observing how swells in New Zealand can translate into giant surf in Southern California, Patzert concluded: "Waves are truly world travelers."

In late March of 1984, Allan Weisbecker, a Long Island surfer, surfed giant swells during a trip to Barbados. He wrote about the incident in his book *In Search of Captain Zero: A Surfer's Road Trip Beyond the End of the Road.* Later that night, Weisbecker phoned a fisherman friend in Montauk and learned the *Wind Blown* had gone missing. Weisbecker knew David Connick — he and others had nicknamed the goofy-footed surfer (meaning that he surfed with his right foot ahead of his left foot) Dave the Wave. After hearing about the *Wind Blown*'s downing, Weisbecker wondered whether the half dozen sets he surfed earlier that day in the Caribbean — "the big, warm-water perfect waves" — had originated from the nor'easter that, only hours before, had swallowed his friend. Apparently, the northern tip of Barbados can catch the tail end of big swells that originate in the North Atlantic.

Henry Uihlein had grown up near Montauk Harbor. On the morning of March 29 he was trying to make it down to the docks — but the wind kept pushing him in the opposite direction. It turned what was typically a one-minute walk into fifteen minutes of sheer agony. Imagining what conditions felt like offshore sent chills up Henry's spine. He shuddered to think.

"Have you spoken to Flappy yet?" Henry asked me. "You have to track him down."

Flappy, or Flap Jaws, a retired commercial fisherman named Joseph O'Connor, was a legendary Montauk character who got his nickname because he rarely stops talking. With crystal-blue eyes, white hair, and a beard the color of snow, Flappy looks like jolly old St. Nick.

"If it's red at night, sailors delight," Flappy explained to me. "If it's red in the morning, sailors take warning." Several times during our conversation, his eyes welled up with tears. At one point, he started to sob. Flappy had been caught in the same storm. In the early-morning hours that Thursday in late March, he disembarked from the *Marlin IV*. He had been out longlining for tilefish in

Atlantis Canyon, and was back on dry land, checking on a small fishing boat he kept at the Star Island Marina. The wind was blowing at seventy-five miles per hour and evergreens bent like Florida palm trees in a hurricane.

As on most mornings, Flappy was nursing a brutal hangover when a familiar voice came over the crackling radio: it was his friend Mike Stedman. Mike described "hellacious conditions" — with thirty- to forty-foot waves coming at them from all directions. On the radio, Mike said the *Wind Blown* was in sight of the Midway Buoy, halfway between Montauk Point and Block Island. It was the same route Flappy and his crew had traversed only hours before. "The boat was hit from the ass in," Flappy surmised. "She pitchpoled. The boat must have come and rolled off a very bad sea."

When the *Marlin IV* finally made landfall early on March 29, Flappy's crew member Mike Vagesse looked over at him and kissed the ground. He felt lucky to be alive. The 1984 storm did him in. Afterward, he stopped commercial fishing altogether. Vagesse now owns the *Lazy Bones,* a fifty-five-foot party boat that escorts day-tripping fishermen in pursuit of bluefish and fluke. They never go much past Montauk Point.

Now in his midsixties, Vagesse marvels at the confidence commercial fishing boat captains must possess. Especially the young guys, who don't yet have the experience to know any better. It's an occupation best suited to one's twenties and early thirties — before reason and common sense make the danger of the work all but impossible to ignore.

Long before Vagesse encountered Mike Stedman and Dave Connick at the docks, they were his surfing buddies. They'd ride waves together at Atlantic Terrace and Ditch Plains. Only months prior, he and Dave had taken a surfing trip together to Cape Hatteras in the Outer Banks, a strand of islands off the North Carolina coastline.

Mike Stedman was a go-getter, and Vagesse knew well the tremendous personal pressure he was under — expenses were high, and coming back early with half a catch wasn't an option. Vagesse concluded that Mike made a fatal miscalculation. He pushed the boundaries too far. He stayed out too long. Vagesse wasn't sure that the *Wind Blown* foursome even had real survival suits at their disposal — in his recollection, they were simply using O'Neill and Rip Curl wetsuits left over from surfing.

Tom Gouba, the captain of the *High*

Stakes, an eighty-foot steel long-liner, was about eight to ten miles south of where the *Wind Blown* went down. If he'd been on that boat, he explained, he would have been on VHF channel 16 (the one closely monitored by the US Coast Guard), screaming at the top of his lungs. Midday Wednesday, March 28, as forecasters reported a major storm headed their way and winds reached eighty miles per hour, one of the *High Stakes* crewmen, wearing a green slicker, got tangled up in gear and washed overboard. He was eventually pulled from the sea, uninjured. At midnight, Captain Gouba ordered his crew to cut their gear and headed for port.

"It was wild," Gouba said in a story that appeared in the *National Fisherman.* "There were waves breaking over the boat. I've never experienced anything like that before, and it scared the hell out of me. It was as bad as anything I've ever been in and more than I ever care to be in again." Afterward, Gouba said the experience "changed everybody's minds around." He ordered special life rafts, survival suits, and an emergency position-indicating radio beacon, or EPIRB. Going forward, he mandated that his crew wear bright-orange slickers to make them visible in the water.

The Provider III.

Lance Hallock, who owned the *Provider III,* was caught in the same churning seas in Lydonia Canyon, about two hundred miles offshore. Lance's musty green, leather-bound logbook from 1984 recorded the water temperature on March 27 as 47.6 degrees. His crew caught 5,155 pounds of tilefish on that trip. In the margins, he wrote in pencil: "HOT. BEST DAY IN YEARS. GENERATOR WENT OUT. STAYING ANYWAY."

But after hearing the weather report, Lance decided to head back to Montauk. At fifty-six feet, the *Provider III* was a slow boat; making seven to eight knots, it took him and his crew a solid twenty-four hours to traverse two hundred miles. Conditions worsened overnight. The water turned to solid foam. In the pitch-black of night, the *Provider III* went underwater twice. Seawater turned the vessel 180 degrees and broke open a watertight steel door that had been hammered shut. If stuff wasn't in the fish hold or down below, it was gone. Once they made it back to Montauk, the inlet, a narrow passageway that connects the Long Island Sound with the fishing docks on Lake Montauk, proved impassable. Even the lights were out. Hallock's crew eventually found calmer waters farther west, docking in Montauk's Fort Pond Bay overnight. When the sun came up on Thursday, March 29, Lance realized the *Provider III*'s cast-iron, hydraulic handles had gone missing, along with the deck tiles. There wasn't so much as a fish scale left on the boat.

Captain Hallock had seen worse weather in the US Navy, but never aboard a fifty-six-foot fishing boat. Some captains faulted the National Weather Service for not providing a more accurate offshore forecast. But in the *National Fisherman* story, Hallock had a different recollection: "We knew it was going to blow sixty knots. We wanted to get one more day in."

Tom Roth, who tilefished out of Barnegat Light, New Jersey, aboard the *Vivian III,* a seventy-foot longliner, also anchored up in

Fort Pond Bay on the evening of Wednesday, March 28. It was rare for Tom to stop in Montauk for the night; he was always eager to make it home and sleep in his own bed again. Tom was a Barnegat guy. On the whole of the East Coast, tilefishing exists in two ports: Montauk and Barnegat Light. Theirs was a fierce rivalry. Every offshore trip was a race to see which vessel returned with more tilefish. Tom and his New Jersey–based crew members jokingly called Montauk "Sissy City." But after Tom's boss radioed from Barnegat Light to tell him that a bad storm was headed their way and to get their asses back to the docks, he swallowed his pride and did as he was told.

Joseph Quingert, who went by the name Thumper Joe, was also out longlining for tilefish in the Middle Grounds aboard the *Terri Lei* that week. About a hundred miles offshore, he remembered the conditions as "pancake flat." The water was glassy calm; like a mirror, it reflected the pastel color of the evening sky overhead. But when the weather started to turn midday Wednesday, the *Terri Lei*'s owner called Joe on the two-way radio. He wanted his crew back on land. Obeying orders, Joe reluctantly told his three crew members to stop catching fish and start hauling in their miles of fishing gear. Though their home port was Barnegat Light, the *Terri Lei* sped for Montauk, the closest point of land, hoping to beat the storm.

At one point, Joe recalled, the *Wind Blown* was about an hour behind the *Terri Lei,* both racing against a deadly sea. The *Terri Lei* got caught at Pollock Rip, a powerful rip current about a mile from Montauk Point. A wave shattered the wheelhouse's windows. Joe eventually laid her down sideways. One of his crew members started screaming in pain; during the commotion, he had fractured his spine. Joe sent out a Mayday alert.

A Montauk-based US Coast Guard boat came to the *Terri Lei*'s rescue. Once Joe and his crew made it safely to the docks in Montauk, he put his injured crew member in an ambulance headed for Southampton Hospital and surveyed what later amounted to about $50,000 worth of damage. But the hassle of filing insurance claims became the least of his worries when Joe heard about the *Wind Blown.* One of his friends, Scott Clarke — Oswald, the young kid with his whole life ahead of him — was still out there.

The same *Terri Lei* appeared near the end of Sebastian Junger's *The Perfect Storm: A True Story of Men Against the Sea.* Having survived the 1984 storm, nine years later, in 1993, the *Terri Lei* had an altogether different crew and was out longlining for tuna off the coast of South Carolina when it ran into trouble and vanished. As with the *Wind Blown,* none of the *Terri Lei*'s crew members escaped alive.

By 1993, Joe Quingert had found work aboard another vessel. He died in August 2019; his obituary went right to the heart of things: "Joseph was a commercial fisherman for most of his life. He never considered it a job though, he loved the sea and he loved to fish."

Over the years, Montauk has seen its fair share of bad storms. It pretty much goes with the territory: the town sits on the exposed edge of a long, narrow island at the convergence of two great bodies of water. Even on a calm, cloudless summer day, the trip back into Montauk Point can be treacherous. And the closer you get, the more dangerous it gets. Deep ocean water meets shallower shoals; the swirling tides and powerful swells forcefully comingle. Offshore in lousy conditions, an eight-hour ride can quickly turn into sixteen. Nevertheless, even amid hurricane-force winds, the *Wind Blown* should have made it back to Montauk

Storm-toppled houses.

by lunchtime on Thursday, March 29.

By midmorning when she hadn't returned to the docks, Patrick Wetzel, Mike's brother-in-law, reported the overdue vessel to the US Coast Guard Station in Montauk. The search-and-rescue unit covered calls up to fifty nautical miles off eastern Long Island. Before charting tides and plotting out the missing vessel's potential whereabouts, the Coast Guard phoned marinas from Cape Cod to Fire Island, hoping for news of the *Wind Blown.* "There was none," the *East Hampton Star* reported.

A dark pall soon fell over the South Fork.

Starting early Friday, March 30, every member of the Montauk fleet who wasn't already out looking was back on the water. The close-knit, year-round brotherhood was searching desperately for their lost men in a race against time. By Saturday, the stormy skies had turned a brilliant shade of cornflower blue. Temperatures rose to the mid-fifties. "The wind was a gentle tickle," the *Star* reported. "It was nature's turnabout, soft spring, ideal weather for a search."

A five-day search followed, led by the US Coast Guard and assisted by the Air National Guard and the US Navy. Fifteen to twenty fishing boats, five planes, and three helicopters scoured nearly twenty-five thousand square miles of ocean between Block Island and the Delaware coast.

On Monday, April 2, a Coast Guard spokesman announced the suspension of the search: "If there was something to find, we would have found it by now. There is always a degree of hope, but we feel we've gone past the reasonable amount in this case."

But the fleet refused to give up hope. The docks sat empty for the next week. Living on black coffee and little else, the men spent ten adrenaline-fueled days with their eyes glued to the water. Most retraced the *Wind Blown*'s last-known path between Montauk Point and Block Island over and over. They looked for any piece of evidence they could find.

Once the Coast Guard called off its

Mike Stedman with Bart and Jeb Stuart.

search, family members and friends of the four men rallied to create the Wind Blown Search Fund. Community donations helped fuel the army of private boats and planes that continued searching for another five days. "If I had to sit down and write thank-you cards to everyone who helped, I would be here forever," Maude Vigilant told a *Star* reporter.

Jeb Stuart, Mike Stedman's childhood friend from East Williston, was living up in Maine when Mary called to inform him about the *Wind Blown* going down. After five days, she explained, the Coast Guard had abandoned the search, but the families of the missing foursome weren't ready to

405

give up hope.

"I came down and took one of the boats I used to captain while I was living down there. I tried to figure out if I were in his shoes, where would I go to get back to the nearest harbor. I tracked the wind and the tide and just started going in that direction," Jeb said in a story that appeared years later in the *Surfer's Journal.* "We found all the wreckage in the middle of the night, at two o'clock in the morning, with a single spotlight after the Coast Guard and all their overflights couldn't find it. Oh, man, it was just so intense. We hoped that maybe Mike and his guys were in a life raft nearby and that, maybe, at sunrise, we would see him waving to us saying, 'Hey, guys, it's good to see you, thanks for finding us!' It didn't happen."

Patrick Wetzel, the commercial fisherman married to Mary's sister Margie, was another member of the six-man search crew. He and Jeb were accompanied by two of Mike's brothers, John and Matt; Stu Foley, a surfing and fishing buddy; and Walter Vogt, a member of the Choppess. These were the men, searching from sunup to sundown aboard the *Viking Star,* who had known Mike all his life.

"The whole trip was filled with so much

hope and hopelessness," Patrick recalled. Having fished with Captain Mike on numerous occasions, Patrick knew that he wouldn't have let anyone else take the wheel in rough weather, even if it meant staying tethered to his wheelhouse for twenty-four straight hours. Standing aboard the *Viking Star* during their last day on the water, Patrick looked up and saw four distinct clouds moving, in unison, through the clear blue, early spring sky. Tears streamed down his face. Though Captain Mike, Dave, Michael, and Scott wouldn't be found, there they still were, keeping watch.

The ten-day search turned up small bits of debris — a life ring, sections of the cabin, fish boxes that had been affixed to its deck, pieces of clothing, a white wooden door, two paddles with WIND BLOWN inscribed on them. On April 6, the Coast Guard came upon the boat's EPIRB beacon some fifteen miles south of Montauk. Later that same day, the Metropolitan desk of the *New York Times* reported that the missing foursome aboard the *Wind Blown* were presumed dead: "The Coast Guard and a volunteer search party of fishermen have concluded that there is no prospect of finding either survivors or the vessel."

The men, and their steel-bottomed boat, had vanished.

21.
ON LAND

A car attempting to board Shelter Island's South Ferry as the storm made landfall.

Earl Ewing was driving home from Garden City High School when he heard about a missing fishing vessel on the radio. It was a Thursday afternoon. There had been a ferocious storm overnight and the skies hadn't yet cleared. Rain was still coming down pretty hard.

Though theirs was an unlikely friendship

409

— a high school math teacher and a commercial fisherman — Earl Ewing and Mike Stedman stayed in close touch for the rest of Mike's life. When visiting Nassau County, Mike often stayed with Earl. When they stopped in to see Earl's mother, Mike would say: "Mrs. Ewing, I brought you some tilefish."

Earl had loaned Mike the final few thousand dollars he needed to cover the closing costs to purchase the *Wind Blown.* "I have a tendency to put people under my wing," Earl explained. For years, Mike had dreamed of owning his own boat. He had spoken to Earl of little else.

On Thursday evening, when Earl arrived home, he put his keys down and picked up the telephone. Fearing the worst, he dialed Mike and Mary's number, which he knew by heart.

"I just heard on the radio that there's a missing fishing boat," Earl said to Mary. "Is it Mike?"

"Yes, it is," Mary said.

"Okay, Mary," Earl said. "I'll be right out."

Earl drove the two hours from Williston Park to East Hampton. He stayed there until rescuers called off the search, leaving Mike and Mary's house only to buy new clothes. A substitute teacher covered his classes until he returned home. Time moved at a snail's pace all that next week. At the Stedman home on Stephen Hands Path, candles glowed in the upstairs and downstairs windows, holding silent vigil. Every evening, as sunset approached, a sense of dread filled the house. A steady stream of reporters — from the *New York Times* to *Newsday* to the *East Hampton Star* — kept stopping by for updates, but there was little news to report. Rescuers kept finding debris. But as the days wore on, it grew less and less likely they'd find any of the four men alive.

Mary initially overwhelmed Earl with all of her cosmic, interconnected observations about the nature of things. But the pair soon developed a mutual appreciation for each other. Both liked to read, and both were smart. Mary confided in Earl when she discovered that Mike had planned on changing the boat's name from the *Wind Blown* to *Sinbad.* "Those are two bad words," she insisted, time and again, during their many conversations. *Sin* and *bad.* "How can you have a combination of those two words?" During the search, she worried the name change had cursed the already unseaworthy boat.

Bruce Stedman was sitting at home in Wisconsin when a newscaster on *Good Morning America* announced that a fishing boat off the coast of Montauk had gone missing. A call to Mary confirmed his worst fears.

He next phoned his youngest son, Matt, with the devastating news. Matt was at work, changing tires at a local auto-body shop in Michigan. He hung up the phone and went to his boss, explaining he had to leave and didn't know when he would be coming back. His boss handed him $200, no questions asked. Matt and his pregnant wife drove the thousand miles from Empire, Michigan, to East Hampton, New York, continuing straight through the night, stopping only to use the restroom. Although he tried to convince himself otherwise, some small part of him knew he'd never see his older brother again.

Bruce and Ruth flew to East Hampton within twenty-four hours of hearing the news. Long since retired, Bruce disguised his worry by taking action: he adopted the familiar role of a civil servant fixing a crisis. One afternoon, Bruce grabbed Mary by the shoulders and said: "You better get married immediately." Bruce was worried about his daughter-in-law's stability, financial and otherwise. To this day, someone suddenly touching Mary's shoulders provokes a panicked response.

At five o'clock each evening, the Stedmans retreated to a two-bedroom East Hampton motel suite they shared with Matt and their daughter-in-law for cocktail hour. But during the day, they took care of business. Bruce went through the stack of envelopes piled up in the front seat of Mike's pickup truck, making sure monthly utility bills and mortgage payments stayed up-to-date. John flew up in private airplanes to search for his lost brother and later, though prone to seasickness, joined Matt at sea for five consecutive days to do the same. Matt's wife panhandled for extra change in downtown East Hampton, helping to raise funds for the fleet of private helicopters and airplanes searching the skies offshore for the missing boat.

Ruth, though, receded inward. She stayed back in the motel room and knit.

For Bruce and Ruth, typically impenetrable to emotion, their stiff upper lips were no match for the disappearance of their son. The waiting game eventually became too much to process — too much pain, too much shock. Bruce and Ruth packed up somewhat hastily and departed for Wisconsin, with the excuse of a house repair that simply couldn't be put off any longer. The Stedmans never made it back to East Hampton for their son's memorial service. Jim similarly bolted. John, the eldest Stedman brother, stuck around, reluctantly playing the role of family patriarch.

Matt and his wife also returned home. With a baby on the way, they were unable to continue living out of their suitcases. But even when Matt went back to his familiar routine, it was hard not to obsess about his lost brother.

Although they were not overly close, Mike had been Matt's road map, his North Star; he had mimicked his older brother's every move. Mike was the man Matt wanted to become. Ever since his brother was lost at sea, a part of Matt has felt lost as well. And thirty-two years after the downing of the *Wind Blown,* John and Jim Stedman died within six months of each other. "I'm the last of the Stedman boys," Matt told me. "All my brothers are dead."

Chris Stedman was sitting in Mr. Geehreng's fourth-grade classroom at John M.

Marshall Elementary School in East Hampton, eagerly waiting for the school bell to ring at three o'clock that afternoon. His dad would finally be home.

There was a break-dancing competition planned for later that day. But Chris never had the opportunity to show off his dance moves, which he had been perfecting for weeks. Instead, an administrator whisked him away to the front office. And from that moment on, everyone in East Hampton knew who the Stedman brothers were. They were the three boys with the dead father.

Chris grew up practically overnight. The eldest, at nine, he became the man of the house. "I am not a child," Chris said to Mary, eager to assert his newfound responsibility. "I'm going with the men to go and look for my dad."

A few days into the search, he accompanied Ray Charron, a close family friend, in a four-seat private plane to look for wreckage. They sat in the rear of the airplane, their eyes glued to the choppy seas. But the writing was on the wall. By sundown each day, the chances of rescuers finding any of the four crew members alive dwindled further.

While the men searched in private planes and fishing vessels from dawn until dusk, there was a separate vigil, populated mostly by women, at Mary's house — fretting, worrying, praying. They made sure she was never alone. They fixed her continuous plates of food that sat untouched. Donna Charron, Ray's wife, was one of the friends who kept Mary company as she flitted about, taking walks, unable to be contained. She couldn't sit still.

In 1971, Ray and Donna Charron had opened one of Montauk's first surf shops: He'e Nalu (Hawaiian for "wave sliding," or surfing). Mike Stedman was a regular customer. And shortly after they started dating, Mike brought Mary over to the Charrons' Montauk apartment. Friday nights were reserved for friends, who stopped by to play guitar, sing, and drink Gallo wine.

"One night, Mary was on a little LSD trip," Donna recalled. She and Mike gently laid her down on the couch to rest. Mary wore a long cape with a hood; she looked like a sleeping Snow White, her long, dark hair splayed out across the couch like a fan. Mike was already a beloved close friend. As Donna looked back and forth, from Mary to Mike to Mary, she couldn't help but wonder about this mysterious girl who had stolen Mike's heart.

Back in those days, Montauk was a sleepy

little fishing village; for a hundred days in the summer, things got a little crazy, but from September to April, the locals had their town back. A close-knit tribe of predominantly young families had started to form. It was the beginning of a community love story, of friends coming of age, a little slice of idyllic, small-town life. They bonded over the surf, played music, and celebrated life's big and little occasions. The Charrons were a few years older than Mike and Mary and already had three sons. And once the Stedmans had three sons of their own, their bond intensified.

Shortly before he acquired the *Wind Blown,* Mary casually mentioned to Donna that Mike planned on buying a Gulf-based boat. Donna knew that Gulf water differed from North Atlantic water. And later that fall, she had a dream that Mike's boat went down. Donna filed the dream away, attributing it to generalized anxiety. A few weeks later, she ran into Mike in downtown Sag Harbor. He was walking out of the Bank of the Hamptons.

"I got the money," Mike said to Donna. "I just bought the boat." He was so excited, he practically skipped across the sidewalk.

Donna's mind raced back to the dream. *How do you say, "That's not the right boat for*

417

Ray and Donna Charron with their son Jay; Jeb Stuart is in the background.

you?" she wondered. So she smiled back, and kept her mouth shut.

"It wasn't that Mike was irresponsible," Donna explained to me. "Mike was a believer that nothing bad could happen to him. And he took a risk, and that risk wasn't a good one."

A week or so into the ten-day search, Donna and Laura, another close friend, accompanied Mary to Smithtown to see a psychic who'd been recommended to them. Supposedly, the New York Police Department had used the same psychic to help

418

solve difficult cases. The women were desperate for answers. They figured it was worth a shot.

The three women borrowed Matt Norklun's Volvo P1800 to drive the sixty miles that separate East Hampton from Smithtown. Matt had loaned his car to Mary after the tree branch landed on her Subaru. Driving west on the Long Island Expressway, Donna sat in the driver's seat, holding on to faith and hope. Every so often, she'd look in the rearview mirror and watch Mary in the backseat, staring out the window, silent and expressionless. If the men weren't going to come back alive, Donna prayed rescuers would at least find a body. Closure felt like the closest thing to a happy ending.

The psychic was an obese woman with bleached-blond hair. She wore an ornate, embroidered caftan and a heavy layer of makeup. Seated at her formal dining room table, she motioned for the three women to sit down directly opposite. Mary sat in the middle, holding the green-framed mirror from aboard the *Wind Blown* that rescuers had found floating at sea.

Before the session began, the psychic warned the women that she would enter an altered state and could say or see things that might prove hurtful.

Shortly thereafter, she started to wail.

"Michael, Michael, David, Scott," she said aloud, over and over, until it sounded like one continuous name.

The psychic blinked her eyes and turned her head from side to side. The women stayed silent, not wanting to break the spell. The psychic asked Mary to put aside the green mirror she was holding. "I thought that it was red," she said to the three women, who hung on her every word. "The mirror in the wheelhouse was definitely red."

"Michael didn't want to die," the psychic said. "And at the moment before he died, he reached out to Mary."

Mary's mind flashed back to the tree landing smack across the hood of her car, shattering her windshield.

"The boat was laden with fish and a big wave overtook them," the psychic said. "The four men drowned and died quick, relatively painless deaths."

Next, she looked over at the other two women.

"You have to stop being a cheerleader," she said to Donna, looking her square in the eye. "If you're going to help Mary, you have to help her come to terms with her husband's death. He's gone, and he's not coming back."

On April 9, a few hours after the extended ten-day search had officially been called off, Mary gathered her sons at the Jericho House, an East Hampton bed-and-breakfast on Montauk Highway run by Ray and Donna. It had five bedrooms, and every summer the Charron family moved up to the attic to make room for paying guests. After the *Wind Blown* went down, the Jericho House functioned as ground zero for daily search efforts. Marked-up nautical charts covered the kitchen table. The coffee-maker stayed on. Adrenaline and hope fueled everyone's efforts.

Mary led her boys into a small bedroom and sat them down together on a bed. Three sets of blue eyes stared intently back at their mother. Mary took a deep, sharp inhalation. She filled her lungs with courage.

"You are the first people of all your friends who have lost your father," Mary explained. "Death happens to everybody, and at some point, all the people you know will watch their fathers die. You have been chosen to be first and to be strong."

The bedroom door creaked open, and friends and family members poured in. They formed a tight circle, embracing Mary and the three boys. It was this same community who helped raise the Stedman boys as their own kin.

Afterward, the Jericho House became a second home, a safe harbor, to the Stedman boys. Chris memorized its every nook and cranny — from the paintings on its walls to the contents of its well-stocked pantry. On Friday nights, it was where Chris and Will would stop in for a big bowl of Donna's chili or corn chowder. They often stayed through the weekend, no questions asked.

The McGivern home was another hideaway. A picture of Will from that era, taken by Morgan McGivern, shows a wooden cross hanging on the bedroom wall. A surfboard leans on the wall directly opposite. A shaggy dog is asleep on the floor. In the middle of the picture, Will lies facedown, fast asleep. He hadn't even bothered to crawl beneath the patterned quilt. Someone, probably Joan McGivern, had covered his sleeping body with a blanket. Looking at the photograph, you can't help but want to rewrite history: you want Mike to come swooping in, lift up his son, and carry him home.

Out in Montauk, Maude Vigilant sat tethered to her telephone, praying. "This is hor-

Will Stedman fast asleep.

rible — it's like a repeat performance." On
April 6, the day the *New York Times* declared that the missing foursome were
presumed dead, Maude told the reporter:
"I am not giving up and I have no intention
of ending the search. I am still hoping to
find my son."

Maude believed, however improbably, that
Michael was still alive — still floating
somewhere in the icy, forty-degree seas.
Even wearing a full-body survival suit, forty-
eight hours is the longest amount of time a
person could survive such frigid conditions.

The day of the joint memorial service for
Michael Dexter Stedman and David
McGuire Connick was five days away,

scheduled for April 11 at the Most Holy Trinity Church in East Hampton. But Maude refused to attend. She stayed back in Montauk. Showing up to the church was the equivalent of giving up. Sooner or later, her son would be found. She was sure of it.

Although no one really said as much at the time, the service represented a further demarcation of social class. The two boys aboard the *Wind Blown* — the youngest mates from the so-called "wrong side of the tracks" — weren't eulogized in the same way the whole town of East Hampton came out in support of Mike and Dave.

That day, finding a spot to park, let alone an empty seat in the packed church, was all but impossible. The local press zeroed in on the young father and the rich kid who had died at sea. But the tragedy of losing two working-class deckhands never registered in quite the same way. It was almost as if Michael Vigilant and Scott Clarke, relatively anonymous young crewmen, hadn't penetrated the East End's complex social fabric. To add insult to injury, only the now-defunct *Suffolk Life* spelled Scott's surname correctly (*Clarke*, not Clark), though the same story misspelled Michael Vigilant's name as Mike Vigulant (he never went by Mike). And Scott Clarke was only *eighteen*, not nineteen, as every news outlet reported.

Over the ensuing months, Maude Vigilant and Donna Llewellyn, Scott Clarke's mother, banded together. They refused to give up hope that their sons would be found — dead or alive. In Maude's gut, she knew that Michael was gone. But a recovery meant closure, and the two women kept the search going for nearly a month. On April 26, Maude and Donna cobbled together any donations that remained from the Wind Blown Search Fund and hired a Staten Island–based salvage crew to conduct a search independent of the US Coast Guard. The month after the *Wind Blown* went down, Maude told a *Star* reporter that a fishing boat, the *Captain Johnny,* had gotten hung up where a private search plane spotted an oil slick about a dozen miles south of Montauk Point. "He got his nets all ripped apart," Maude said. "We're pretty sure that's where the hull is." But even the salvage crew turned up empty-handed. No remains of the four crew members were ever found.

Afterward, Maude donated what remained of the search fund to the town of East Hampton so it could set up an emergency relief account, "if, God forbid, there's another disaster like this and the families want to keep searching after the Coast Guard has stopped." She couldn't stomach the idea of money getting in the way of a mother finding her lost son.

■ ■ ■ ■

Mourners gathered outside the Most Holy Trinity Church.

22.
THE MEMORIAL

In late March of 1984, Olivia Brooks was sitting inside her in-laws' house, in the heart of East Hampton Village, when her husband, Jim Brooks, came bursting through the kitchen door.

"Michael Stedman is gone," Jim said.

"What do you mean, Mike's *gone*?" Olivia asked. "Did he leave town? Did he leave Mary and the boys?"

Olivia, who had grown up in East Hampton, was a teacher at John M. Marshall Elementary School. She knew the Stedmans well. Olivia also knew the Connicks. Her mother, Amelia Hagedorn, had worked as a seamstress in town when Olivia was growing up, altering and sewing clothes for many Maidstone Club members. Every summer, Alice showed up at their house to retrieve the cocktail dresses Olivia's mother had altered. Alice had a sweet tooth and it was only a matter of time before she made her way to the family's cookie jar, quickly devouring one or two cookies.

"Livy," Alice would ask little Olivia, "am I average or skinny?" Even as a young girl, Olivia knew there was only one acceptable response.

One summer, Amelia recommended her daughter as a possible babysitter for Alice's two young boys. At the time, Peter was a toddler and David was a baby. Whenever Big Pete and Alice wanted a night to themselves, Olivia became a regular fixture at the Connick home on The Crossways.

Alongside so many East End locals, Olivia Brooks will never forget the day the *Wind Blown* went down. Like President Kennedy's assassination or the fall of the World Trade Center towers, the date of the *Wind Blown*'s downing sits lodged deep inside her memory bank. Once she discovered Dave Connick was also lost at sea, the tragedy hit her especially hard. The summer after the boat went down, Olivia had a difficult time being near any body of water. Both the Atlantic Ocean and the Long Island Sound seemed unforgiving, haunted, and cruel.

On the blustery, raw April day of the joint memorial service for Mike and Dave, Olivia sat in one of the wooden pews, a few rows behind Pete and Alice Connick. The entire community — the locals and the summer people — had turned out in droves. At one point during the mass, Olivia watched as Pete put his arm around Alice to comfort his grieving wife. By then, Olivia had two young children of her own. Her heart split in two. It ached, for Alice and for Mary, in different ways.

Seamus Mahoney flew home to East Hampton for the memorial service.

Locking eyes with Alice during the service, even though no words were exchanged, Seamus sensed her resentment of Mahoneyville and all it had represented. *You stole our son,* her look seemed to say, *and now look what's happened.*

"Mary was completely out of her mind, understandably," Seamus recalled. "Dave was one of her best friends too."

Earlier that morning, Mary had her sons picked up and brought to the church. She planned to meet them there. She was sitting at home when Tom Talmage, a close friend and state trooper who lived in Springs, knocked on her door. She was wearing a white silk blouse, gray pants, and a mauve suede jacket, bought at a high-end boutique in Water Mill. At the urging of the boutique's owner, before the reception began,

429

she would change into a white angora sweater. The suede jacket wouldn't hold up, the shopkeeper had explained, with so many people hugging her.

The bill totaled $800. "Mike would have never let me have this, so I bought it," Mary confided to a close girlfriend.

Tom showed up at Mary's doorstep wearing a light-gray suit with a pink oxford shirt and a pink, paisley-printed tie. Mary didn't know whether to laugh or cry. She had expected Tom, tasked with escorting her into the church, to wear a black or navy-blue suit. Here, Mike was dead. And Mary and Tom, wearing matching pastel outfits, looked like the Bobbsey Twins.

At noon, inside the church on Buell Lane, it was standing room only. Some four hundred people showed up, a mixture of men wearing jeans and heavy work boots, and city people dressed to the nines. Sunlight streamed in through the more than three dozen stained-glass windows. Those who didn't get seats stood outside, listening to the service through open doors. The American flag stood at half-staff. Everyone held copies of the lemon-yellow mass cards. Two caskets, strewn with flowers, stood at the front of the church. But they were mere placeholders. There were no bodies inside.

Earl Ewing sat in the front row alongside Mary and the boys. Chris, Will, and Shane all wore brand-new outfits from a Bridge-hampton boutique. Mary considered it a necessary expenditure; others viewed it as a frivolous waste of money. Living in East Hampton was like living under the glare of a microscope. Surely Mary could have gone to the Ladies' Village Improvement Society of East Hampton and borrowed three blaz-ers from their thrift store, or driven to River-head and gone to Sears. But she paid any criticism little mind. She figured her boys were being christened for a new life without their father, and stained playclothes simply would not do. At the age of three, Shane was far too young to grasp the day's signifi-cance. He fiddled with his baby bottle, filled with orange juice, and smiled at mourners who sat nearby.

Five priests concelebrated the mass. It began with a reading from Isaiah, which set a somber tone. Monsignor George Deas read from Matthew the story of Jesus walk-ing on the Sea of Galilee. Despite their boat being tossed around by a roiling, relentless surf, Jesus quieted the storm and saved his disciples. During the homily, Monsignor Deas explained that Jesus had a predilec-tion for fishermen: "We are, all of us, ships

431

O alas for the hero
whom the sea-wave is hiding;
to the mountain-chase now
'tis not thou shalt be riding.

Ne'er I feared 'twould betide thee,
(vain O vain is my weeping)
that in ocean's wide depth
though shouldst ever be sleeping;

While her rudder should stand
and thy hand be to guide her,
though the tempest should rave
and the wave crash beside her;

While her timbers and gear
should cleave stoutly together,
with thy hand on the helm
any storm she might weather.

But fierce was the gale
and thy sail it hath tattered,
it hath roused the black waves
and thy brave boat is shattered.

Translation by J. C. Watson (1916-1948) of a Scottish Gaelic song attrib. to Mary McLeod (c. 1615-1706)

Memorial Mass
Most Holy Trinity Church
East Hampton, New York
April 11, 1984
for
Michael Dexter Stedman,
Captain
and
David McGuire Connick,
Mate
Lost at Sea
March 29, 1984

First Reading : Isaiah 40:12,26,28-31
Second Reading : Romans 8:31-39
Holy Gospel : Matthew 14:22-35

"Lord, if it is You, bid me come
to You on the water."
He said, "Come."

R.I.P.

Memorial mass card.

on the storm-tossed sea of life."

The service concluded with a tape recording of Donovan singing the popular 1968 folk song "Atlantis." Its chorus — "Way down below the ocean, where I wanna be, she may be" — brought everyone to tears. The lyrics about the beautiful sailors hit too close to home. There wasn't a dry eye in the house.

Katie Dove, an East Hampton summer kid who'd met Mike and Mary Stedman while hanging out at Mahoneyville, sat next to Mary during the ninety-minute church service. Katie had a genuine fondness for Mary. "She had taken care of everyone back then, and people loved her for it," she told

432

me. Katie, whose mother had died when she was nine, kept looking over at Chris with tears in her eyes. She wanted to rewind the tape, to shield him from the years of heartbreak that were sure to derail him when he least expected it. "I think back on that time and the tragedy quite a lot. The boat going down defined the time in many ways," Katie later wrote to me. "They were lost at sea and we were lost. Lost youth. Lost lives."

In a photograph that ran in *Newsday* the following day, Mary looks off to one side, her hands clasped together. Flanked by her three sons, who are wearing matching khaki pants, white oxford shirts, navy sport coats, and brown boat shoes, Mary looks the part of a well-attired widow. But the expensive new clothes, for both herself and her sons, didn't blunt her grief in the way she hoped they might. The day after the memorial service, Mary wanted the shiny new clothing out of her house. She eventually gave it all away.

The memorial service marked a turning point. Afterward, nothing again was quite the same.

The Lost at Sea Memorial at Montauk Point.

23.
LOST AT SEA

Two months later, in June of 1984, after conducting an investigation into the circumstances surrounding the *Wind Blown*'s disappearance, the US Coast Guard issued a two-page report.

The report concluded that the missing vessel and its four personnel had gone down "in the approximate position of Latitude 40 degrees 30.1 minutes North, Longitude 72 degrees 21.4 minutes West."

That was it.

Since 1999, the Lost at Sea Memorial has sat adjacent to Montauk Point Light, the lighthouse President George Washington commissioned on January 2, 1796, proposing that it stand for two hundred years. At the time, Congress authorized $22,300 in construction costs. Oil from sperm whales, harvested from Sag Harbor, first lit the octagonal structure made of sandstone.

Whale oil was replaced by lard oil and then by kerosene and finally by electricity. The original beacon shone steady and fixed; in 1858, it became a flashing white light, visible some twenty nautical miles away. Every ten seconds it sends a bright beam of light out to sea.

On a clear day, when standing at Montauk Point Light, you can see Plum Island, Gardiner's Island, Fishers Island, Block Island, and parts of Rhode Island and Connecticut. Overlooking the Atlantic Ocean, on a bluff called Turtle Hill, about eighty feet above the rocky, churning sea, the Lost at Sea Memorial is a holy spot and one of deep reverence. For the survivors of men lost at sea, there is no grave to visit. The shared memorial is all they have left.

In 1993, Joseph Hodnik, a Montauk fisherman, went down off the coast of Martha's Vineyard along with his best friend, Edmund Sabo. Anne Hodnik, Joseph's young widow, recalled the pain of having no physical place for her and her young son to mourn. Mary Stedman and Alice Connick could relate. The Lost at Sea Memorial Committee formed shortly thereafter, with Mary and Alice lending their support. In short order, the committee raised $225,000 to build the memorial, soliciting donations from local celebrities who had personal ties to the East End.

Two dozen artists entered the subsequent design contest, with Malcolm Frazier's rendering chosen as the winner. The selection committee was drawn to Frazier's sculpture of a fisherman pulling in the day's bounty because his design emphasized the daily toil, rather than the pain of loss. To help raise additional funds, Ralph Lauren designed T-shirts that included Frazier's design with "Lost at Sea Memorial Montauk" written in a circular logo.

Standing eight feet tall, the massive 2,600-pound bronze statue rests atop a seven-foot granite base. For Alice, watching Malcolm Frazier work on the sculpture proved cathartic. "He used to come and work in my garden. It was a healing experience," she told me. "It helped me get back on track."

Arnold Leo, a committee member, told a *Daily News* reporter, shortly after its unveiling: "We originally were going to inscribe the names, dates, and ships of just the fishermen lost from the five East End towns, then we thought we'd open it up to all those who died at sea on the island." The monument's only rule: "People must have made their living at sea, like charter and commercial fishermen, and their bodies have not been found."

Etched in granite are the names of the four *Wind Blown* crew members. Their names appear alongside 120 Long Island fishermen who have similarly been lost at sea, joining a brotherhood that dates back to the 1700s. The first name is Jeremiah Conkling. He was a twenty-four-year-old from East Hampton who froze to death on February 24, 1719, along with three unidentified crew members after a pod of whales capsized their boat. A quick scan of the memorial reveals that multiple losses of life aboard the same vessel were a relatively rare occurrence.

The 1984 loss of the *Wind Blown* was the worst nautical disaster suffered by a Montauk-based vessel since Labor Day weekend of 1951, when the *Pelican,* an overloaded party boat, capsized in the Long Island Sound. Forty-five of its passengers and crew drowned within sight of the lighthouse. Day after day, helicopters hovered near the water, trying to locate the bodies of the *Pelican*'s victims, most of whom were city folks who had planned a celebratory end-of-summer day on the water. A US Coast Guard investigation reported that the forty-two-foot *Pelican* should only have allowed a maximum of twenty passengers aboard. Going forward, the downing of the *Pelican,* which carried sixty-two anglers (plus a captain and his mate), prompted the US Congress to pass stricter regulations governing vessels carrying six or more passengers.

Thirty-three years later, in 1984, the *Wind Blown* went down about thirteen miles, as the seagull flies, from where the *Pelican* capsized. Shipwreck history tells us that even the largest and most seaworthy vessels are vulnerable to the shoaling and rocky terrain near Montauk Point, where the Long Island Sound empties out, and the Atlantic Ocean rushes in.

■ ■ ■ ■

Offshore.

24.
SHIPWRECK HUNTERS

Even after the advent of lighthouses, which provided some degree of navigational assistance, Long Island's shores were the scene of thousands of shipwrecks. In the years since, a small group of fishermen have hunted obsessively for them. In members-only online fishing forums, they post periodic updates about their exploits. For such fishermen, their main goal is to be the first to fish each wreck, not only off Long Island but throughout the mid-Atlantic and New England region. Among such shipwreck hunters, the sinking of the *Wind Blown* still represents a great mystery.

Some local wreck fishermen believe the *Wind Blown* did not, in fact, go down east of Montauk Point in the vicinity of Block Island — but farther to the south, in an area known as the Butterfish Hole. Before he died, Tim Coleman, a fishing writer who also shared in the wreck-finding obsession, supplied the coordinates of where he believed the hull of the *Wind Blown* could still be found to Steven Cannizzo, a retired marine law enforcement detective who lives in Brooklyn, and whom I eventually tracked down in one of the online fishing forums.

Though the official position in US Coast Guard records lists the *Wind Blown*'s last-known location as latitude 40 degrees 30.1 minutes north, longitude 72 degrees 21.4 minutes west, Coleman proposed a slightly different location after several commercial dragger fishermen kept ripping their nets on a "new hang" near the coordinates in question. Coleman's suggested position: latitude 40 degrees 54.7 minutes north, longitude 71 degrees 43.7 minutes west. A tenth of a minute can be the difference of about six hundred feet.

Cannizzo decided it was high time to go investigate. During a fishing expedition a few years back, he went out with a well-known East End charter boat captain and came upon what he believed was the profile of the damaged hull of the *Wind Blown* on his Garmin GPS Fishfinder. Since Coleman had provided Cannizzo with a rounded-off location, it took some patience to finally locate the hull itself — or so he thought — some 1,000 to 2,000 feet away. A color photocopy he scanned and mailed to me showed thick bands of red and orange bars, which he believed indicated the presence of the sixty-five-foot, steel-hulled vessel. It sat at a depth of roughly thirty fathoms (or about 180 feet) below the surface.

After revealing the precise coordinates, he swore me to secrecy. "The exact location is a closely guarded secret since it is rare to have a shipwreck so close to a major fishing port," Cannizzo explained. "The *Wind Blown* was one of those 'have-to-find' spots, and many fishermen who target codfish and black sea bass would love to know where it sank." Cannizzo believes the *Wind Blown* now rests on the bottom of the Butterfish Hole, just east of the CIA Grounds. Based on his conversations over the years with highly skilled wreck and salvage divers, Cannizzo cautioned that "until a diver can descend to the bottom and return with either a photograph or physical evidence from the wreckage, it is the only way in which one can make a positive identification."

Besides the investigative allure, such fishermen seek out wrecks because there is generally good fishing to be had. Among local fishermen, the Butterfish Hole is known as "the Aquarium" because of its tendency to attract a variety of baitfish, which in turn attract game fish — everything from bluefin tuna to a wide variety of large sharks that are targeted by top- and bottom-water fishermen.

The Butterfish Hole is one of the unique ocean anomalies off the south shore of Long Island. Created during the last ice age, it contains a large depression where both warm- and cold-current eddies form throughout the calendar year. Divers who have previously visited other nearby shipwrecks report a dramatic change in water temperature. For instance, during the summertime, while the surface water temperature may read seventy degrees or more, as divers make their way down they start to feel a noticeable chill, especially on the small exposed areas of their faces not covered in neoprene. At the spot where Cannizzo believes the *Wind Blown* rests, the water temperature averages in the forty-degree range during the summer.

Some shipwrecks come alive during winter; others peak for fishing in the summer. The Butterfish Hole runs hot during the beginning and end of southern New England's offshore fishing season. Located south of, and within eyesight of, Montauk Point Light at the easternmost tip of Long Island, it's near the extremely busy inbound and outbound Nantucket shipping lanes. Before either commercial or recreational fishermen knew about the existence of the Butterfish Hole, sailing ships in prior centuries crossed the Atlantic Ocean en route to Boston Harbor. They'd then make their way around the dangerous Nantucket Shoals to New York City, unknowingly passing right over a deep, gaping hole within sight of Long Island.

But unlike the Lost at Sea Memorial located at the Montauk Lighthouse, Cannizzo thinks of the *Wind Blown* wreck as a second, secret memorial — its existence known only among a select few fishermen. Though the *Wind Blown*'s wooden wheelhouse and the remains of her four crew members would have long since dissipated, Cannizzo holds out hope that, based on the reports of draggermen who have torn their nets over the years, the *Wind Blown*'s steel hull remains.

All these decades later, Cannizzo likes to imagine the *Wind Blown* at rest, buried thirty fathoms below the surface. He sees her at the bottom of the ocean, joined by generations of lost fishermen, entombed at sea, who never made it home. For Cannizzo, it's a reminder that you're never home from a fishing trip until the lines of your vessel are again lashed to the dock.

The photograph that Maude Vigilant has kept in her wallet since 1984.

25.
THE SURVIVORS

All these decades later, the absence of Mike's body still hits Earl Ewing at unexpected times. The wound has healed, but every so often it still flares up. In 1986, on a trip to England on the *Queen Elizabeth 2,* he finally grasped the enormity of the Atlantic Ocean: the giant swells that come seemingly from nowhere, and disappear just as fast.

Long after Mike was lost at sea, Mary and Earl found themselves on the same flight to Jamaica in search of wintertime relief. As Mary would say, there are no coincidences.

When Earl takes walks along the Long Island Sound, at the edge of the sea, Mike sometimes comes to mind. Now close to eighty, Earl can't quite let go of it. He's sure Mike is dead. And yet, the absence of his body lingers.

"For some reason in our culture, we need closure, and the closure is somehow dealing with the physical remains of a loved one. And if you don't have that, the closure never comes," Earl said. "You need something, even when you're one hundred percent sure."

The lack of that closure has left an unsettling residue. "Are you a body with a soul or a soul with a body?" Earl wondered. "If you have a belief that there's something beyond the physical world, you need a physical piece of proof."

For months after the *Wind Blown* went down, Kim Bowman would go to the docks by herself and just sit there. Sometimes she brought Frankie along to keep her company.

Years later, well into her twenties, Kim couldn't really process that Michael was never coming back. Magical thinking took over. She told herself he was still alive, possibly suffering from total amnesia. She imagined the *Wind Blown* had washed up on Bermuda. This became her coping mechanism, the idea Michael was still out there, simply living an alternate life.

Every March, on the anniversary of the *Wind Blown*'s downing, Kim dives into the ocean. Immersing herself in the salt water — no matter how cold — fills her with a tremendous sense of relief.

"On land, I'm a woman," Kim explained.

"But in the water, I'm a mermaid." When she dies, Kim wants her ashes spread off Montauk Point, hoping some part of her physical body might join whatever particles remain of Michael, way down deep, like the golden tilefish they were hunting, at the bottom of the sea.

For Catherine Cederquist, the loss of Dave Connick is always present.

On March 29, 1984, Catherine was twenty and living with her father in Manhattan, when her doorbell buzzed. It was the doorman, asking if her friend Kristen could come up. Minutes later, Kristen sat on the edge of Catherine's bed and told her Dave was missing.

Three days later, on April 1, Marvin Gaye, who had supplied the soundtrack to her love affair with Dave, died in Los Angeles.

Catherine felt paralyzed. She didn't leave her father's apartment, not even to go to the grocery store or to her classes at Hunter College, until she made her way out to East Hampton some ten days later for Mike and Dave's joint memorial service. Catherine and Alice sat together in the back of a limousine. Alice recalled her son's girlfriend with particular fondness: "She was lovely. She was beautiful. She was *real.*" For years,

448

whenever Catherine ran into Alice, she teared up. Alice and Dave had identically shaped hazel eyes. It was impossible to look at her and not see her son.

When Dave died, Catherine kept most of his clothes. She can still remember the way he smelled. He had the perfect mix of pheromones, overlaid with the faintest trace of fish guts. His skin tasted like salt water.

Catherine's drug use, which began during high school after her parents divorced, intensified after Dave's disappearance. In May of 1986, after completing a stint at Hazelden, Catherine walked into her first Alcoholics Anonymous meeting at a nearby fellowship house. By then, she went by Cat. Over the years, she's taken on various nicknames — each one a fresh chapter, a chance to start anew. "It's funny that Dave only knew me as Nana. He only knew me for four years," Catherine said. Dave is frozen in time. Forever the twenty-two-year-old first love of her life. "Who knows what we would have become. We were just kids."

Harry, Catherine's husband, sent me a photograph of her at Georgica Beach when she was sixteen: a beatific young woman wearing a scoop-necked, one-piece swimsuit. Her trademark mane of dark, curly hair remains the way Dave would remember it,

Catherine at Georgica Beach.

though her cheeks and lips, she said, have thinned with time.

Like many survivors in this story, for the first few years after the *Wind Blown* went down, Catherine wasn't entirely convinced Dave was dead. Because of it, she doesn't shy away from death. "I've kissed many a dead corpse," Catherine said. She wants to see the bodies of the people she has loved. She needs to *touch* and *feel* them dead. The way the physical body changes shape once the soul resides elsewhere. Her need — practically a compulsion — for closure.

Christmas of 1983: Scott and his mother at home in Oceanside.

26.
DONNA

There is no right way to grieve, and each of the survivors in this story adopted a different coping mechanism. Donna Llewellyn, the mother of Scott Clarke, the redheaded crew member about whom the least is known, went to her grave believing that her only child was still alive.

Donna gave birth to Donald Scott Clarke on July 12, 1965, at the Sibley Memorial Hospital in Washington, DC. It was curious that she named him after his father, Donald Nelson Clarke, since they had divorced early on in her pregnancy, not long after they'd married. Donna never even met her ex-husband's extended family. She had grown up in rural West Virginia. Her father was a farmer and drove a truck; her mother stayed at home looking after the couple's five children.

Early on, it was Donna and young Scotty against the world. As a single mother, she was eager to make a better life for her only son. With his mother often away at work, little Scotty grew up quickly. His independent streak became a coping mechanism that grew to serve him well.

A decade or so later, Lee Finley, Donna's brother, was riding home from work on a bus in the Washington, DC, area when he saw a man he was sure was Scotty's estranged father. He had the same long, muscular limbs, and, like Scotty, a freckled, pale face framed by a full head of frizzy red hair. "I almost said something and decided against it," Lee said to me. "I had remembered that Donna did not want him to know that Scott existed."

During Scotty's early childhood, Donna worked as a customer service agent at Trans World Airlines in DC, where she met Thomas Llewellyn, who worked in air traffic control. When Scotty was five or six years old, the couple married and took jobs in New York, transferring from Ronald Reagan Washington National Airport to LaGuardia Airport and John F. Kennedy International Airport, respectively. They made their home on Long Island in nearby Oceanside.

But Scotty's relationship with his stepfather, Tom Llewellyn, was a fraught one, and he soon sought solace anyplace that wasn't home. Dyslexic and frustrated in class, he started cutting school and at fourteen dropped out altogether, eager to get as far from Oceanside as he could. Donna contacted the local police, even filing a PINS (Person in Need of Supervision) petition with New York State to intervene on behalf of her missing son. Scotty, however, was long gone. He later moved to Freeport, where he started working on commercial fishing boats, rising up through the hierarchy.

Scotty and Donna eventually reconciled — but on his terms, this time. "I'm not coming back home. I'm not finishing school. I'm becoming a fisherman," his cousin recalled Scotty saying of his newfound autonomy.

Already studying for his captain's license, Scott was a tireless, formidable presence around the docks. Montauk was an insular fraternity, not especially keen on admitting outsiders. But Scott soon proved his worth. It didn't hurt that surfing was also a passion of his. By sheer force of will, Scott hustled as a young mate, not afraid to get his hands dirty or bust his ass. "He was the biggest, strongest, and the hardest working. I always said when I get my first boat I want him on it," William Campbell, a fisherman

Scott Clarke with his stepfather and cousins on Long Island.

friend, said in a *Star* story. "He loved the sea, he worked hard. He never hurt anybody and he could have. He was six-foot-four and plenty powerful. He was nice, though, and gentle."

When the *Wind Blown* went down, rescuers came across one of Scott Clarke's shoes. It was a brown, size thirteen dress shoe, acquired by way of the free airline passes his mother had given him. In late December of 1983, he had used some of his mother's complimentary airline miles to fly down to Texas to meet up with Mike, Tom, and Dave, and escort the *Wind Blown* back to

Montauk. In those days, airlines required voucher holders to dress up; Scott's usual uniform of sneakers and hooded sweatshirts was forbidden. Hoping to blend in with the other passengers, he had worn a pair of brown dress shoes for the occasion, and apparently stashed them aboard the *Wind Blown,* forgetting to remove them from the boat.

After Scotty disappeared, Donna continued putting her free airline mileage to use. She took trips around the world whenever vacation time presented itself. South America. Australia. Hawaii. St. Thomas. St. John. But Donna wasn't keen on going sightseeing. Walking through crowds, she searched, endlessly, for her son. In every exotic new location, Donna posted flyers with pictures of her missing son, asking if anyone had seen him. Her obsession wasn't confined to air travel: Donna put hundreds of thousands of miles on her car, looking everywhere for her lost boy.

In one of the few photographs I've seen of Scott, his arm is wrapped around his mother. At eighteen, he stood two feet taller than Donna. Both have curly hair and identical bowl-shaped haircuts. A Christmas tree, covered in tinsel, is in the background. "Three months before death," is written on the back. Tom Llewellyn stood on the other side of the camera. After taking the photograph, the three of them sat down to their last meal together. Scotty cooked them lobster.

In 2010, at the age of sixty-nine, Donna Llewellyn died from a respiratory illness. Or maybe the cause of death was a broken heart. She went to her grave believing her son was still out there. Donna and Scotty now share a joint gravestone at a cemetery in Sardis, West Virginia, next to Donna's parents. No matter the season, Aunt Zandra, a relative, keeps the granite vases filled with freshly cut flowers. Passersby don't know that the son who died isn't buried beneath the gray tombstone. He was lost at sea. It's a kinder revision of history. The horizontal headstone is all visitors see: son and mother, together at last.

Scott Clarke and Donna Llewellyn's joint headstone.

27.
SECRETS AND LIES

Chris, Shane, and Will Stedman at Uncle Albie's 1994 wedding.

Maybe it was Mary's destiny to repeat the destructive patterns of her childhood.

"Has Mary told you the secret yet?" Chris asked me, in the spring of 2018.

He went on to say that the three Stedman sons had survived two tragedies.

"*Two* tragedies?" I asked.

"Two tragedies," Chris said.

The first one I obviously knew about, when their father, Michael Stedman, was lost at sea.

But a second tragedy, Chris told me, occurred about a decade later.

It was Easter Sunday, April 11, 1993 — a cold, rain-drenched night — when Mary sat her sons down together around the dinner table. Chris was in his freshman year of college at nearby Stony Brook University. Will was a junior at East Hampton High School. And Shane was in the seventh grade at East Hampton Middle School.

Holidays were tough. Whenever possible, Chris slept over at a friend's house. But it was Easter, and Chris was counting the hours until he could finally, in good conscience, escape.

"Your mom has something she wants to say," the boys' stepfather, Paul, who had wed Mary the year prior, announced at the end of dinner. Chris recalled it being the first and last time that Paul had addressed all three sons together, as a unit.

Mary stood up, while the rest of the family stayed seated around the dinner table. There was a thousand-yard stare in her eyes.

"Shane is not Mike's son," Chris recalled

her saying. "And Will isn't Mike's son either."

Shortly afterward, Chris walked outside and sat down in the backyard, in the same spot where his father had planted those marijuana plants for his wife all those years before. The rain poured down on him until his hands and feet were frozen and numb. Chris felt like the odd man out, suddenly thrust out of the equation. In the span of thirty seconds, the fairy tale of marriage, of love, of trust — everything he held most dear — had gone up in flames. Despite the chaos, one thought rang out loud and clear: *His father had been spared.*

Mary remembers the conversation a little bit differently.

"My kids know, and it's ruined their lives," she told me, when I looped back around to corroborate the stories. Up until then, she had not mentioned the incident. Mary said the conversation occurred at Thanksgiving dinner. The year? 1995.

"Shane is not Dad's child," Mary recalled blurting out. "And by the way, I don't know about you either," she said, looking over in Will's direction.

The revelation — possibly true, possibly not — separated the sons from that moment forward. The ground beneath them had cracked open. It was a conversation that no one in the family has ever recovered from. Things never went back to the way they were before.

"I never meant to be this eternally fucked-up mother," Mary said as she began to explain this new piece of the story. "It's a double standard," Mary added. Her mind flashed back to her aunt Peggy, who used to work in Manhattan as a secretary for Wall Street bankers. On her lunch hour, Aunt Peggy would stop into Bergdorf Goodman on Fifth Avenue to purchase expensive bottles of perfume for her bosses' mistresses. Their wives were never the wiser. "Men can do whatever they want," Mary said. "Women can do nothing."

About a month before she and Mike were set to marry in June of 1973, she came to him with a startling revelation: she was pregnant.

"I will not marry you if you're pregnant. I will only marry you if you have an abortion," Mary recalled of Mike's response. Although New York State had legalized abortion in 1970, the January 22, 1973, decision by the US Supreme Court in *Roe v. Wade,* declaring abortion a constitutional right, had fundamentally altered the political landscape. Even though Mary hadn't technically broken any laws by going through with it, her conscience, deeply rooted in years of Catholicism, told her otherwise.

On a Monday morning in early June of 1973, Mike drove Mary into Manhattan. She had an abortion on the fiftieth floor of a midtown skyscraper. Though she would have three healthy sons, her first abortion in 1973 and a second one in 1978 (when Will, her second son, was two years old) filled her with resentment. The rebellious streak of her childhood had found another target in her husband. When Mike made her do something against her will, Mary felt an uncontrollable urge to retaliate against him. "Every time I was made to have an abortion, I acted out," she said.

Throughout her marriage to Mike, Mary strayed on a number of occasions. Mary said Mike knew, that the two of them had come to an understanding, and that he had forgiven her trespasses. (Whatever Mike knew of her affairs, based on my interviews, it does not appear that he spoke of them to even his closest friends.)

Mary told me she had an affair with Walter

Vogt, a close friend of Mike's dating back to his childhood, during the time that Will, her second son, was conceived. As Mary explained, it was less about giving in to attraction or desire — and more about exacting revenge. Walter was one of the original fifteen Choppess. In high school, he was among four of the Choppess who had played in a band together (Mike was the drummer). On page ninety-seven of the Wheatley School's 1968 yearbook, Walter, wearing a Kalamazoo College sweatshirt, sat directly in front of Mike. Thirty pages earlier, the two boys stood side by side in the varsity wrestling team picture.

When I phoned Walter, he wanted to know the purpose of my inquiry. Before hanging up on me, he said that *The Perfect Storm* had already been written.

A few years after Will's birth, Mary told me she had a one-night fling with Pete Connick, Dave's older brother, during the time that Shane, her youngest son, was conceived.

"Only one of the children was Mike's," Pete said to me, the first and only time we met. "Mary thinks Shane is mine. I don't know if Shane is mine. We're all Irish Catholics and we all look like each other."

■ ■ ■ ■

"What do we inherit, and how, and why?" Dani Shapiro wrote in *Inheritance* that many people feel or look different from their parents or their siblings. "Biology doesn't promise similarity. Traits skip generations. Characteristics emerge, seemingly out of nowhere." Nevertheless, genetics play an undeniably powerful role in the people we become.

As far as the three Stedman sons are concerned, their father, Mike Stedman, died at sea. Any revelations, no matter how true, only tarnish the memory of the man who was their father. From a nurture perspective, Captain Mike passed along his love of the ocean and his love of fatherhood.

Sigmund Freud said that the death of a father is "the most important event, the most poignant loss of a man's life." For Michael Stedman's sons, the early, unexpected death of their father was a catastrophic loss. The tremors continue unabated. It has left them with a void they've been trying to fill, with varying degrees of success, ever since.

Erna Furman, an expert on grief in children, explained the key difference between losing a parent in childhood versus adulthood. An adult distributes his love among several meaningful relationships — say, a spouse, parents, children, friends, and colleagues. A child, by contrast, focuses all of his love on one primary bond: his parents: "Only in childhood can death deprive an individual of so much opportunity to love and be loved." Furman's book *A Child's Parent Dies: Studies in Child Bereavement,* which came out in 1974, challenged the prevailing notion that children who lose a parent don't need the same therapy that can benefit adults. Even toddlers, she explained, can be helped to mourn a dead parent.

In 1992, after twenty-five years on the South Fork, Ray and Donna Charron sold the Jericho House and moved to Kauai, five thousand miles away. A diagnosis of Raynaud's disease, which causes extreme sensitivity to cold, made the harshness of East Coast winters all but unbearable for Ray. An avid marathon runner and triathlete, he now runs an art gallery; Donna works as a marriage and family therapist. The three Stedman boys eventually followed, one after the other. Chris told me, borrowing a line from John Crescenzi, a Montauk transplant and fellow Kauai resident, "Hawaii was the farthest place we could move from Mary and still live in the United States."

It was May of 2018 when I sat down with Ray and Donna. The previous day, I had interviewed Chris. We met in Ray's art gallery after closing one night. Brightly colored paintings, mainly of sea life, covered all available wall space.

At first, the Charrons spoke warily of Mary. Somehow, they had fallen from grace. Before they ran into Mary two years prior at Shane's wedding, it had been twenty years since the two women had spoken.

All three arrived at the wedding at the exact same time. Ray and Donna were cautious as they stepped out of their car, wondering how Mary would greet them. They prepared themselves for the worst. But Mary, always full of surprises, smiled and hugged them. It was as if no time had lapsed since they last embraced.

One of their last meetings took place in Mary's East Hampton home. Donna was visiting from Kauai — she makes periodic visits to the East End for her "love fix" — and Mary and her husband, Paul, had invited her over for dinner.

As they were eating, Mary looked over at Donna. "You're the one," she said happily, as if she were announcing a winning lottery ticket. "They chose *you* as their *mother.*"

There was more than a grain of truth to what Mary had said. Still, the acknowledgment left Donna speechless. Right or wrong, she didn't know quite what to say in response.

Over the years, though, the Charrons have become surrogate parents to the Stedman sons. They freely and openly talk about Mike. His deep, roaring laugh that brought a room to life. How his beautiful exterior matched his soulful interior. They try to keep his memory alive — especially for Shane, who has no recollection of his father.

As a therapist, Donna views Mary through an altered lens. She can see now that Mary suffered from post-traumatic stress disorder. In the early 1970s, such a diagnosis didn't yet exist. She had survived a pretty difficult childhood; becoming a young widow with three sons only magnified that early trauma.

"Our mind is a wonderful thing and takes care of us," Donna explained. When recalling a traumatic event, survivors often block out the details entirely or replay them, over and over, in excruciating detail. Mary's photographic memory put her in the latter category. Even with the passage of time, the horrific events of 1984 hadn't been bleached of their power. Over the years, when the memories became too much, Mary's sur-

The Stedman and Charron sons at Ray and Donna's 1991 vow renewal.

vival mechanism was to disassociate, or disconnect. Ray and Donna did what they could to help pick up the slack.

The Charrons, their own sons included, were like an umbrella in a storm. Donna likes to think that Mike looks down on all of them. The three Charron boys and the three Stedman boys make six sons. Together, Donna likes to think they did good enough.

All three Stedmans now have children of their own. In subtle and obvious ways, the early loss of their father has embedded itself into the fabric of the men they became.

Like their late father, they are avid watermen. The ocean is their common denominator. Mary believes that children whose parents die when they're young unconsciously try to achieve the dreams of their dead parent. For her, it's no mystery that her sons all built lives centered on the sea — just as Mike Stedman would have done.

For the blue-eyed Stedman brothers, booking one-way tickets to paradise was a way of living out the endless summer version of life that their father had pioneered decades before and thousands of miles away. The warm ocean water. The humid tropical air. The soft caress of the Mother Island that envelops you, like a fragrant lei placed around your neck, when your plane touches down at Lihue Airport.

It's May of 1984 on Georgica Beach, about two months after the *Wind Blown* went down. Chris is nine. Will is seven. Back then, the two brothers were inseparable. Chris and Will put on Mike and Dave's Rip Curl wetsuits and wore them into the water to catch some waves.

For vacationers sitting on towels beneath beach umbrellas, it must have been a sight to see: the two oldest Stedman boys wearing the floppy wetsuits of grown men twice their size. Riding boogie boards and going under and over waves, the brothers would lock eyes. This was the same beach where

470

Mike and Chris at Georgica circa 1980.

they had bodysurfed alongside their father only the summer before. (Some thirty years in the future, their younger brother, Shane, would name his first daughter Georgica — forever cementing the East Hampton beach in the Stedman bloodline.)

Unknown to them then but clear to them now, their grief was being washed clean in the water. Though rescuers had stopped looking for Mike Stedman months before, his sons would never stop returning to him.

28.
PETE

On March 29, 2013, Pete Connick updated his profile picture on Facebook to a black-and-white photograph of him and his brother, Dave, standing on a frozen pond in Central Park. In the picture, the boys are maybe eight and six years old. Pete stands a full foot taller than Dave. Holding hands, the two brothers wear matching mittens and leather ice-skates that lace up the front.

Later that fall, in October of 2013, Mary sent an e-mail to Pete. Shortly thereafter, she forwarded the e-mail to Chris, who eventually sent a copy to me. Apparently, Mary had been trying to get Pete to own up to his paternal responsibility for quite some time. For far too long, the burden had been hers — and hers alone. "It is not something, the fathering of a child, that one dismisses for that child's entire life," Mary wrote to Pete about Shane.

■ ■ ■ ■

It was March 30, 2018, one day after the thirty-fourth anniversary of the *Wind Blown*'s downing, when Pete and I met at Bobby Van's, a Bridgehampton bar and restaurant. Pete's nerves seemed understandably frayed.

For the survivors in this story, the anniversary of the boat's sinking isn't the only difficult day. Birthdays are tough too; singed into Pete's memory bank: 12/18/61.

"The ocean's a big thing for me, since I'm still looking for my brother," Pete said to me, by way of introduction. The loss of his brother comes to mind every time he's near the water. Most days when Pete is out east, he makes his way to the Atlantic Ocean. He walks. He surfs. He swims. For the past few years, he has divided his time between an apartment in Manhattan and his mother's house in Bridgehampton. Now divorced, he has two grown sons. Or three, I guess, depending on how you want to look at things.

"I don't blame anyone for Davey's death," Pete said. "Blame is such an old energy." And yet, Pete explained, if his parents hadn't created such an inhospitable atmosphere in which to grow up, Davey might still be alive. His brother, Pete thinks, went looking for the kind of unconditional love he never found at home.

It was difficult, Pete explained, being the children of two larger-than-life parents. The Connicks were social, charismatic creatures and their children often felt like unwanted afterthoughts. The two brothers adopted different strategies for navigating their isolated upbringing. Petey submitted; Davey rebelled. Petey was the golden child who wore ironed shirts and white tennis shorts. For the most part, he did whatever Alice told him to do. Davey, meanwhile, ran as fast as he could in the opposite direction. He refused to become a Park Avenue gentleman. He was a carefree bohemian who contentedly marched to his own beat.

Maybe five years before Dave died, Pete went in search of the people who had become his brother's surrogate family. He recalled stepping foot inside the Stedman home for the first time in the late 1970s. At the time, the Stedmans were living on Newtown Lane, right around the corner from East Hampton High School. "I ended up going over there to rescue my relationship with my brother," Pete said. He wanted to find out where, exactly, Dave had been spending all of his time. "He went where he was wanted."

Mary had recently given birth to Will, her second son. She had an intoxicating air, all soft edges and long, flowing skirts. She looked like a living, breathing version of Mother Earth. Attentive young men — handsome, strapping Irishmen (not unlike himself) — orbited around her, as if in a trance. Mary was like a witchy seductress who had cast a spell on them. And Pete, needing no convincing, soon joined their ranks.

"I showed up looking to have a relationship with my brother, and Mary Stedman fell in love with me and wanted to fuck me," Pete said. "A lot of people on my side think Mary saw these blue-blooded sons coming out of New York."

Earlier in our conversation, I had mentioned Barbara Mahoney's memoir about her husband's alcoholism, which I had recently read. Much like the Mahoneys, various members of the Connick family have suffered from similar demons. "What we do is drink," Pete said, in between sips of a vodka cranberry cocktail. The irony wasn't lost on him. Pete squirmed in his seat. Rather than make eye contact, he stared out the window as we spoke.

"Dad was a drunk. Dad was fucking around. My mother lived through the same thing as Barbara — but Dennis Mahoney didn't fuck around as much." Pete explained that, for a solid decade, his father was one of the most successful attorneys on Wall Street. The elder Pete Connick was handsome, charismatic, and insanely funny. "It's what got himself into everyone's pants." Big Pete oozed money, sex, and power. "He was the charm of the party and an absolute slut," his son recalled. "He was the greatest father you could have until you got to be an adult and you finally realized what had been going on."

As Pete told it, underneath all the glitz and glamour lurked something darker and more sinister. Alice had a knack for interior design and she had created a beautiful, elegant space in their new penthouse apartment, where the brothers shared a bedroom with matching navy-blue velvet couches that pulled out into beds. The bedrooms faced Central Park. Alice had a closet of floor-length gowns waiting to be worn a second time. But Davey rejected the elegant façade. To him, the opulence felt shallow and empty.

The move to PHB coincided with a troubled time. The spirit of the Connick family had started to crack. Mental illness ran in the Lamm family. In 1978, Alice's sister, Roberta Lamm Curtis, who suffered from bipolar illness, overdosed on sleeping pills. A few years earlier, her brother, Harold, also took his own life. After Roberta's death, two of her three children came to live with the Connicks for a time. By then, Alice and Pete had decided to separate, with Big Pete tasked with keeping an eye on Davey, who was still in high school, and his two cousins.

William Gale Curtis V, or Billy, was Roberta's eldest son and Pete and Dave's first cousin. As boys, they grew up half a block apart on the Upper East Side and had attended St. Bernard's together. Billy's family had a weekend house in Southampton and were members of the Bathing Corporation of Southampton (the town's equivalent of the Maidstone Club). Once summer rolled around, Billy and his family frequently visited the Connicks at their Crossways home — a twenty-five-minute drive east along Montauk Highway.

Billy, now a successful real estate developer living in the Boston area with his wife and three sons, is a self-made man. He had to be. Shortly after his mother's suicide, the silver spoon was yanked out of his mouth.

At sixteen, he no longer had a bed to call his own. Looking back, the loss of any inheritance and his father's subsequent abandonment may have actually saved young Billy's life. In subsequent years, he witnessed the ambition of the trust fund kids in his peer group fall by the wayside. Their inherited wealth had rendered them impotent. Few possessed any drive or determination. "Most of the kids with any money became fucked up," Billy explained. "Everything had been handed to them."

Sitting in Bobby Van's, near the end of our conversation, Pete kept looking at the table next to ours, where four people had sat down for drinks, his eyes darting back and forth. Pete thought they were eavesdropping.

"Stop looking at me!" Pete eventually yelled to one of the men. Deep in conversation, the man looked up, startled.

"What are you talking about?" the man shouted back.

Pete swallowed the last of his second cocktail and ended our interview on an abrupt note. He kissed me on the cheek, put on his jacket, and headed out into the cold March night.

Over the coming weeks and months, as I

478

looped back around to corroborate stories, he eventually stopped responding to me altogether.

About a year later, after I had moved back to Sag Harbor with my family, our paths crossed once more. Pete was with Alice and her caretaker. Alice looked remarkably frail, and I didn't want to disturb them.

"You're the writer, aren't you?" Pete asked, from maybe ten feet away. Before I could respond, he turned his back and walked away.

It was the last time I saw him. Alice, too. On September 13, 2020, at the age of eighty-eight, her heart finally gave way. Pete stayed by his mother's side until the very end.

Mary at the beach with sunscreen.

29.
MARY

For Mary, now in her midsixties, the winter's never over until March has come and gone. Even daffodils and forsythia, the yellow blooms that typically signal the start of springtime, can't be trusted.

Within two years of the *Wind Blown* going down, the shock of grief had turned Mary's dark brunette hair a bright shade of white. She now dyes it pale blond. She wonders, sometimes, if Mike would even recognize her.

When we were first becoming acquainted, Mary suggested I read James Agee's *A Death in the Family.* In the book's first few pages, Agee describes a scene of haunting beauty. It's written from the perspective of a child, joined on a quilt in the wet grass by his mother and father, his aunt and uncle. Everyone is making idle chitchat, contentedly talking about everything and nothing at all. "By some chance, here they are, all

Mary, Mike, and Chris circa 1974.

on this earth; and who shall ever tell the sorrow of being on this earth, lying on quilts, on the grass, in a summer evening, among the sounds of night." The boy asks God to bless his people, to "remember them kindly in their time of trouble; and in the hour of their taking away."

Since 1984, the Stedmans have been trying to find their way back to a time, even in their mind's eye, when their family quilt contained all five of them. A father. A mother. And three sons.

On March 26, 2009, Mary wrote another letter to the *East Hampton Star* to commemorate the twenty-fifth anniversary of the *Wind Blown*'s downing. In the letter, she shared with readers a poem she had written. In her poem, Mary repeated the same phrase seven times: "in the deep blue ocean you vanished."

Michael Stedman has been dead for nearly forty years now — longer than the thirty-two years he was ever alive. He never had the privilege of watching Chris, Will, and Shane become men, get married, and become fathers. Or watching Georgica, his fearless, pint-size granddaughter, learn how to surf.

On most anniversaries of the *Wind Blown*'s downing, Matt Norklun, the close friend who loaned Mary his car during the search for wreckage, calls her to check in. If Scott Geery, Mike's childhood friend from East Williston, is out in Montauk, he usually rides over on his motorcycle and drops off a small bouquet of flowers on her driveway. Paul, Mary's third husband, likes to give his wife plenty of space. It's a day of quiet reflection for Mary — a holy day, a sacred day — usually involving the lighting of

483

candles and saying of prayer. Depending on the weather, she might take a walk in the woods. She finds solace in the ritual of walking the same paths she traversed during the endless search for wreckage.

Every year on March 29, the memories come flooding back. Some of them are beautiful and some of them are traumatic. All of us, Mary explains, have sacred days — days marked by births, deaths, or anniversaries. In this way, all of humanity becomes linked by these private occasions.

On March 29, 2018, when we walked into Rowdy Hall, an East Hampton restaurant, for a bite to eat, the other patrons didn't recognize the day's significance. Mary walked slowly and deliberately. We sat down and ordered two pints of thick, dark Guinness. Mary frequently described our conversations, which stirred up the sediment, as "heavy-duty." I didn't disagree.

Falling in love with Mike meant falling in love with fishermen. Their work ethic. Their smell. The autonomous parts of themselves, forever out of reach, that come alive elsewhere. It's a profession that requires a level of comfort with one's interior life. The *Wind Blown* became Mike's mistress. As soon as he returned home, he was already planning his next voyage out. Mike was forever thinking about the *Wind Blown* and tending to her needs — a part of his brain he could never quite shut off. "There was never a time when Mike was injured or sick," Mary said. "His work ethic was his religion."

His perpetual coming and going, their long-distance marriage, grew to suit her. It's no accident that Mary's husband, Paul, is also a commercial fisherman. "Of my three husbands," she remarked, "they all had one thing in common: they were never around." (In 1989, she and Dan Weinstock exchanged vows; shortly thereafter, the marriage was annulled.)

All these years later, the grief comes and it goes. Over time, Mary has trained her mind to sit with feelings of discomfort. During the nineties, she studied at Peter Matthiessen's Zendo, formerly housed in a converted horse barn, on the same six-acre property as his Sagaponack home. When Mary closes her eyes, she's transported back to the rows of black meditation cushions on which practitioners sat cross-legged, their spines stretched tall and erect. A giant Buddha kept watch over the room. Mattheissen had a commanding, watchful presence. The students sat together in silence. When the mind raced, as it always did, practitioners

485

gently directed their attention back to the breath in the here and now. Some days the meditation technique works better than others.

Mary finds great comfort living in East Hampton. The memories safely tucked away inside the house Mike built for them. The local cemetery, where she discovered that Mike's ancestors from a prior century are laid to rest. The thirty-foot elm tree planted across the street from the Most Holy Trinity Church. The bronze plaque beneath it reads: IN MEMORY OF MICHAEL STEDMAN. 1952–1984. LOVED BY FAMILY AND FRIENDS. New York State Route 114, which connects East Hampton with Sag Harbor, and which was later renamed the Lost at Sea Memorial Pike. The four distinct seasons. The shifting clouds and changing light. The water that surrounds her on all sides. She's never more than a few minutes from either the Atlantic Ocean or the Long Island Sound.

The reminders don't appear accidental. Mary has put herself in the way of them. Wherever she goes, there they are.

The plaque for Mike on Buell Lane in East Hampton.

30.
Chris

Chris and Mary circa 1974.

When Chris Stedman and I sat down together in Kauai in May of 2018, the resem-
blance between father and eldest son was
uncanny. When Chris visits the East End
and runs into family friends who knew his
father, he often sees tears in their eyes. It's

impossible to look at Chris and not see Mike. The same hair. The same teeth. The same smile.

Over the years, I worried that my arrival and my questions — turning over rocks and pebbles, picking apart debris — had created an unintended atmospheric disturbance. Partly to assuage my fears, Chris wrote: "I chose to share the truth with you because I recognized two things: the pervasive 'tide,' which brought about this book, and your authenticity. I believe in you."

In February of 2019, after months of being unable to sleep, Chris sought the help of a skilled therapist. He soon discovered his post-traumatic stress disorder symptoms were off the charts. His therapist made an immediate assessment: "There was no way you could have grieved as a child. There was too much chaos. You were always in survival mode."

Growing up, Chris felt the need to pull himself up by his bootstraps. It was a survival instinct. Then as now, he feels his mother was a ticking time bomb, her mood mercurial and impossible to predict. Mary, he says, gaslighted everyone who crossed her. Even simple disagreements ended in a permanent severing of ties. The guilt and anger, Chris thinks, had overtaken her. The specter of having three sons with three different fathers. In Mary, Chris perceived a cognitive dissonance of the highest order.

Trauma has a life-span of its own. Since he was nine years old, Chris has been trapped in the storm. The trauma had lodged itself so deep within his psyche that he couldn't remember a time when it hadn't been there. It had rewired his nervous system. He was perpetually stuck in fight-or-flight mode, bracing for the next traumatic event to come his way. His parasympathetic nervous system never took over. He couldn't let his guard down. At any moment, he had learned, his life could be turned upside down.

"A person is suddenly and unexpectedly devastated by an atrocious event and is never the same again," Bessel van der Kolk wrote in *The Body Keeps the Score: Brain, Mind, and Body in the Healing of Trauma*. "The trauma may be over, but it keeps being relayed in continually recycling memories and in a reorganized nervous system."

Like hair and eye color, mental illness can pass from one generation to the next. Chris thinks we inherit the sins and the stories of our mothers and fathers. He wanted to finally break free of the cycle, to finally right the ship. Telling the truth felt like freedom,

490

like he could finally move on with his life, once and for all. He could leave the trauma in the past, where it belongs.

Twelve years ago, Chris married Joy, a native Hawaiian. They now have two daughters: Mikaela and Keely. He shared with me a concept called *Ho'oponopono*. It's a Hawaiian practice of reconciliation and forgiveness that prioritizes familial well-being. A family is only as sick as its secrets. "When bad things happen that need to be addressed, you address it as a family. You have to get it out," Chris explained. "It's the exact opposite of how we were raised." Growing up, Chris tried to be the hero child, to raise his brothers, to get straight As. But trying to be the perfect son wasn't sustainable. Eventually, the suppression morphed into aggression and rage.

Chris thinks the story of Captain Mike Stedman going down aboard the *Wind Blown* is akin to a classic Greek tragedy. The hero is a beautiful, kind guy, but he possesses a tragic flaw. He knows something is wrong, but rather than confront the problem, he escapes into the ocean.

He has come to believe that out in the deep blue, Mike communed with the divine. He drank in the beauty of the ocean and it

491

filled his eyes and his soul. He brought that beauty back to shore, sharing it with his smile. But Captain Mike's smile hid his pain. Something was wrong. On land, life was not the same. Mike and Mary never have the *Ho'oponopono*. Mike was duped. He was tricked. Mike vanished, leaving his descendants to make sense of the unfathomable deception he couldn't bring himself to face. Mike was too good-natured. Mike was too trusting. But deep down, Chris believes his father knew that things weren't as they appeared.

To help Chris process the trauma — and hopefully heal from it — his therapist, who studied eye movement desensitization and reprocessing, guided Chris through a few sessions. EMDR involves the recollection of traumatic memories combined with rapid, side-to-side eye movement; data has shown it can have tremendous efficacy in helping patients recover from PTSD. It doesn't erase the trauma, but it can help patients process disturbing memories by making them seem like they happened in the distant past, and consequently feel less immobilized by them.

When Chris first met with his therapist, it felt like he was being guided through the

Chris and his great-grandfather, Alfred Stedman, during a summer visit to Minnesota in 1984.

woods in the pitch-black of night. Thankfully, his therapist shone a bright flashlight, illuminating the path underfoot — as if to say: *It's safe to step here, beware of a fallen branch there.* During the EMDR sessions, Chris time-traveled, back to when the trauma first began.

It's the first week of April of 1984. Chris is nine years old again. His brother Will is next to him. They are in the driveway of their house on Stephen Hands Path, standing beside the evergreen tree their father had recently planted, when Jeb Stuart, who had led much of the search for wreckage, walks up to them.

"Your father is gone. Your father is dead," Jeb says. "He's not coming back. He's been declared lost at sea."

"Can I have a new skateboard?" Will asks. At seven, he couldn't comprehend the weight of Jeb's words.

"I understand," Chris says.

"You're going to have to take care of your mother and your brothers," Jeb says to Chris. "You're the man of the house now."

"I got it," he answers.

Now in his midforties, Chris walks over to that nine-year-old boy and lifts him up. Chris holds him in his arms. He hugs him. He doesn't let go. He tells him he won't abandon him.

"You are loved, just as you are," Chris tells his boyhood self.

But progress isn't always linear. Four decades' worth of grief are a tough habit to break.

Each morning, shortly after waking up, Chris thinks of his father, and he's catapulted back to his childhood. The nine years when he and his father were inseparable: bodysurfing together at Georgica, cruising down the Napeague stretch after a day of fishing, or charging down the trail above

Will Stedman selling fish in front of the McGivern home on Dunemere Lane circa 1983.

Turtle Cove on a dawn surf patrol outing, when the sun hadn't yet risen and all he could hear was the sound of the churning sea crashing against the rocky shore.

Some mornings, Chris is on the bow of the *Marlin IV*. Captain Mike, standing watch in the wheelhouse, smiles down on his son.

495

Dave is there. The Grateful Dead are serenading them: "Like I told you, what I said, steal your face right off your head."

Other mornings, it's March 29, 1984. Like a record with a scratch on it, the needle is stuck on the same groove. He's back in the abyss. It's the last voyage and Chris is in the wheelhouse of the *Wind Blown* standing alongside his father. He feels the impact of a wave hitting the boat. Chris takes the hit. Adrenaline courses through his body. His pulse races. His breathing becomes shallow. And just like that, the flashback is over. A sense of calm, of surrender, washes over him. It's dark and tranquil at the bottom of the ocean.

After reliving the imagined memory of his father's vanishing, gratitude and serenity overtake him. The heaviness eventually gives way to light. "It's a wave of love. Love breaks the cycle," Chris said. "The act of remembrance is what makes me *me*. It's the hefty price of understanding the impermanence, the fragility of life."

Many people have this idea that grief eventually subsides. But it never really does. The loss of his father has lodged itself deep within his armor. Chris wears his grief, which has opened a gateway to vulnerability, like a badge of courage.

The bond between father and son lives well past the grave. Alongside so many survivors in this story, the loss of his father will accompany Chris Stedman until he takes his last breath. But that's as it should be: grieving is the last way we get to love someone.

And yet, the downing of the *Wind Blown* continues to ricochet, in new and unexpected ways, through the next generation. At each undulation, there's a promise for a certain kind of reconciliation, a reckoning with the past. With each passing year, another layer of the story reveals itself. Every so often, a glimmer of hope rushes in.

After Bruce Stedman died in 2013, Chris became estranged from both Mary and his two brothers. Granddad was like the last knot in the net — the container — that had unknowingly held them together. Once he was no longer alive, their bond started to fray.

Despite their estrangement, Chris and his family send Mary flowers every Mother's Day. In May of 2020, while the world was under quarantine from Covid-19, they sent her a particularly magnificent bouquet.

A few weeks later, sitting inside his mailbox halfway around the world, Chris received a thank-you card with an East Hampton return address.

His mother's perfect calligraphy was unmistakable.

It had been years since he'd heard anything in response.

Mary wrote: "The door is open and the light is always on."

ACKNOWLEDGMENTS

"Mama, how long have you been working on your book?" my daughter asked me in the fall of 2020, as I sat huddled over my laptop, poring over last and final line edits. At the time, Violet was five. My mind raced back to the fall of 2017, three years prior, when a germ of an idea first started gaining momentum. "Honestly, for most of your life," I answered back.

Years from now, when my children are finally old enough to sit down and read this book, I hope they can see their mother enthralled in the telling of an incredible story, the uncertainty of knowing where it would all lead, and the joyfulness of the pursuit. Books, though commendable, outward accomplishments, don't love you back. Theo and Violet, make no mistake: you're the best thing I've ever done.

Nonfiction books, I've come to appreciate, are the product of a great many gracious souls.

My first debt of gratitude goes to Biddle Duke. For better or worse (he would probably say worse), it was Biddle's introduction to Mary Stedman that set this whole thing into motion. For that initial introduction, and his guidance and counsel throughout several complicated junctures in the years since, I am profoundly thankful to call him not only a colleague but a trusted friend.

Mary Stedman deserves a second, but equal, thanks. She bore the great inconvenience of opening the doors of the heart better than anyone I have ever had the pleasure of interviewing.

Chris Stedman's vulnerability and candor knew no bounds. I will forever be in awe of his courage. As the years wore on, Chris became the North Star of this book: a constant reminder that the only way out is through.

Lance Hallock possessed a genuine kindness and eagerness to help. Probably, I later learned, because his wife, Heather, was a small-town newspaper reporter. Understanding the finer points of commercial fishing was like learning a foreign language. The learning curve was steep. Though any technical errors are mine and mine alone, this book is stronger because of Lance's stewardship.

From family members to friends to commercial fishermen to surfers, each interview added an unexpected layer of depth to the story in these pages. Thank you for sharing your stories, your memories, and your expertise with me: Colin Ambrose, Kelly Anderson, Dave Arapatch, Barry Augus, Lee Beiler, Russell Bennett, Phil Berg, Dave Berwald, Frank Bowman, Kim Bowman, Bonnie Brady, Donnie Briand, Mary Bromley, Olivia Brooks, Laurene Campbell, Steven Cannizzo, Tony Caramanico, Al Cavagnaro, Catherine Cederquist, Donna Charron, Jay Charron, Matt Charron, Ray Charron, Susan Collins, Alice Connick Ryan, Peter Connick, Susan Coursey, Bill Curtis, Vincent Damm, Jo Davidson, Christy Davis, Eugene DePasquale, Jamie DePasquale, Greg Donohue, Katie Dove, Diane Duca, Rick Etzel, Earl Ewing, Linda Faatz, Lee Finley, Thom Fleming, Stu Foley, Paul Forsberg Jr., Paul Forsberg Sr., Barbara Friedman, Jay Fruin, Gary Fuschillo, Walter Galcik, Scott Geery, Brian Gladstone, Susan Goodwillie Stedman, Andrew Greenebaum, Brian Halweil, Frank Hammer, Peter Hewitt, Jack Irving, Barbara Johnson, Richard Jones, Serge Kovaleski, Nathaniel Kramer, Bill Kurtz, Betsy Lashin, Thomas Llewellyn, Brian Lonegan, Kevin Maguire, Dennis Mahoney, Seamus Mahoney, Harry Matthews, Alex Matthiessen, Maria Matthiessen, Tom McGivern, John McHugh, Mary Anne Miller, Francis Minor, Francis Mott, Jeanne Nielsen, Kenneth Nolan, Matt Norklun, Joseph O'Connor, Henry Osmers, Susan Pollack, Tom Powell, Cathy Pradié-Connick, Joseph Quingert, Barry Raebeck, John Raymond, Thorson Rockwell, Steve Rosen, Tom Roth, Sam Rotis, Kevin Schaefer, Chris Schumann, Paul Seeth, Jon Snow, Philip Sprayregan, Kim Tiernan, Carol Stedman Johansen, Joy Stedman, Madonna Stedman, Matt Stedman, Tom Talmadge, Charlie Tarbet, George Tweedy III, Henry Uihlein, Mike Vagesse, Cathy Vedder, Gary Vigilant, Linda Vigilant-Holdeman, Walter Vogt, Chuck Weimer, Margie Wetzel, Patrick Wetzel, Brad White, Dick White, and Marge Winski.

Morgan McGivern's phenomenal photographs help tell a story my words could never convey. Thanks also to Tom Ford, James Brill, Jaime Frankfurt, and William Neal for sharing your pictures with me. Finally, to the family members who sent along photographs of your lost men, you deserve a wholly separate recognition.

Laura Dail, my literary agent, read my book proposal and saw in that first iteration the many complicated layers I dared to convey. Thank you for exhorting me, time and time again, to go for greatness. I trust this is the first of many collaborations together.

At Gallery Books, Jackie Cantor became a champion of this story within minutes of our very first phone call. A writer is only as good as her editor, and Jackie, over the course of several painstaking drafts, helped coax this story into a form I only dared to dream. A further thanks to Molly Gregory for her photo-wrangling prowess; to Joal Hetherington for her masterful copyedit; to Stephen Breslin for his eagle eye; to Elisa Rivlin for her fastidious legal read; and to Aimee Bell for swooping in at the eleventh hour with her journalistic microscope. Finally, on the publicity and marketing front, I have Sally Marvin, Anne Jaconette, and Sammi Sontag to thank for getting my first book into the hands of reviewers and other early readers, despite my trepidation of all things Zoom.

All hail librarians! Gina Bardi, a research librarian at the San Francisco Maritime Library, Kelly McAnnaney, an archivist with the National Archives in New York City, and

Victoria Triplett, an archives specialist with the National Archives at College Park, all played essential fact-finding roles. But Andrea Meyer, an archivist who oversees the Long Island Collection at the East Hampton Library, deserves a gold medal for her superhuman email response time and ability to locate *every single query* I sent her way.

Closer to home, my gratitude extends to the Rattray family: Helen Rattray, David Rattray, and Bess Rattray. Were it not for my years at the *East Hampton Star,* this story would never have become mine to tell. Your vast archive (and incredible photographs from 1984) saved my bacon in ways too numerous to count.

Stephen Kennedy Smith for providing steadfast encouragement and familiar shelter.

Peter Ragone for wisely insisting, four years ago, that I follow my heart and not sell my soul to a technology company.

Terry Stevens for expertly holding down the fort.

Benjamin Asher and Louise Reiner for keeping me well.

Early readers provided critical, essential feedback: Shay Astar, Marsha McClain, Liza and Joe Tremblay, Jonathan Cranin, and Andy Karsch.

My lady friends, near and far, not previously mentioned, who enrich my life: Zachary McClain, Jessica Chan, Winter Miller, Courtney Sullivan, Rachel Templeton, Cesalee Venema, Melissa Grimm, Amy Reed, Sarah Cohen, Erika Halweil, Mia Ljungberg Nevado, and Kristen Abboud.

Robert and Judy Millner, my parents, gave me the best gift imaginable: the freedom to choose whatever it was I wanted to do with my life — even when it became abundantly clear that print journalists were a dying breed. My mother, in particular, helped ensure that book deadlines didn't get in the way of clean clothes and baked goods and happy grandchildren.

And last, but certainly not least, Sudhir Venkatesh has my heart. He observed the first spark, the endless books about maritime history arriving at our doorstep, and gently nurtured my obsession along, every step of the labyrinthine way. It's a lucky thing to marry not only your first reader, but your best one.

Sag Harbor, New York
December 2020

NOTES ON SOURCES

The bulk of this narrative came from extensive personal interviews conducted over the span of three years. The material below was also essential to the writing of this book.

Articles

Ashby, Neal. "A Baedeker for the Hamptons Beaches." *New York Times,* July 29, 1973.

Barbanel, Josh. "Minimum Size of Striped Bass Raised by State; Commercial Fishermen Argued against Bill." *New York Times,* August 10, 1983.

Barons, Richard. "The English Cometh." *East Hampton Star,* April 30, 2020.

Berliner, Uri. "Art for Rescue Benefit." *East Hampton Star,* May 10, 1984.

———. "Fishermen Feared Lost in Storm off Montauk." *East Hampton Star,* April 5, 1984.

———. "No Trace of Crew." *East Hampton*

Star, April 19, 1984.

Berliner, Uri, and Linda Sherry. "Service for Crew." *East Hampton Star,* April 12, 1984.

Bleyer, Bill. "Finding the Unknown Fishermen." *Newsday,* February 14, 1999.

———. "On the Water: Remembering Those Lost at Sea." *Newsday,* May 9, 1993.

Bock, Eileen. "A House Topples." *East Hampton Star,* April 5, 1984.

Brasley, Patrick. "Service Scheduled for 2 Lost at Sea." *Newsday,* April 8, 1984.

Bryan, C. D. B. "1-A or 2-S — the Draft and the Student." *New York Times,* March 19, 1967.

Bryant, Nelson. "Outdoors: Going for Tilefish Is a Far-Out Experience." *New York Times,* May 5, 1980.

Buder, Leonard. "1980 Called Worst Year of Crime in City History." *New York Times,* February 25, 1981.

Carlson, Jen. "In the 1960s, You Could Buy a Montauk Home at Macy's for $12,000." *Gothamist,* May 18, 2015.

Coleman, Tim. "Last Reported Position — the Loss of the F/V *Wind Blown.*" *Long Island Boating World,* July 2010.

Cornell, Chris. "A Pro Provides Tips on Longline Deck Gear." *National Fisherman,* August 1985.

Crowe, Kenneth C. "Sea Search Unsuccessful." *Newsday,* April 2, 1984.

de Jonge, Peter. "Barbarian at the Tee." *New York Magazine,* August 18, 2005.

D'Mello, Judy. "A Funky Modernism." *East Hampton Star,* May 25, 2017.

Drudi, Dino. "Fishing for a Living Is Dangerous Work." US Bureau of Labor Statistics. Summer 1998.

Drumm, Russell. "A Handful of Montaukers Take On the Tilefish." *East Hampton Star,* May 29, 2003.

———. "Remembering the *Wind Blown.*" *East Hampton Star,* April 1, 2004.

———. "When the *Wind Blown* Went Down." *East Hampton Star,* March 26, 2009.

Duginski, Paul. "A Record 75-Foot Wave off California Coast Was Produced by Big Storm." *Los Angeles Times,* December 6, 2019.

East Hampton Star. "Alice Connick-Ryan." October 8, 2020.

———. "Andrew Connick." September 22, 2011.

———. "Charge Theft at Maidstone." January 25, 1979.

———. "Cletus Cavagnaro." March 15, 2007.

———. "Cottage List for Season of 1927."

May 20, 1927.

———. "Fishermen Drown." November 16, 1978.

———. "Miss Lamm to Marry Andrew J. Connick." March 17, 1955.

Edwards, Everett J. "Montauk Was Great Place for Gunning." *East Hampton Star,* October 24, 1935.

Fabricant, Florence. "No Striped Bass? There Are Other Fish in the Sea." *New York Times,* February 15, 1987.

Farrington, S. Kip, Jr. "Train Service Improves on L.I. Since Year 1925." *East Hampton Star,* October 24, 1935.

Firstman, Richard C. "East Coast Storm Leaves Swath of Destruction." *Newsday,* March 30, 1984.

Frye, John. "Scientists Ponder Dwindling Striper Stocks." *National Fisherman,* July 1979.

Gatewood, Dallas. "Shared Embrace for Lost Sailors." *Newsday,* April 12, 1984.

Gatewood, Dallas, and Steve Wick. "Tanker Rams LI Boat Off La. Coast; 3 Die." *Newsday,* November 14, 1978.

Gifford, Mary-Elizabeth. "Evacuated by Dory." *East Hampton Star,* April 5, 1984.

———. "Four Young Men." *East Hampton Star,* April 5, 1984.

Giovanni, S. D. "Barnegat Light Fishermen

Honor Radio Operator Mary Louise Cook." *National Fisherman,* October 1982.

Graves, Jack. "Skateboard Tilts." *East Hampton Star,* May 3, 1984.

———. "The Town Is Battered." *East Hampton Star,* April 5, 1984.

Haberstroh, Joe. "Solace by the Sea; Montauk Memorial Honors 110 Lost Fishermen." *Newsday,* October 6, 1999.

Hampton Chronicle-News. "Four Lost on Montauk Boat." April 4, 1984.

Interland, Peter. "Northing Instinct." *Surfer's Journal* 13, no. 1 (Early Spring 2004).

Jones, Kim A. "Assessing the Impact of Father-Absence from a Psychoanalytic Perspective." *Psychoanalytic Social Work* 14, no. 1 (September 25, 2008).

Junger, Sebastian. "The Storm." *Outside,* October 1, 1994.

Kirkman, Edward, and Don Singleton. "Seek 4 Lost in Stormy Atlantic." *New York Daily News,* March 31, 1984.

Kocher, Robert L. "A Beginners' Guide to How Loran C Navigation Systems Work." *National Fisherman,* January 1980.

Mackay, John William. "Paradise for Sportsmen on Historic Isle." *East Hampton Star,* October 24, 1935.

Mason, Bill. "Barge, Not Tanker, Hit Boat:

Report." *Newsday,* November 15, 1979.

Maynard, Joyce. "Choate-Rosemary Hall — Boys and Girls Apart." *New York Times,* December 17, 1976.

McAward, Mary. "Search for *Windblown* Turns Up Wreckage, but Four Still Missing." *Suffolk Life,* April 4, 1984.

Mermelstein, Susan. "Assessing the Damage." *East Hampton Star,* April 5, 1984.

Moore, Kirk. "Search for Boat Turns Up Nothing." *Asbury Park Press,* April 10, 1993.

Morning Call. "New Memorial at Montauk Is for Those Lost at Sea." October 10, 1999.

National Fisherman. "Boat Quality Rests with Buyer as Much as Builder." July 1980.

New York Times. "Alice Lamm Wed to Law Student." April 17, 1955.

———. "Bright and Tasty Tilefish Never Attained Popularity; Species Discovered in 1879 Was Exploited in Vain by the Bureau of Fisheries." April 21, 1929.

———. "College Enrollment Linked to Vietnam War." September 2, 1984.

———. "Four on Missing Boat Presumed to Be Dead." April 6, 1984.

———. "Mass Is Said for 2 Fishermen Lost off Long Island in Storm." April 12, 1984.

————. "Parties Planned at East Hampton." July 17, 1941.

————. "Weddings; Catherine Pradie, Andrew Connick." June 14, 1998.

Newsday. "Art Show to Help Lost Fisherman's Kin." April 17, 1984.

————. "Fishermen Pressing Search for Crew of Missing LI Boat." April 4, 1984.

————. "Search for Boat Called Off." April 3, 1984.

Palmer, H. V. R. "Crewman Lives to Tell of Pitchpoling in 55-Footer." *National Fisherman,* February 1981.

Pauly, Daniel. "Anecdotes and the Shifting Baseline Syndrome of Fisheries." *Trends in Ecology and Evolution* 10, no. 10 (October 1, 1995).

Pitcher, Michael W. "Four L.I. Crewmen Lost at Sea in Storm." *National Fisherman,* June 1984.

Planz, Allen. "Fish Diplomats." *East Hampton Star,* August 23, 1984.

————. "Left Early." *East Hampton Star,* April 5, 1984.

————. "On the Water." *East Hampton Star,* July 12, 1984.

————. "Storm-Tossed Boats Struggle to Port." *East Hampton Star,* April 5, 1984.

Pollack, Sarah. "Search for Fishing Boat Continues." *Newsday,* April 1, 1984.

Pollack, Susan. "A Captain's Wife Talks about Her Life." *East Hampton Star,* January 29, 1976.

————. "Long Islanders Want Total Ban on Foreign Longliners." *National Fisherman,* June 1983.

————. "Longliner Crew Makes Quality Its Business." *National Fisherman,* August 1984.

————. "More Bad News." *East Hampton Star,* January 19, 1978.

————. "N.Y. Commercial, Sport Fishermen Renew Battle." *National Fisherman,* May 1980.

————. "Ocean Haulseining on Long Island — Can It Survive Much Longer?" *National Fisherman,* April 1984.

————. "On the Water." *East Hampton Star,* March 2, 1978.

————. "Tell of Sinking." *East Hampton Star,* February 8, 1979.

————. "Tilefish Vessel Has a Close Call off New Jersey." *National Fisherman,* June 1984.

Portland Press Herald. "R. Bruce Stedman." February 15, 2013.

Potter, Job. "The Week of the *Wind Blown.*" *East Hampton Star,* March 26, 1987.

Raebeck, Barry. "End to Rural East Hampton." *East Hampton Star,* November 29, 1984.

Rosenbaum, Susan. "Owen McGivern." *East Hampton Star,* July 9, 1998.

Sherry, Linda. "For Captain's Family." *East Hampton Star,* May 24, 1984.

Stewart, Barbara. "Owen McGivern, 87, Dies; Judge Led Appellate Court." *New York Times,* July 8, 1998.

Stutz, Bruce. "Two Are Convicted of Racketeering at Fulton Market." *National Fisherman,* January 1982.

Sullivan, Tim. "N.Y.'s Fulton Market Linked to Organized Crime." *National Fisherman,* July 1981.

———. "Sane Management Is Possible." *National Fisherman,* March 1981.

Sullivan, Walter. "Burrowing Fish Found Shaping Seafloor." *New York Times,* July 22, 1986.

Tough, Paul. "A Speck in the Sea." *New York Times Magazine,* January 2, 2014.

Townes, Brooks. "Weather: You Can't Change It . . . but You Can Get a Reasonable Facsimile." *National Fisherman,* August 1983.

Virag, Irene. "She Prays the Sea Doesn't Win Again." *Newsday,* March 31, 1984.

Waldmann, Steven M. "Pulling Together."

East Hampton Star, April 12, 1984.

Welch, Laine. "Commercial Fishing Remains One of Most Dangerous Jobs in the U.S." *Juneau Empire,* May 9, 2018.

White, E. B. "Beautiful upon a Hill." *New Yorker,* May 12, 1945.

Winerip, Michael. "Beach Erosion: Nature vs. Shortsighted Man." *New York Times,* June 12, 1983.

Wiscasset Newspaper. "Richard Bruce Stedman." February 11, 2013.

Books

Agee, James. *A Death in the Family.* New York: Penguin Books, 2008.

Aldridge, John, and Anthony Sosinski. *A Speck in the Sea: A Story of Survival and Rescue.* New York: Weinstein Books, 2017.

Berwald, David H. *Chinese Buffet: A Journal of My Life and Career.* Self-published. 2020.

Bradford, Gershom. *The Mariner's Dictionary.* New York: Weathervane Books, 1952.

Brown, Daniel James. *The Boys in the Boat: Nine Americans and Their Epic Quest for Gold at the 1936 Berlin Olympics.* New York: Penguin Books, 2013.

Carson, Rachel. *The Edge of the Sea.* New York: Houghton Mifflin, 1998.

————. *Lost Woods: The Discovered Writing of Rachel Carson.* Boston: Beacon Press, 2011.

Chethik, Neil. *Fatherloss: How Sons of All Ages Comes to Terms with the Deaths of Their Dads.* New York: Hyperion, 2001.

Clavin, Tom. *Dark Noon: The Final Voyage of the Fishing Boat* Pelican. New York: McGraw-Hill, 2005.

Cole, John N. *Striper.* Boston: Little, Brown, 1978.

DiBenedetto, David. *On the Run: An Angler's Journey Down the Striper Coast.* New York: William Morrow, 2003.

Field, Van R. *Mayday! Shipwrecks, Tragedies, and Tales from Long Island's Eastern Shore.* Charleston, SC: History Press, 2008.

————. *Wrecks and Rescues on Long Island: The Story of the U.S. Life Saving Service.* East Patchogue, NY: Searles Graphics, Inc., 1997.

Finnegan, William. *Barbarian Days: A Surfing Life.* New York: Penguin Books, 2016.

Frankel, Adam P. *The Survivors: A Story of War, Inheritance, and Healing.* New York: Harper, 2019.

Friedan, Betty. *The Feminine Mystique.* New York: W. W. Norton, 1963.

Furman, Erna. *A Child's Parent Dies: Stud-

ies in Bereavement. New Haven, CT: Yale University Press, 1981.

Greenberg, Paul. *Four Fish: The Future of the Last Wild Food.* New York: Penguin Books, 2010.

Gruen, John Jonas. *The Sixties: Young in the Hamptons.* Milan: Charta, 2006.

Junger, Sebastian. *The Perfect Storm: A True Story of Men Against the Sea.* New York: W. W. Norton, 2009.

Keating, Céline, and Ed Johann, eds. *On Montauk: A Literary Celebration.* Sag Harbor, NY: Harbor Electronic Publishing, 2016.

Kurlansky, Mark. *Cod.* New York: Penguin Books, 1997.

Mahoney, Barbara. *A Sensitive, Passionate Man.* New York: David McKay, 1974.

Malcolm, Janet. *The Journalist and the Murderer.* New York: Vintage Books, 1990.

———. *The Silent Woman: Sylvia Plath and Ted Hughes.* New York: Vintage Books, 1994.

Matthiessen, Peter. *Men's Lives: The Surfmen and Baymen of the South Fork.* New York: Vintage Books, 1986.

Perel, Esther. *The State of Affairs: Rethinking Infidelity.* New York: Harper, 2017.

Philbrick, Nathaniel. *In the Heart of the Sea:*

The Tragedy of the Whaleship Essex. New York: Penguin Books, 2000.

Rattray, Jeannette Edwards. *Montauk: Three Centuries of Romance, Sport, and Adventure.* New York: Star Press, 1938.

————. *Ship Ashore! A Record of Maritime Disasters off Montauk and Eastern Long Island, 1640–1955.* New York: Coward-McCann, 1955.

Sahre, Paul. *Leisurama Now: The Beach House for Everyone.* New York: Princeton Architectural Press, 2008.

Shapiro, Dani. *Inheritance: A Memoir of Genealogy, Paternity, and Love.* New York: Alfred A. Knopf, 2019.

Slade, Rachel. *Into the Raging Sea: Thirty-Three Mariners, One Megastorm, and the Sinking of* El Faro. New York: Ecco, 2018.

Stein, Jean. *Edie: American Girl.* New York: Grove Press, 1982.

Strong, John A. *The Montaukett Indians of Eastern Long Island.* Syracuse, NY: Syracuse University Press, 2001.

Thompson, Ed. *Ice Cream Headaches: Surf Culture in New York and New Jersey.* Bologna, Italy: Damiani, 2018.

van der Kolk, Bessel. *The Body Keeps the Score: Brain, Mind, and Body in the Healing* of Trauma. New York: Penguin Books, 2014.

Van Dorn, William G. *Oceanography and Seamanship.* Centreville, MD: Cornell Maritime Press, 1993.

Warner, William W. *Beautiful Swimmers: Watermen, Crabs, and the Chesapeake Bay.* Boston: Little, Brown, 1994.

———. *Distant Water: The Fate of the North Atlantic Fisherman.* Boston: Little, Brown, 1983.

Weisbecker, Allan C. *In Search of Captain Zero: A Surfer's Road Trip Beyond the End of the Road.* New York: Penguin Putnam, 2001.

Wilder, Thornton. *The Bridge of San Luis Rey.* New York: HarperCollins, 1998.

Primary Sources

Geery, John, Mike Stedman, and Bart Stuart. "Zee Baja Safari." Undated.

Marine Safety Information System (MSIS), 1981–2001. Extracted Record for Marine Casualty Case MC84906665. National Archives and Records Administration. Prepared on July 27, 2018.

Provider III Record Books: 1978–1984. Courtesy of Lance Hallock.

Stedman, Alfred D. "The Stedman Story." 1964.

Stedman, Michael D. Arrest Report. Town of East Hampton Police Department. October 23, 1983.

———. File Number: 239A85. Suffolk County Surrogate's Court. Riverhead, New York.

Stedman, R. Bruce. "Book II: The Bruce Stedman Story (A Personal History)." 2003.

US Department of Transportation. US Coast Guard records and correspondence. Seventy-three documents related to Official Number 506876 (F/V *Capt. Scotty, Wind Blown, Sinbad*) from years 1966 to 1984.

Vigilant, Richard H. File Number: 968A1978. Suffolk County Surrogate's Court. Riverhead, New York.

Vigilant, Richard Michael. File Number: 711A84. Suffolk County Surrogate's Court. Riverhead, New York.

The Wheatley School Yearbook, Class of 1968. Old Westbury, New York. Courtesy of Gary Fuschillo.

PHOTO CREDITS

398 Courtesy of Lance Hallock

403 Courtesy of *The East Hampton Star*

405 Courtesy of Chris Stedman

409 Courtesy of *The East Hampton Star*

418 Photograph by Tom Ford

423 Photograph by Morgan McGivern

426 Photograph by Mary-Elizabeth Gifford/ *The East Hampton Star*

432 Courtesy of Albert N. Cavagnaro

434 Photograph by Morgan McGivern

439 Photograph by Morgan McGivern

445 Courtesy of Maude Vigilant-Hastings

450 Photograph by Dave Connick

451 Photograph by Thomas Llewellyn

455 Photograph by Donna Llewellyn

458 Photograph by Betsy Lashin

459 Courtesy of Chris Stedman

469 Courtesy of Chris Stedman

471 Courtesy of Chris Stedman

480 Courtesy of Chris Stedman

482 Courtesy of Albert N. Cavagnaro

487 Photograph by Morgan McGivern

488 Courtesy of Chris Stedman

493 Courtesy of Chris Stedman

495 Photograph by Morgan McGivern

ABOUT THE AUTHOR

Amanda M. Fairbanks has worked in the editorial department of the *New York Times,* as a reporter for *HuffPost,* and as a staff writer at the *East Hampton Star.* Her writing has also appeared in the *Boston Globe, Newsweek,* the *Atlantic,* and the *San Francisco Chronicle.* A graduate of Smith College and a former Teach for America corps member, she has two master's degrees from Columbia University's Graduate School of Journalism, and currently lives with her family in Sag Harbor.

The employees of Thorndike Press hope you have enjoyed this Large Print book. All our Thorndike, Wheeler, and Kennebec Large Print titles are designed for easy reading, and all our books are made to last. Other Thorndike Press Large Print books are available at your library, through selected bookstores, or directly from us.

For information about titles, please call:
  (800) 223-1244

or visit our website at:
  gale.com/thorndike

To share your comments, please write:
  Publisher
  Thorndike Press
  10 Water St., Suite 310
  Waterville, ME 04901